T0202104

Social Media in Northern Chile

WHY WE POST

PUBLISHED AND FORTHCOMING TITLES:

Social Media in Southeast Turkey
Elisabetta Costa

Social Media in Northern Chile
Nell Haynes

Social Media in Rural China
Tom McDonald

Social Media in an English Village
Daniel Miller

Visualising Facebook
Daniel Miller and Jolynna Sinanan

How the World Changed Social Media
Daniel Miller et al.

Social Media in South Italy
Razvan Nicolescu

Social Media in Trinidad
Jolynna Sinanan

Social Media in Emergent Brazil
Juliano Spyer

Social Media in South India
Shriram Venkatraman

Social Media in Industrial China
Xinyuan Wang

Find out more: www.ucl.ac.uk/ucl-press

Why We Post

Social Media in Northern Chile

Posting the Extraordinarily Ordinary

Nell Haynes

First published in 2016 by
UCL Press
University College London
Gower Street
London WC1E 6BT

Available to download free: www.ucl.ac.uk/ucl-press

A CIP catalogue record for this book is available
from The British Library.

ISBN: 978–1–910634–57–8 (Hbk.)
ISBN: 978–1–910634–58–5 (Pbk.)
ISBN: 978–1–910634–59–2 (PDF)
ISBN: 978–1–910634–60–8 (epub)
ISBN: 978–1–910634–61–5 (mobi)
DOI: 10.14324/111. 9781910634592

Introduction to the series Why We Post

This book is one of a series of 11 titles. There are nine monographs devoted to specific field sites (including this one) in Brazil, Chile, China, England, India, Italy, Trinidad and Turkey – they will be published in 2016–17. The series also includes a comparative book about all of our findings, published to accompany this title, and a final book which contrasts the visuals that people post on Facebook in the English field site with those on our Trinidadian field site.

When we tell people that we have written nine monographs about social media around the world, and that they all have the same chapter headings (apart from Chapter 5), they are concerned about potential repetition. However, if you decide to read several of these books (and we very much hope you do), you will see that this device has been helpful in showing the precise opposite. Each book is as individual and distinct as if it were on an entirely different topic.

This is perhaps our single most important finding. Most studies of the internet and social media are based on research methods that assume we can generalise across different groups. We look at tweets in one place and write about 'Twitter'. We conduct tests about social media and friendship in one population, and then write on this topic as if friendship means the same thing for all populations. By presenting nine books with the same chapter headings, you can judge for yourselves what kinds of generalisations are, or are not, possible.

Our intention is not to evaluate social media, either positively or negatively. Instead the purpose is educational, providing detailed evidence of what social media has become in each place, and the local consequences, including local evaluations.

Each book is based on 15 months of research during which time most of the anthropologists lived, worked and interacted with people in the local language. Yet they differ from the dominant tradition of writing social science books. Firstly they do not engage with the academic literatures on social media. It would be highly repetitive to have the same discussions in all nine books. Instead discussions of these literatures are to be found in our comparative book, *How the World Changed Social Media*. Secondly these monographs are not comparative, which again is the primary function of this other volume. Thirdly, given the immense interest in social media from the general public, we have tried to write in an accessible and open style. This means we have adopted a mode more common in historical writing of keeping all citations and the discussion of all wider academic issues to endnotes. If you prefer to read above the line, each text offers a simple narrative about our findings. If you want to read a more conventional academic book that relates the material to its academic context, this can be done through engaging with the endnotes.

We hope you enjoy the results, and we hope you will also read our comparative book – and perhaps some of the other monographs – in addition to this one.

Acknowledgements

This book is a product of my postdoctoral research as part of the Global Social Media Impact Study. Of course, no book is entirely an individual project, but this book in particular has been nurtured through collaboration and assistance from many individuals. The Global Social Media Impact Study team, who welcomed me, shared with me and taught me so many important lessons has been invaluable to this work. Elisabetta Costa, Tom McDonald, Razvan Nicolescu, Jolynna Sinanan, Juliano Spyer, Shriram Venkatraman and Xinyuan Yang have been the greatest colleagues, collaborators and friends anyone could hope for. Daniel Miller, our fearless leader, has been especially important to the development of this book. But my postdoctoral research fellowship was housed at the Interdisciplinary Center for Intercultural and Indigenous Studies at Pontificia Universidad Católica de Chile, funded by the Chilean CONICYT - FONDAP15110006, to which I am grateful for financial and academic support. I am also grateful to have benefitted from the project's primary funding from European Research Council grant ERC-2011-AdG-295486 Socnet. At the Universidad Católica I have been fortunate to work with Jaime Coquelet, Helene Risør, Marjorie Murray, Piergiorgio di Giminiani and longtime friends and collaborators Paula Seravia, and Jorge Montesinos.

This research would not have been possible without the help and support of the people of Alto Hospicio, Chile. In particular Jorge Castro Gárete's help as my research assistant in July and August 2014 was invaluable. I also will be forever indebted to individuals who gave their time and knowledge, and often offered their homes, food, vehicles and any number of other resources to me. First I must thank Jair Andres Correa Garamuño, who provided all of these as well as great emotional support during some of the hardest times of field work. Guillermo Lopez and Cristian Schlick also provided instrumental emotional support and an occasional necessary respite from field work. I would also like to thank the Correa Garamuño family, the Cornejo Ferrest family and

Michelle Cornejo in particular, as well as José Vilches, Eduardo Callo, Marcela Rojas, David Urrea and Alex Vilches.

I would also like to thank a number of colleagues who read drafts of various chapters and provided helpful feedback. I am grateful for the support of Matthew Thomann, Elijah Edelman, Joowon Park, William Leap, Bryan McNeil, Adrienne Pine, Dylan Kerrigan, Harjant Gill, Luis Landa, Rebecca Stone Gordon, Gregory Mitchell and Mark Cartwright. Former mentors Helen B. Schwartzman, E. Patrick Johnson, and the late Dwight Conquergood deserve thanks too. I cannot fail to mention those friends I have met in South America, who in different ways have been present and supportive, including Mauricio Salazar Jemio, Gustavo Palacios, Carlos Mendoza Martinez, Kicho Jimenez Ross, Rodrigo Jimenez Ross, Raquel Canales Molina, Roger Durán, Lysanne Merkenstein, Michael Poteet, Alex White, Juan Carrizo Ibarra, Orlando Compton, Lorenzo Dolcetti and Andrés Sánchez. But most importantly, I must thank my parents, Mary and Thomas Haynes, and my sister, Ida Haynes, who have always encouraged me to explore new places and try new things. They have also been a lifeline during the hardest times of field work and most stressful times of writing and editing. Without their support this book would not have been possible.

Contents

List of figures

1
Introduction: Online and on the margins in Alto Hospicio, Chile

On 18 September 2014 – Chile's national holiday, the *Fiestas Patrias* – 24-year-old Nicole work up early in her family apartment. She looked out the window at Alto Hospicio, in the north of the country. Her mother was in the kitchen preparing food for the occasion and her father had just arrived home from a week-long shift as a heavy machine operator at a large copper mine a few hours away from the city. She could hear her younger brother still snoring through the thin walls of their small apartment. As usual she grabbed her second-hand iPhone 4 to send Martin, her boyfriend of five years, a Facebook message wishing him a good morning. Then she began skimming through Facebook. After reading a number of posts wishing everyone a fun-filled holiday, she wrote her own post related to *Fiestas Patrias*.

> *Primero, soy HOSPICEÑA, Después, soy NORTINA, y último, soy Chilena. . .así qué viva Alto Hospicio! Viva el Norte!*

> First I am HOSPICEÑA [from the city of Alto Hospicio], next I am NORTHERN and finally I am Chilean . . . so Hooray Alto Hospicio! Hooray the North!!

In this short post Nicole declared her loyalties – first to her city, next to the region and only then to her country, even on the national holiday. In many ways she used this post to establish how she imagines her position in the world, and the way she understands herself in relation to various larger communities to which she belongs. Alto Hospicio is considered a marginalised city, and the far north of the country a peripheral region. By emphasising these more local ways of identifying rather than her national pride, she highlights her own marginality as a citizen. Particularly during *Fiestas Patrias*, a time invested with national symbolism, when she writes 'Viva Alto Hospicio! Viva el Norte!' she leaves the much more common phrase 'Viva Chile' notably absent.

Nicole's proclamations of loyalty to city, region and nation are particularly poignant as conveyed through social media, a form of communication often imagined as existing beyond any borders. Social media has become associated with global networks, unfettered by nation-states, geographical differences or even cultural variation. Yet Nicole used this medium precisely to declare certain kinds of place-based citizenship.

Citizenship, in its colloquial use, is generally understood to mean an individual's membership in a political and geographic community. It includes that individual's legal status in relation to a governing body, but also her or his participation within the public defined by that governing body. These range from small-scale, local, face-to-face communities, in which an action such as picking up litter makes one a 'good citizen', to the much larger communities such as the nation – or even a sense of 'global citizenship' where most members do not know one another face-to-face, yet individuals still feel obligations to contribute to a collective good.

The specific meaning of citizenship varies considerably in different historical, physical and cultural contexts. Bosniak suggests that we conceive of citizenship as a collection of interwoven strands including legal status in an organised community, rights within such communities, public participation and feelings of belonging.[1] Considering these different conceptions of citizenship allows us to differentiate between them, while also recognising that they are always (en)tangled. These various meanings at times complement one another; at other times there may be tension between them. As Nicole's post makes clear, citizenship is often deeply connected to people's understanding of who, where and how they exist in the world.

Traditional treatments of citizenship acknowledge the role of mass media in its construction, particularly in terms of belonging and nationalism. For example, in tracing the spread of print media beginning with the Industrial Revolution, Benedict Anderson suggests that speakers of different varieties of a language such as English or Spanish may have found it difficult to understand people from another region, even if they nominally spoke the 'same' language. With the rise of national newspapers, however, people began to see themselves as similar to others in the rest of their country, who were readers of the very same paper, and began to understand the nation as an 'imagined community'.[2] With the emergence of internet communication, and particularly the interactive features of social media, we can see how these imagined communities are now likely to cross national borders quite easily.

Anderson indeed suggests that the local alignment of social habits, culture, attachment and political participation are being unravelled, in part, by modern communications. However, virtual spaces also allow for conceptions of citizenship that move beyond formal, legal and constitutional definitions in order to emphasise the 'everyday practices of belonging through which social membership is negotiated'.[3] As we see from Nicole's Facebook post, in some instances global forms of communication become the very space in which individuals use place-based ways of expressing the self. And Nicole is not alone. Though not always as explicit, the residents of Alto Hospicio, Chile often use social media to express various forms of citizenship related to the city, region or nation. Much like the 'public sphere', described by Habermas[4] as a domain of social life in which public opinion may be formed and debated, social media provides a space for discussion, for expressing opinions – and thus creates a public for discussing and contesting what citizenship means.

Because this new public sphere of social media is, in theory, open to and viewable by people almost anywhere in the world, we often find it easy to assume that it fosters forms of cosmopolitan citizenship, privileging the view that all people, regardless of geographic location or political affiliations, are citizens in a single community. As borders become increasingly porous, with capital, goods, people and ideas flowing practically unimpeded by geographic boundaries,[5] citizenship takes on new meaning. Within such a context, the way Nicole and many other Hospiceños place importance on locally based forms of citizenship becomes all the more meaningful, particularly as residents of a marginalised area. Social media provides an ideal medium for studying these types of self-expression, rendering them visible both to other Hospiceños and to the ethnographic observer.

Hospiceños contrast their experiences with the types of national or global citizenship that often accompany movements of people and ideas, promoting a sense of solidarity within the community rather than emphasising distinctions. These individuals identify in ways that highlight local affiliation connected to family, social networks, work and community politics. When Hospiceños express these identifications through social media it often reinforces their values of normativity in surprising ways. This book elucidates the ways in which Hospiceños use social media as a conduit to highlight certain discourses and erase others, in the service of sustaining normativity and redefining citizenship from a a marginalised position.

These themes of citizenship, marginality and normativity are pertinent to the discussion of social media in this book. This is because, particularly in a marginalised area, social media has become the most prominent public sphere in which claims to and contestations of citizenship may be made. In Alto Hospicio most of what people post on social media is in some sense connected to the performance, maintenance or examination of what it means to be a good citizen.[6] Of course not all postings explicitly announce that they are about citizenship, as Nicole's did on the national holiday. Instead most of Hospiceños' posts masquerade as funny memes, silly videos, mundane photographs or banal recounting of the day's events in a status update. When framed as claims that their marginality actually represents a normative form of citizenship, however, the extraordinary potential of an ordinary post is revealed.

Viva Alto Hospicio!

When Nicole wrote her Facebook post, declaring 'First I am Hospiceña', she communicated the importance of her connection to Alto Hospicio. She positioned herself as one of the roughly 100,000 residents who occupy this city near the geographic centre of the *Norte Grande*, or 'Great North' region of Chile. Alto Hospicio, literally translated as 'High Accommodation', sits high on a sand dune overlooking the Pacific Ocean, but at first glance there is little that seems hospitable about the place.

The Great North is enveloped by the Atacama Desert, the driest in the world, and the natural landscape is barren. Sand permeates everything. Most roads in the city are paved, but covered with a layer of sand, giving them the same neutral colour as the empty lots that host beds of discarded rubbish. Cars line the streets from one end to another, also covered in a thin layer of sandy dust. Homes are usually constructed of painted cement blocks or bricks, with flat roofs, and surrounded by security fences. Dogs lie by the side of the street, often with a coat of sand covering their fur. Average annual precipitation is about 1 mm, so plant life is almost completely absent, apart from a few plazas with artificially grown palms, flowers and grass. Playgrounds and cement basketball courts are common, and well used, leaving them with peeling, faded paint. The wares sold at corner shops spill out into the street, alongside faded poster advertisements that look as if they were printed in the mid-1980s. On busy streets and plazas vendors lay out wares on blankets, selling everything from fresh produce and prepared lunches to school supplies and used clothing.

Despite its 100,000 residents, Alto Hospicio feels like a small city that continues to sprawl. The central business area occupies only three blocks of busy road, and includes city government offices, the cultural centre, several banks, two supermarkets and what seems like

Fig. 1.1 Map of Chile showing Alto Hospicio, nearby Iquique and the national capital, Santiago

100 barbers shops. The city began to grow in the early 1990s, jumping from 9,000 residents in 1992 to over 90,000 a decade later, and has been officially recognised as a municipality only since 2004. Although it is a new city, there is something that looks faded and used about almost everything. Nothing seems to be shiny or fresh in Alto Hospicio.

Glancing at the social media profiles of young Hospiceños makes this clear. They snap selfies in front of their dusty school buildings or inside their homes, usually decorated with furniture and textiles purchased second-hand at the city's outdoor market. Even the humorous

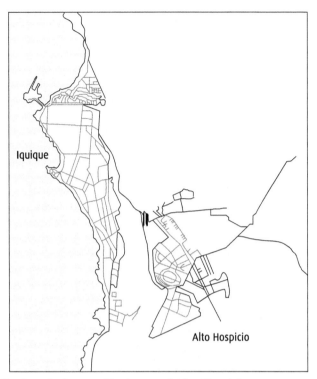

Fig. 1.2 Detailed map of Iquique and Alto Hospicio

memes so popular among Chileans are passed from page to page like reused goods.

Though the majority of this young generation grew up in Alto Hospicio, most of their parents did not. The population boom of the 1990s was a result of strong economic conditions in the region. Alto Hospicio sits between the port city of Iquique, with its tax-free import zone, Zofri, and copper mining operations in the Altiplano, the high plain of Chile's interior. So, despite the seemingly barren surroundings, the region teems with natural resources, from fishing and importation on the Pacific coast to the copper reserves in the Andes mountains. Because of these resources, the region attracts migrants from central and southern Chile, as well as international migrants from Bolivia, Peru and Colombia, all looking for better work opportunities.

The entire Norte Grande[7] region is essential to Chile's economy. The port in Iquique is one of the most important in western South America, and employs about 20,000 people, loading and unloading cargo,

Fig. 1.3 A view of Alto Hospicio from a hill in the central eastern part of the city

shipping goods and selling tax-free items in Zofri. Even more influential is the mining industry, which employs over 150,000 people throughout Chile, most of whom are concentrated in the Great North. Copper exports alone make up about 20 per cent of the country's GDP and 60 per cent of its exports.[8] Yet while the people who consider Alto Hospicio their home make up a significant proportion of workers in both these industries, they rarely experience the true economic benefits of this industry.

The economy of this mining region in Chile is a study of contrasting juxtaposition, in which vast mineral wealth is surrounded by a seemingly endless desert void. In Iquique's new southern neighbourhoods high-level managers and international engineers buy mini mansions and park their Hummers in the driveway. At the same time the majority of mining workers and their families live in modest neighbourhoods in northern and central Iquique or in Alto Hospicio, often inhabiting homes with cement floors and lacking conveniences such as hot water. In Alto Hospicio some entire neighbourhoods are *tomas* [takings], in which residents simply claimed the land without any title by building their own houses there.

Iquique is surrounded by water to the west and a 600-m sand dune to the east. The latter curves toward the ocean to close off the city in the north and south, dropping almost directly into the sea. As both the mining and importation industries boomed in the 1990s and huge numbers of migrants arrived to the region from other parts of Chile and abroad, Iquique simply could not accommodate more people: moving to Alto Hospicio was the only option. The sand dune had long been home to a mining train depot, dating from the early twentieth century, and a few indigenous peoples' settlements that had been there since the 1950s. Migrants began staking claims to land on the dune, simply by beginning to build on the area that later became known as the *Auto Construcción* [Self-Construction] neighbourhood.

As the city continued to grow, new neighbourhood developments became more organised, with homes and large apartment buildings funded by government programmes. Alto Hospicio continued to be officially part of Iquique until 12 April 2004, when President Ricardo Lagos Escobar signed Law No. 19943 declaring Alto Hospicio a separate municipality. Today most reports suggest that Alto Hospicio has about 100,000 inhabitants, though no census results have been made public since 2002.

Residents describe the city as marginal and disenfranchised, calling it *fome* [boring] and ugly. Because almost all residences in the city are modest – either self-constructed or part of government social housing systems – a uniform and utilitarian aesthetic pervades the

Fig. 1.4   A self-constructed home in a *toma* neighbourhood

Fig. 1.5 'Alto Hospicio occupies last place in ranking of quality of life in cities'

landscape. Those in the port city of Iquique, just 10 km down the sand dune to the east, often describe Alto Hospicio as impoverished, dangerous and 'uninhabitable'. In 2014 and 2015, during which I conducted the majority of my field work, the *Indice de Calidad de Vida Urbana* [National Index of Quality of Urban Life] ranked Alto Hospicio last among cities in Chile. The rankings took into consideration working conditions, business climates, sociocultural conditions, transportation connectivity, health, environment and housing.[9] Hospiceños certainly recognise these stereotypes about the city, and do not necessarily disagree. However, they see their marginalised city as part of the way they perceive themselves – not as victims, but as an exploited community that continues to fight for its rights.

When the quality of life ranking appeared in the news, many Hospiceños shared a link to the article on Facebook, commenting with both pride and sarcasm. Commentaries ranged from '*Díos mío, como sobreviven???*' [My God, how do they survive?] to '*Vengan a visitar a nuestro paradiso*' [Come visit our paradise]. No one contested the ranking or listed things that they felt could be assets for the city. Instead they employed sarcasm to highlight both their pride in being from Alto Hospicio, as well as calling attention to their marginalised subjectivity that comes as part of being a Hospiceño. They knew most people who would see their comments on the post were Hospiceños as well, but still felt it was important to comment. Within the local public sphere, these types of public comments about marginality were important to express belonging and community cohesion.

Viva El Norte!

Alto Hospicio's quality of life ranking clearly marks the city as marginal. Yet it also calls attention to the fact the entire northern region is in many ways a peripheral zone. Indeed, this positioning was important to Nicole's declaration of northern pride as well. Despite a few high-ranking mining professionals who make their homes in Iquique, the wealth and prestige of Chile is concentrated away from the North. At the same time, however, this wealth and prestige very much depends on the northern region's natural resources.[10] Copper exports from the Great North make up about one-third of the country's income, significantly contributing to the fact that Chile's economy expands by about six per cent annually while unemployment and inflation remain very low.[11] In fact it was the natural resources of the Great North's Atacama Desert that brought the region into the Chilean nation in the first place.

　　The Inca were the first to exploit the natural resources of the Atacama, developing silver mining after they colonised the Chango indigenous people of the region in the early sixteenth century. Spanish colonists, who conquered the area and its people a few decades later, further exploited silver deposits and built up the city of Iquique as a social and economic centre. When Peru won independence from Spain in 1821, Iquique and the surrounding mining towns became part of this new nation. It was not until the 1830s, when prospectors discovered deposits of the natural fertiliser sodium nitrate in the Atacama, that the governments of Bolivia, Chile and Peru began to consider the land valuable. All three nations hoped to profit from mining, and began negotiating what was previously an undefined border. After decades of dispute,

Fig. 1.6 Map of territory changes as a result of the War of the Pacific

and encouraged by British financiers, Chilean president Aníbal Pinto sent troops to capture the resource-rich desert that was under Bolivian rule. In accordance with a previous treaty Peru came to the defence of Bolivia, joining in combat against Chile. Pinto declared war on both nations in April 1879, thus beginning what became known as the War of the Pacific (1879–83). By the end of the conflict in 1884 Chile had taken Bolivia's entire coastline and Peru's southernmost province of Tarapacá, thus moving its northern border more than 700 km north. The area of

Iquique and Alto Hospicio, as well as Antofagasta (more than 400 km to the south), had both previously been Bolivian areas. Arica (300 km to the north), formerly part of Peru, also now came under Chilean rule. Most importantly, the resource-rich Atacama Desert had become Chilean territory. The border has remained as such, though the area is still disputed; Bolivia and Peru continue to file challenges with the United Nations International Court of Justice.

When Chile finally firmed up its claim to the Atacama territory, the government quickly set about a process of 'Chileanisation' to cement their sovereignty. Military units were stationed in the area, not only as deterrents to Peruvian and Bolivian forces, but also to remind the populace of their new nationality. To mitigate resentment towards the military, and the new nation as a whole, the Chilean government launched projects aimed at incorporating the northern population into the nation-state. It mounted projects in religion and education for both children and adults, projects which Frazier calls 'key vehicles for promulgating official memory'.[12]

Modernisation was at the core of the country's nationalist discourse. The newly won northern region of Tarapacá was home to nitrate exports that provided economic means to sustain such an image. A new class of wealthy citizens emerged from the nitrate industry, strengthening Chile's reputation as a country of wealth, culture, progress and modernity, but most were based in the capital, Santiago.

Nitrate mining, particularly as backed by foreign investment, created a boom in the region. Though most of the new-made nitrate barons settled in Santiago or abroad, those who settled in Iquique quickly set about constructing the city in European style; a municipal theatre was included among many stately buildings of colonial architecture, made of Oregon pine. Migrants began arriving from Southern Chile, Bolivia, Peru and other South American nations to fulfil the need for labour in the mines and processing plants. The nitrate industry proved short-lived, however; a German-made synthetic substitute was created in 1909, causing the Chilean industry to collapse by the 1940s.

Cycles of economic boom and bust have characterised the area since the nitrate era. The most recent mining boom, beginning in the 1980s, has been in copper exportation, and it continued through the time of my field work. In the current decade (2010s) northern Chile supplies one-third of the world's copper, which makes up 60 per cent of the country's exports and 20 per cent of its GDP. Large multinational companies such as Phelps Dodge and Sumitomo have partnered with CODELCO, the state-owned copper company. Much of the profit is sent abroad, to Japan, the United States and the United Kingdom, while the Chilean government averages about 11.5 billion US$ per year in profits from mining.[13]

The influence of mining also made Tarapacá the 'birthplace of the Chilean labour movement'.[14] In the early nineteenth century most of the labour force in the sodium nitrate fields was composed of migrants from southern Chile, Argentina, Peru and Bolivia. Despite very different backgrounds, these workers overcame ethnic and national differences to organise their demands for better working conditions. Such solidarity was in part a consequence of their labour and lives being so thoroughly controlled by the nitrate industry. Mining companies often paid wages in tokens usable only at company-owned stores, and most workers had no family resources on which to rely. The nitrate fields were also so distant from workers' homes that it was almost impossible to return to their communities with any regularity. With the mobility of the workforce restricted, the companies found it easier to enforce adherence to work schedules and rules. As Frazier suggests, these conditions gave workers the sense that 'solidarity among the miners was their sole means of protecting themselves against the ups and downs

Fig. 1.7   Iquique's Municipal Theatre, decorated for *Fiestas Patrias*

of the mining cycle and exploitation by the foreign companies'.[15] The labour movement, increasingly important until the early twentieth century, organised not only for better working conditions, particularly in response to times of economic depression: it also supported the creation of schools, adult education programmes, cultural centres and women's centres, and has been noted as providing a foundation for Chilean socialism.[16]

The Great North was a strong region for the socialist party in Chile through the 1960s, making it a particularly prominent target when Augusto Pinochet's United States-backed neoliberal regime overthrew Salvador Allende's socialist government in 1973. General Sergio Arellano flew by helicopter from Santiago to the northern provinces in what came to be known as the 'Caravan of Death'. He visited the prisons filled with 'subversives' – socialist party sympathisers – and singled out the highest profile prisoners for execution, sometimes as many as 26 at a time.

Of those who were not imprisoned, tortured or disappeared, many Northerners fled the country. The area was already well equipped with tunnels into Peru. They had been used to smuggle food into Chile during the preceding US-led embargo designed to weaken the socialist party, paving the way for a leadership more sympathetic to neoliberal reforms. When, despite the embargo, Chileans reaffirmed their faith in socialism by electing Allende, the United States backed Pinochet's violent military coup. The food-smuggling tunnels were then transformed into escape routes, and at times, into living quarters. Overall the brutal regime executed or disappeared 3,200 Chileans. It imprisoned an additional 80,000, while more than 200,000 fled the country.[17]

The influence of the Pinochet regime was multifaceted, resulting in huge economic impacts on the region as well. Indeed, the United States backed the regime specifically as a means to install Milton Friedman's neoliberal economic theories as a test case. These policies centred on privatising state-owned companies and resources, deregulating business, cutting social services and opening the country to unimpeded imports.[18] As a result inflation spiralled to 374 per cent. More than 400 state-owned companies were privatised and tariffs were brought down by an average 70 per cent. Chileans working in manufacturing and related industries quickly lost their jobs as cheaper imports flooded the market. Unemployment under Allende had been about three per cent, but under the new 'economic shock' dictated by Friedman it reached 20 per cent. In 1975 Pinochet's finance minister reduced government spending by 27 per cent and continued to cut: in 1980 government spending reached just 50 per cent of what it had been under Allende, leading to further unemployment and fewer social resources at a time when they were acutely needed. The government almost entirely defunded social services. The social security system was privatised, health care changed to a pay-as-you-go system and public schools[19] were replaced with vouchers and chartered schools; even cemeteries were privatised.[20]

Pinochet's government maintained these policies until 1982 when the Chilean economy crashed – debt exploded, hyperinflation took hold and unemployment rocketed to 30 per cent. Pinochet was forced to re-nationalise several companies. Naomi Klein points out that in retrospect Pinochet's saving grace was that he had never privatised the state copper mine company CODELCO, which generated 85 per cent of Chile's revenue from exports. Copper from the Great North saved the country from complete financial ruin.

However, those profits went to the government and wealthy investors, while workers in the north felt the brunt of economic problems created by extreme 'free market' reforms; they were in large part among the 45 per cent of citizens who had fallen below the poverty line by 1988. Pinochet's regime was finally defeated in a democratic election in 1989. However, subsequent democratically elected administrations intensified the export-oriented neoliberal reforms, though with less violent and totalitarian control.

These histories of exploitation and violence give Northerners a certain character, particularly in terms of their sense of citizenship. For many Chileans, the legacy of the Pinochet regime has left a void in political life in the North, as people try to distance themselves from national politics. Yet at the same time memories of the labour movement that began with nitrate workers remain a strong organising principle for Northerners, who understand themselves as similarly exploited for the benefit of those living in Santiago or who take the profits abroad. Nitrate-era imagery even figures prominently in memes that declare northern pride. Such memes that reference local historical politics are popular and posted by social media users in order to highlight their identification as Northerners. These memes differ drastically from those that comment on national politics, which often involve Photoshopped pictures of current politicians in ridiculous situations, overlaid with funny text and commentary. Being Northern is thus often about claiming political citizenship on a local level while eschewing national politics, and Hospiceños use social media as a key place to express this kind of citizenship. Citizenship is about more than politics, however, and this history equally affects how Hospiceños see their participation within the nation–state in a variety of formations – among them sociality, economy, politics and legal rights.

Viva Chile?!?

In many ways the legacy of the Pinochet regime made Chile precisely what Friedman hoped – a neoliberal example. Following the vote to end Pinochet's rule, subsequent democratically elected administrations have maintained neoliberal economic policies, through export promotion strategies and continued privatisation. The government's role in the economy is mostly limited to regulation, although as noted the state continues to operate copper giant CODELCO and Banco Estado [State Bank]. Since 2006 Chile has boasted the highest per capita income in Latin America, with a purchasing power parity value of $21,948 between 2010–14,[21] demonstrating the apparent success of these policies.

As economic anthropologists point out, neoliberalism is not just about faith in the 'free market'; it also includes the reconfiguration of ideological assumptions about the role of individuals in society.[22] These ideologies become embedded in normative social scripts.[23] Rather than people expecting the government to provide for their basic needs, they expect government to act merely as a referee for private business. Individual responsibility often becomes a cultural value, promoted by political rhetoric which suggests those in need of social safety nets are failing to contribute to society, as well as similar but more subtle forms of discourse within education and advertising.[24]

Advertising in fact plays a major role in the adoption of neoliberal ideologies as cultural norms.[25] When governments deregulate markets, they often become saturated with consumer products. Companies hope to distinguish their goods through advertising, which often appeals to certain forms of identification – middle class or luxury, masculinity or femininity, family or regional values, alternative lifestyles or youthful enjoyment. Specifically neoliberalism shifts the meaning of 'citizenship' so that citizens often participate in the political process through the purchase of commodities, in ways that reinforce privatisation and eroded citizenship rights.[26]

These values are often evident on social media as well. From motivational memes which encourage viewers to take responsibility for achieving their goals despite difficult life circumstances to selfies that conspicuously display the trendiest brand-name accessories, neoliberal ideology has pervaded even this seemingly unencumbered media form. This is not the case for the majority of social media users in Alto Hospicio, but is certainly true of most users in Santiago and even Iquique.

Given the ways in which the private mining industry and tax-free imports have bolstered Iquique's economy, it could be considered a poster city for neoliberal policies. Private industry continues to thrive in the area. Private banks and healthcare companies provide infrastructure, while nationally and internationally known private businesses such as Walmart (known as Lider in Chile), Home Depot (known as Sodimac) and McDonald's provide commercial outlets for residents. The main attraction in Iquique is the beach flanked by restaurants and nightclubs. The Dreams Casino is a popular spot not only for slot machines and craps tables, but also for weekly concerts. Of course the Zofri on the north side of the city is popular for buying imports, ranging from children's toys and clothing to new HD flat-screen televisions and cars from China, Japan and the United States. Iquique even boasts an 'American-style' mall with over 100 shops and a ten-screen movie theatre. The food court offers international favourites such as KFC and Yogen Fruz, as well as national chains such as Doggis serving *completos* [hot dogs]. In contrast to Alto Hospicio, a handful of cafes, restaurants and bars offer free Wi-Fi to patrons.

The absence of Wi-Fi in Alto Hospicio may be indicative of a more extensive difference. Alto Hospicio is a city built within, and because of, the economic outcomes of neoliberalism, but the consequences of this ideology have been quite different here than in most places. Businesses of the sort that can afford extensive advertisement have never placed importance on attracting Hospiceños as potential customers. This has lessened the influence of 'keeping up with the Joneses'-type class consciousness; Hospiceños generally see little value in conspicuous consumption and feel no shame in seeking assistance from social services. Consequently Hospiceños retain their expectation that the government should provide services such as housing, healthcare and education. The lack of large-scale advertising has also left the market open for the types of small, family-owned companies that are often eclipsed by larger businesses. In Alto Hospicio this trend promotes the valuing of community over 'outsiders', and means that to a large extent the association of consumer products with certain forms of identification has never taken root.

In contrast most Chilean cities, including Iquique and Santiago, represent a neoliberal system as it was intended by economic architects such as Friedman – one in which private businesses provide for most

Fig. 1.8 Billboard advertisement in central Iquique for Zofri Tommy Hilfiger shop

needs and people are 'free' to consume products that they see as con-tributing to their sense of self. And this neoliberal system is central to the fact that most middle- and upper-class Chileans see their country as more 'Europeanised' or 'Americanised' than its neighbours, citing the stable government, military and economy, as well as the world-class cos-mopolitan city of Santiago.

The International Monetary Fund and World Bank have used Chile's free-market economy as a model for the region.[27] Santiago, in particular, provides proof that the 'modernity' associated with neoliberal econom-ics places Chile among the most highly developed nations of the world.[28] Santiago is home to the best Chilean universities, which represent some of the highest ranked educational institutions in Latin America.[29] It is also home to the national football team, which presents a serious challenge to the best teams in the world. In terms of art and literature Chileans have made contributions to world-renowned collections, and Santiago boasts museums and historical sites showcasing the lives of well-known Chileans such as Pablo Neruda and Isabel Allende.[30] Musicians such as Victor Jara and Violeta Parra are still revered, and recent popular acts such as Gepe have gained international fame. Chile is also home to annual music festivals such as Lollapalooza Chile, which attract musicians from around the world and hundreds of thousands of their fans.

Most Chileans in central urban areas conceptualise the nation not as *mestizo* [mixed race] nor multi-ethnic, but as homogenous, and in fact homogenously white.[31] This homogeneity and claims to modernity 'bind the nation with a sense of "exceptionalism", as most Chileans look at their country as a beacon of stability amidst a rather chaotic set of neighbouring countries'.[32] Yet many Chileans in central urban areas also identify the poor living conditions in places such as Alto Hospicio as a symptom of national decline that conflicts with with a more prevalent national narrative of modernity.

Life on the margins

While Santiago appears comparable to cosmopolitan cities on any continent, Alto Hospicio looks and feels like another world. To travel the 2,000 km between Alto Hospicio and Santiago takes about 30 hours by bus. Hospiceños experience this profound distance as both physical and figurative. Rather than perceiving themselves to be a part of this developed nation, Hospiceños view themselves as representatives of the country's inequality. Chile's high per-capita income is mitigated by its standing in 2015 as the developed nation with the highest inequality in the world.[33] So while median income may be around US$20,000, even the most prosperous Hospiceños – those who work in mining – make only about US$8,000 a year. Those working outside the mining industry usually earn about half of that. Residents of Alto Hospicio watch as most of the profits from their region are funnelled back into economic transactions in the national capital or sent abroad. Many Hospiceños feel ignored by national politicians and exploited by international industry.[34] To them Santiago often appears as a symbol of the economic exploitation of the region, and of the nation's economic inequalities in general.

Lessie Jo Frazier suggests that a unifying force for northern Chileans is their 'profound sense of abandonment and persistence'.[35] This sense of abandonment in many ways conditions the ways in which Hospiceños understand their position within the nation-state. Through a lens of marginality, many Hospiceños see themselves as peripheral, defined in contrast to the perceived centre of Santiago. Marginality is often used as a category of analysis within the social sciences, generally to describe the conditions of people who struggle to gain societal and spatial access to resources and full participation in political life.[36] In this view marginalised people are socially, economically, politically and legally excluded, and therefore vulnerable to a host of forms of structural violence.[37]

Marginality is defined and described along both societal and spatial axes. The societal axis focuses on demography, religion, culture, social structure, economics, politics and access to resources, emphasising the underlying causes of exclusion, inequality, social injustice and spatial segregation of people.[38] The spatial dimension of marginality is primarily based on physical location and distance from centres of development – areas lying at the edge of, or poorly integrated into, local, national and global systems. The two axes intersect when marginal spaces are considered dirty and unhealthy, dangerous, disorganised and threatening to the established order, leading to depictions of the inhabitants of marginal *barrios* themselves as marginal people: 'backwards, aggressive, and primitive or uncivilized in nature, qualities that their geographical position on the urban periphery supposedly reflects'.[39] In both senses marginality is not a static state, but a process that emerges and evolves with time in various types and scales in socio-economical and geo-political environments. Thus a person or group is not marginal, but *marginalised*, actively positioned as such through the deployment of power.[40]

Yet, as Goldstein points out, anthropological writing about marginal areas – sometimes referred to as *barrios, favelas, barriadas, colonias populares*, shantytowns, encampments or *tomas* – have contested assumptions that marginal urban citizens are alienated and lacking agency to effect change over their circumstances.[41] Instead anthropologists have pointed out the ways in which marginalised peoples and places are economically and culturally integrated into larger urban society, effectively engaging in struggles to improve their living conditions.[42] Yet despite this work the idea of marginality continues to figure prominently in popular and official ideologies of spatial and cultural identification and categorisation in urban Latin American society.[43]

I use marginality here then not as a theoretical principle, but as a way that Hospiceños identify.[44] In actively distancing themselves from Santiago – both in daily life and through their online activity – Hospiceños identify as marginalised citizens through visual modes, discourses about personal relationships, ways of configuring their associations with production and consumption and, perhaps most importantly, in their engagement with politics and national citizenship. In this sense marginality is neither an analytical term nor a static identity, but something collectively and actively produced.[45] Through this production Hospiceños categorise themselves as that which is 'unlike the centre', while also instantiating a self-understanding[46] that includes their social location as peripheral.

Evelyn, who moved to Alto Hospicio from Antofagasta in the early 2000s, often used social media to express her experiences as ones of abandonment by the state. Having lived in a *toma* for almost a decade, she often complained about the lack of social services available, blaming their absence on the national government. Evelyn's husband Marco worked a seven-day shift in a mine about four hours from Alto Hospicio, leaving her alone with her ten-year-old son every other week. During this time Evelyn devoted most of her time to local campaigns, for example opposing a sewage plant in her new neighbourhood or advocating for more children's playgrounds. She had also been involved in recent mayoral campaigns and helped with the 2012 census. She explained to me:

> I know that if I want something done, I have to do it. The politicians aren't going to help me. Santiago isn't going to help me. But I'm a fighter and even though they are absent I persevere.

In this complaint Evelyn both identifies herself as speaking from the periphery and distances herself from 'Santiago' as a symbol of the centre. These sentiments are reflected in her social media use. Evelyn created a Facebook group to unite 'outraged' Alto Hospicio residents for social justice causes. These include the sewage plant and playgrounds mentioned above, as well as simply spreading information about corruption in the regional and national governments. She also uses WhatsApp extensively to organise citizens' meetings, most recently focused on bargaining collectively for better electricity rates. Although her personal Facebook page is peppered with funny videos and pictures of her young son, it also has a strong base in political memes and videos that denounce hypocrisies and inequalities perpetuated by the national government.

Through her online presence Evelyn both claims identification as a marginalised citizen as well as speaks back to the types of institutional and governmental power she believes lie at the root of these inequalities. Evelyn identifies herself in contrast to what she sees as an exploitative Chilean government and positions herself alongside her neighbours as 'outraged', marginalised citizens advocating for their rights. In doing so she positions committed individuals as 'good citizens' while positioning the government, and those who support or benefit from its corruption, as part of a national problem. She demonstrates that her allegiance is to the local community rather than a form of national citizenship. By doing so through social media she positions Facebook and similar platforms as the appropriate space in which these public-sphere debates should take place.

Erasing difference, highlighting normativity

To return to Nicole, her Facebook post declaring herself *Hospiceña, Nortina* and only then *Chilena* did much more than highlight her allegiances. Perhaps more importantly, it erased certain other possible forms of identification that might have been salient. Her gender is implicit in the Spanish noun formation, in which personal descriptors ending in 'a' indicate a woman as antecedent (i.e. Nortina-feminine vs. Nortino-masculine, or sometimes used as a gender-neutral form). Yet she does not draw attention to her gender here, as she could have done by saying 'Soy una mujer Nortina' [I am a northern woman]. Equally she emphasises location, rather than a particular political party or stance. Location also replaces the possibility of identifying her Quechua indigenous origin in this post, which in many contexts, even in other regions of Chile, would be relevant to themes of citizenship and nationalism. I only learned that Nicole had Quechua ancestry after knowing her for more than a year, when she filled out a survey and I watched her enter 'Quechua' into the ethnicity box. For many Hospiceños, the elements of their personal experience with which they identify are distilled both on social media and in daily life.

Of course, all people at all times erase aspects of themselves that could form the basis of a particular way of identifying. Identification is an active process, which often involves highlighting certain aspects of the self and reducing the emphasis on others, sometimes in ways that exceed conscious awareness.[47] The point is not that Nicole neglected to mention some of these aspects, but rather that there was a clear trend in Alto Hospicio to ignore or erase particular forms of identifying – those commonly connected to 'identity politics' – such as indigeneity, non-traditional gender ideologies and class differences. And these erasures are further amplified on social media.

Rather than aiming to distinguish themselves from others, many individuals in Alto Hospicio highlight their desire for normativity. Viewed from an anthropological perspective, the concept of normativity refers to the everyday assumptions individuals make in a particular context, and the way in which they consider these assumptions to be natural. These assumptions have to do with what is considered correct or incorrect, just or unjust, appropriate or inappropriate, right or wrong. Hospiceños have a sense of what their neighbours consider to be appropriate, and they generally follow those guidelines rather than challenge them. Of course such guidelines exist, and are followed by, most people in any context. These guidelines change according to the society or situation in which they emerge, but the fact that most people abide by them is precisely what makes them normative.

In Alto Hospicio, however, those guidelines often encourage individuals to fit in rather than seek to distinguish themselves from others. Bourdieu famously argued that those with assets such as education and cultural knowledge create a sense of 'distinction' for themselves by determining what constitutes taste, and thus naturalising differences between 'high culture' and 'low culture'.[48] Upward mobility, then, is about not just economic means but expressing distinction through taste as well. Yet residents of Alto Hospicio actively reject attempts at distinguishing themselves from others in the community. The norm of Alto Hospicio then, is doubly normative: most individuals abide by 'correct' behaviour which requires them to refrain from overly distinguishing themselves from others.

In looking at Hospiceños' online media, it is clear that a general sense of being marginalised is highlighted; forms of identifying that could compete, in contrast, are often left in the background or even erased. In fact the erasure of ideologically discordant elements from identification is key to its social utility. This erasure is particularly important in Alto Hospicio because identifying as marginalised, rather than more specific subaltern forms of identification, excludes those who are most marginalised in favour of a more general, normative sense of marginality.

For Chileans living in Alto Hospicio, people are rarely categorised as anything other than *mestizo*,[49] or of mixed Spanish and indigenous ancestry. Many Hospiceños in fact expressed sentiments such as 'pure races do not exist here'. Southern and central Chileans who have moved to the city quickly integrate with those born in the north. Census projections suggest that around 2,000 individuals from the Mapuche indigenous group of southern Chile live in Alto Hospicio,[50] but they are essentially absent from public discourses and understandings of race and racial relations,[51] as are Afro-descended Chileans. Both groups are considered merely Chileans, blending into the tapestry of brown *mestizo* shades that make up the human landscape.

However, certain other nationalities are racialised instead. Bolivians and Peruvians living in Chile often do not conform to the idealised *mestizaje* (*mestizo*-ness). While their skin colour does not differ significantly from darker Chileans they often have phenotypic differences evident from their Aymara ancestry, for example a shorter, broader stature and what many refer to as 'indigenous facial features' including close-set eyes and a large nose. In contrast to Mapuche, who are considered to be phenotypically closer to the *mestizo* standard, Aymara are thought to appear more indigenous, falling outside of the *mestizo* spectrum. Bolivians and more indigenous-looking Peruvians are also characterised as speaking slowly and softly, and many Hospiceños claimed they have a particular unpleasant odour. 'It must be their food!' one older Hospiceña woman explained.

Iquique boasts a *barrio boliviano* [Bolivian neighbourhood], several Colombian social clubs and countless Peruvian restaurants which often function as Peruvian social centres as well. Alto Hospicio by contrast has very few public clubs or social spaces dedicated to foreign migrants. While some immigrants such as Colombians and Peruvians from urban areas integrate more easily into social life, Bolivians are

Fig. 1.9 Graffiti reading '*Cholos fuera! Bolis, pata raja! Monos culiao*' [trans: 'Cholos (urban indigenous Andeans) get out! Dirty feeted Bolivians! Fucking monkeys']

excluded from the collective sociality and subject to discriminatory discourses. Bolivia, a nation in which 60 per cent of citizens consider themselves indigenous (and up to 74 per cent in the Altiplano region that borders Chile), is also ranked as the poorest economy in the continental Americas, outranking only that of Haiti in the hemisphere.[52] Bolivian immigrants are often treated by Chileans as second-class residents of the city.

This discrimination is closely associated with the politics of indigeneity in Chile, and the benefits provided to indigenous Chileans as a 'vulnerable category'. Many Chileans believe that individuals with indigenous surnames (whether citizens since birth or naturalised citizens) have greater access to social services such as public housing, healthcare and even education (although this perception is actually incorrect). In the racial logic of Alto Hospicio, the categories of 'indigenous', 'Bolivian' and at times 'Peruvian' are conflated to mean a foreign racial underclass; terms are often used interchangeably, so that nation of origin stands in for race.[53] By grouping these international migrants into a single category they are racialised and stigmatised, much as local people view economic migrants around the world. Racial tensions rarely manifest in violence, but stigma and outright discrimination against Altiplano immigrants is undeniable. As one informant mentioned to me, 'Racism is the same here as everywhere, except we don't hit them, we just ignore them. We don't insult them to their faces, we do it behind their backs.' Ignoring immigrants often serves to exclude them from public social life and the imaginary of racial homogeneity that dates to the colonial period. As Bosniak notes, notions of belonging have inherently exclusionary tendencies: some individuals must inevitably be constructed as 'outside' the community in order for the 'inside' to have value.[54]

While Colombians, Peruvians and Bolivians often retain strong connections to their countries of birth citizenship, hoping to return home after benefiting from northern Chile's economy, nationality-based groups in Alto Hospicio do not exist in the public eye. Though Colombian men are known to socialise on a particular corner of the central plaza, and in neighbourhoods on the outskirts of Alto Hospicio one can often hear parties playing Bolivian Morenada music on weekend nights, these social groups do not form official organizations or publicise their activities online or offline. They certainly do not use public social media to identify themselves as members of such social groups. While more than 11 per cent of Alto Hospicio residents are of Aymara descent, many of whom are Chilean by birth, they do not organise using indigeneity or Aymara ancestry as a way of identifying. The director of the small

Consejo Nacional Aymara [National Aymara Council] office, which occupies a nondescript building a block from the former city hall office, notes that their services are drastically underused.

This is in part because identifying as Aymara, even for Chileans, aligns oneself with foreignness and is understood as contrary to discourses of progress. In fact many people do not even know that they are indigenous until they discover their surname on a government-published list of names of indigenous origin. As noted above, appearing on this list classifies the individual as part of a 'vulnerable category' allowing them access to indigenous land and university scholarships, although not to government-funded housing and subsidised heathcare, as many assume. But instead of providing a rallying point for political rights, as it does in southern Chile's Mapuche areas,[55] indigenous identification in the North is easily glossed over or utilised in depoliticised ways only to gain access to certain governmental advantages.

Forms of identification associated with gender and sexuality are often similarly de-emphasised. A number of Hospiceños, both men and women, comment that the local women's centre is unnecessary. Indeed most of its programming involves courses such as knitting or health-conscious cooking classes in which anyone could enrol. Many Hospiceños consider the centre to be unnecessary because they believe most women feel empowered in their families and community; they see issues related to poverty and violence as affecting men and women equally. In their perception men and women have similar economic problems and face similar rates of intimate violence. Both are equally likely to be assaulted if walking alone at night. Popular discourses value women as mothers, as well as recognising women's need to have friends and a social life outside of the family. Many men also comment that they feel their wives and girlfriends are more empowered than themselves, as women generally manage finances and organise shared time within the relationship. Several young men even joke that women see girls' nights as a human right, whereas a man going out with his friends is considered highly suspicious and is often regulated by his female partner.

For lesbian, gay or bisexual individuals in Alto Hospicio, identifying as such may cause a stir within the family but is not generally publically shamed. A number of young men and women are quite open about their identification as lesbian or gay on Facebook and Instagram, often using hashtags such as #lesbichile or #instagay in their posts. Most are open with their families as well and maintain a normative lifestyle, with expected forms of wage labour aligned with their gender. It seems that only when individuals – whether they identify as gay, lesbian, bi or straight – adopt roles that cross or confound gender lines are they considered to breach social conventions.

For example, when 18-year-old Michelle told her friends that she was interested in women they initially teased her, asking if she would cut her hair, stop wearing skirts and give up studying graphic design to work in construction. The group continued to invite her along for their outings to Iquique and weekend parties, however, and after a few months hardly any of her friends thought of Michelle any differently than before. Even when she used the #lesbichile tag on Instagram, it was hardly worthy of note by her friends. In contrast lesbians who take on a 'butch' appearance and seek employment in what are considered masculine forms of work, such as mining or construction, are generally rejected by both their male colleagues and by women's social circles.

Men are subject to similar gender constraints. Pablito, a gay man in his late twenties, is happily open about his sexuality with his family. However, his mother has no idea that he is involved in organising a weekly drag performance show in Iquique. He manages performers through a separate Facebook profile using his stage name, and vigilantly controls the privacy of those posts to ensure his mother never discovers this aspect of his life. So gay and lesbian Hospiceños are generally accepted in the community, as long as they do not upset the apparent homogeneity of the community or call too much attention to themselves.

Perhaps most importantly, class distinctions in Alto Hospicio are also downplayed in an attempt to homogenise. Most people consider themselves to be in the bottom half of income in the country, but very few place themselves in the bottom 25 per cent (though official figures suggest that poverty in the city may be as high as 40 per cent). Key to this sense of class homogeneity is a collective rejection of conspicuous consumption. People who do make expensive purchases often become targets, judged and viewed with suspicion by their neighbours.

I often ate lunch with Vicky, a 50-year-old woman who had lived in Alto Hospicio for 20 years. She and her husband Jorge, a miner, moved in during the first major wave of new residents in the 1990s, along with their two young children, Alex and Gabriela. By the time I met them Gabriela had a son, Samuel, and her fiancé José had moved in with the family as well. One day, as I ate some of Vicky's famous pesto noodles, she mentioned that her neighbours across the street were building a third storey on to their home. 'They've only lived there a year,' she told me. 'Where are they getting the money? They must be narco-traffickers,' she conjectured sincerely.

On another occasion she and Gabriela spoke about another neighbour, an example of someone who had recently moved up the sand dune from Iquique and did not conform to the norms of Alto Hospicio. 'I see her Facebook posts and she's always buying expensive clothing, wearing jewellery, new shoes, new furniture. It just seems like a waste of money to me, always posting pictures, always showing off.' Gabriela jumped in, 'It's like she's *flaite* but not *flaite*.'

Flaite was a term I heard often, either in warnings or in jokes about slang terms. Something akin to 'gangsta' or 'ghetto' in English, *flaite* is both a noun and an adjective; it describes young people from poorer families, who speak in uneducated slang and are considered aggressive if not dangerous (for example, 'That *flaite* might steal your wallet' or 'Don't use that word, it's really *flaite*'). What prompted Gabriela to make the comparison with their neighbour, however, is the idea that *flaites* are known for wearing flashy brand-name clothing. In fact, that is usually how they are identified.[56] Particularly because their neighbour often posts pictures of her purchases, her 'showing off' is considered just as tactless and flashy as *flaites*. Both Vicky and Gabriela thus clarified the boundaries of what was acceptable to them in terms of home architecture, as well as self-presentation, by pointing out instances of going beyond the norms. Affronts to normativity have social consequences, most of which are reflected in moments such as Vicky and Gabriela's gossip at lunch.

Individuals such as Vicky's neighbours, with new-looking, pressed clothing from department stores in Iquique, reveal their relative affluence. Almost everyone in Alto Hospicio wears mostly second-hand clothing, bought at the local Agro market, though individuals of lower income use the same few worn T-shirts for years. Only their tattered state distinguishes them from the sea of people in simple T-shirts paired with jeans, khaki work trousers or shorts. It is rare to see a woman in high heels or a formal skirt, even when at work, while in the winter fleece jackets are common. Shoes are most often athletic styles such as Converse, Reebok or Nike brands, and in the colder months most women wear faux leather boots. Some teens adopt 'heavy metal' or 'punk' styles, but this usually means that they wear more black than colour, and occasionally have visible tattoos. Even haircuts rarely stand out from the crowd, with men sporting trimmed cuts and women long wavy styles.

Similarly, most homes conform to one of a few standard styles. In contrast to the three-storey home nearby, Vicky's house was like those of most established families with a steady income in Alto Hospicio. These houses have between three and five bedrooms on two levels, one

Fig. 1.10 Women's clothing styles for sale in Alto Hospicio's Agro market

bathroom and tiled floors. In a middle bracket, newer families often live in small, three-bedroom apartments in large complexes, such as the one where I lived. Though the apartments are quite spacious for one or two people, most families have at least three generations in the same apartment, often with five to seven members of the family sharing the three small bedrooms. In poorer neighbourhoods homes are more likely to be built by the families who live in them, sometimes without legal right to the land. These houses have concrete floors and one or two bedrooms into which they fit multiple beds like the pieces of a jigsaw puzzle.

Fig. 1.11 A barber's shop display of possible hair styles

Living arrangements clearly vary widely and are usually organised by neighbourhood: the relatively wealthier families live in homes in the central, oldest parts of the city, and the poorest live on the outskirts of the city in *tomas*. In part, however, architecture helps to homogenise even these differences, as almost all homes, whatever the neighbourhood, have a high fence or wall surrounding them, with some sort of sharp points deterring unauthorised entry. These fences serve not only to provide security; they also obscure views of the home, making differences in quality and size hard to perceive from outside.

Within the home, certain material goods also help to identify social class. Electronics are considered necessary, even as prevalent cultural norms in Alto Hospicio eschew the types of consumerist ideals that characterise the middle classes of middle and higher income countries. A computer of some sort is essential for all but the very poorest of families, while a new Xbox is a true sign of means. While the prevalence of somewhat new technology may seem at odds with identification as marginalised citizens, they buy these items relatively cheaply from the Zofri mall. They are prioritised over other consumer goods, including clothing, new furniture and even seemingly basic necessities such as hot water or repairs to damaged ceilings and walls.[57]

Aside from electronics, most home goods are purchased secondhand. Families buy appliances such as used refrigerators and stoves at the outdoor market of Alto Hospicio, or online through Facebook groups such as 'Buy and Sell Alto Hospicio'. For most families televisions, stereos, video game systems and smartphones are among the few expensive consumer goods that are considered important despite a family's limited financial resources. These represent a significant expenditure in a community where many people support a family on the national minimum salary of $210,000 CLP (Chilean Pesos) a month, or about US$340. As social media has become ever more important to daily life, these devices that Hospiceños use to connect are now considered essential.

Homes are especially important because there are few social spaces for entertainment and consumption in Alto Hospicio. While neoliberal economic contexts are usually characterised by a proliferation of businesses catering to entertainment and lifestyle, most businesses in Alto Hospicio are family-owned, and few of these families have ambitions for a business any larger than that which will sustain their single family on its profits. Most restaurants operate as take-away windows, though the city's eight Chinese restaurants are popular for a sit-down meal. The city has one pool hall, two bars and one strip club (for men only). There are no gourmet restaurants, nor any department stores, cinemas, bowling alleys or casinos. Nor, in contrast to many Latin American contexts, is the central plaza used much as a social space for meeting and conversing with neighbours. Instead the private home is the hub of social life.

In most families, meals are especially important for spending time together. Breakfast is less formal, but the whole family returns to the house for lunch, the largest meal of the day. Over dishes such as rice and meat or noodles with tuna and tomato sauce, the family takes a break from daily work to share an hour together. Usually only the miners, working several hours away from the city, are absent. There are plenty of small lunch restaurants in the centre of Alto Hospicio, but these usually cater to men from other towns who work in Alto Hospicio doing construction. Residents prefer to pick up popular pre-made meals of fried chicken and fried potatoes, or *colaciones* of noodles, vegetables, meat and salad, available at small take-away windows all over the city, to eat at home with the family.

Evening tea, known as *once* [pronounced 'own-say', like 11 in Spanish], is also a family affair, accompanied by bread and cheese, avocado or sandwich meat, while the radio or television relays the day's news. The family, as well as friends or extended family who often come from another neighbourhood in the city to partake, traditionally linger for hours at the table, a time called *sobremesa* in which they discuss the news or family and neighbourhood gossip. In recent years, however, adolescents often race away from the table after eating to return to Facebook, and even younger children ask to be excused in order to continue a game of Angry Birds. With the ubiquity of social media, public spaces are no longer necessary for socialising. One can be connected to any number of friends and family without leaving the home.

These customs also reveal the ways that social class bears on daily life in terms of economic resources and comparable social standing. Social class also helps to shape cultural norms and cultural outlook.[58] In this respect most Hospiceños are quite similar, subscribing to the same unassuming normativity as most of their neighbours. They identify with a general, locally based sense of marginality, which deemphasises neoliberal accoutrements of big homes and fancy clothes in favour of commonalities shared by all members of the community. Almost all individuals in Alto Hospicio, even with their personal differences, still fit into this scene. Their life plans rarely involve exploits other than finding a job and a partner, making a home together, raising children (and maybe a pet) and enjoying cable television in the evening on a large flat screen, while chatting with friends on a Samsung smart phone.

Very few people finish a university degree. For young men the mining industry is more lucrative and has more job stability. Although contracts usually last between six months and three years, there always seems to be another mining operation in need of workers. Most are content to remain in Alto Hospicio, rarely expressing desire to move to Iquique, let alone to another region. Few people aspire to the types of higher education or employment beyond options available in the region. Though most young people can quote from Hollywood films, few have a desire to become proficient in English or Portuguese. Younger adults particularly love making fun of the Open English commercial for language learning on television, mockingly repeating English words from the advertisements such as 'hospitalisation' and 'Mr. Fitzpatrick'.

Though travelling within the region is common, taking a trip of more than a few hours by bus is considered a rather big deal. Trips to other parts of Chile usually involve bus rides of more than 24 hours and cost at least $60,000 CLP or US$100 for a round trip (about one-third to one-fifth of the cost of flying). While some young people hope to move to Santiago (particularly those who have family there), most Hospiceños who grow up in the North see Santiago and other large urban areas as full of crime and chaos. While they do not necessarily believe Alto Hospicio to be ideal, they think of it as a middle ground that offers the conveniences of urban life (as opposed to the small mining villages) without the annoyances of crowds on the Santiago metro, *barrios* full of petty criminals and the pollution and dirt associated with city life. In fact many at times refer to the national capital as 'Santiasco' (*asco* is the Spanish word for disgusting).

One popular meme, shared as simple text on a white background, portrays the vision many Hospiceños have of Santiago. The text says:

Living in Santiago is. . .1) Wake up at 5 am, kiss your children while they sleep and arrive at work at 8am while trying to avoid being assaulted. 2) Stop working for half an hour to eat crappy food or drink coffee while trying not to be assaulted. 3) Leave work at 6:30 and arrive home at 9, while avoiding assaults. 4) Kiss your children while they sleep. 5) Shower, eat something, and try to sleep for 6 hours. Thanks but I think I'd like to stay here in my region.

Through actions that portray all Hospiceños as similar, and those that distance them from or express distaste for Santiago, they create a binary between the normative, marginalised people with whom they identify and a wholly different, consumerist, cosmopolitan, exploitative and 'disgusting' world of Others. Ariztia[59] points out that in Santiago both the location of a newly purchased home and the consumer items residents use to decorate it are closely connected to a sense of 'distinction',[60] as well as belonging and identity.[61] These are 'points at which [class] categories are actually negotiated and performed'.[62] The general anti-consumerist discourses and aesthetics of Alto Hospicio combine with tendencies to group all within a general sense of marginality rather than appeal to subdivided senses of identity politics. In so doing they construct a binary between the good, hard-working but exploited and marginalised population of Alto Hospicio and the superficial, consumerist, capitalist, exploitative imagined residents of Santiago.

By conforming to the aesthetic and (non)aspirational normativity of Alto Hospicio, residents socially locate themselves as belonging to a marginal place, content with a marginal lifestyle, and even express pride in identifying as marginal. They do not highlight their autonomous individuality, but rather present themselves as closely connected to networks based on family, friendship, work relationships and community engagement. In terms of race and class, individuals in Alto Hospicio put forth a great deal of effort to maintain a sense of homogeneity, rather than emphasising distinctions between different social groups.

They achieve this, to a large extent, by highlighting ways of identifying that support ideals of community and working-class pride, rather than forms of identification that distinguish between nationality, race or ethnicity, or forms of lifestyle that are rooted in consumption. So while a place with so much migration and mixture might easily display significant cultural clash, jostling and juxtaposition of histories, traditions, customs and concerns, these differences are neutralised in Alto Hospicio into a visible normativity. Such normativity is particularly visible through Hospiceños' use of social media. Identifying with a general sense of marginality is especially highlighted, while other more particular forms of identification are erased.

Ordinary people, extraordinary citizenship

These normativities, both online and offline, are key to citizenship in its various strands. Being a 'good' citizen in most neoliberal contexts involves blending into the population, as a 'proper' member who reproduces, finds employment and aspires to 'possessions, property and wealth'.[63] Yet in Alto Hospicio residents place importance on distinguishing themselves from what they see as a dominant yet exploitative form of mainstream citizenship, instead positioning their marginalised citizenship as that which represents 'real' Chileans.

Like many Hospiceños 30-year-old Francisco does not post much original content on his Facebook page. His infrequent status messages rarely even amount to a full sentence. More than half of his profile pictures are photographs of celebrities, cats or cartoons, rather than images of himself. Those that do feature Francisco portray him in his work uniform from a loading dock at the port or in fatigues from his time in the military. However, he does post multiple memes, videos and music every day. Most of the memes in particular play on themes of marginality and difference with a sense of humour. One meme he posted portrays Adam and Eve in the Garden of Eden. Eve asks, 'Adam, where do you think we are?' to which Adam responds, 'We are in Chile, Eve. Don't you see that we're without clothing, without food, without a house, without education and without hospitals? And they still tell us we're in paradise!'

In posting such memes Francisco uses his Facebook page not only to identify himself as being marginalised, but to position this marginality as central to his sense of what it means to be Chilean. This particular meme positions the real Chile and real Chileans as those who go without things such as hospitals and education. Rather than suggesting that Alto Hospicio is not included in the imagined icon of Chileanness, Francisco, like many Hospiceños, repositions his marginality as true Chileanness. The political and economic elite of places such as Santiago, meanwhile, are positioned as outside of this sense of belonging – those who *tell* others that they're in paradise.

In a sense Francisco here redefines what Chilean citizenship looks like from a marginal perspective. When Hospiceños oppose themselves to their imaginary of Santiago residents, they claim being marginalised as the norm, the condition of the *real* Chile. In doing so they mark their own citizenship as that of 'good citizen-subjects' – contrasted with those who claim citizenship based on identity politics rather than identifying in solidarity, consumption rather than hard work and working-class identification and, of course, political power rather than marginalised subjectivity. They move beyond identifying with legal status and political rights to highlight public participation and feelings of belonging instead. They privilege the city above the region and the region above the nation, and emphasise cultural citizenship above political citizenship. The majority of Hospiceños also prioritise a normative sense of being marginalised above the identity politics of gender, sexuality and indigeneity.

In identifying themselves as marginalised and in portraying this marginality as ordinary, Hospiceños reverse the logic of centre and periphery. They seek to position themselves as 'true' Chileans, while those in the 'centre' of the country – symbolised by Santiago – are cosmopolitan Others. This is possible in part because of social media, which allows them a space to express such a reversal in which theoretically those in Santiago or other world centres may see their posts. Hospiceños overwhelmingly concentrate their social media use on local concerns in which normativity rather than distinction is valued. Hospiceño normativity emphasises unassuming aspirations and utilitarian life goals focused on the local community, with very little emphasis on anything that could be considered fantasy. Thus there is something quite extraordinary about the ordinariness of Alto Hospicio.

The form of this project

The extraordinary nature of the ordinariness of Alto Hospicio is something that I came to recognise over time. Colleagues and acquaintances in Santiago, and even Hospiceños themselves have questioned my choice of such a marginal city as a field site for this project. In response, I usually explain that studies of social media are most often based in metropolitan centres, including New York, Madrid, Cairo or indeed Santiago, where new forms of capitalism, cosmopolitan identities or mass demonstrations are forged in online spheres. In looking at the use of social media in these already cosmopolitan contexts we see digital technologies as forces of global citizenship, homogenisation, democracy and modernity. Yet looking at social media in peripheral places reveals how individuals' adoption of social media in everyday life contests these grand narratives of homogenisation. This book explores the ways in which Hospiceños use social media – ways that conflict with and challenge assumptions about such media's cosmopolitan and revolutionary powers.

While some critics suggest that a project on social media might be successfully carried out entirely online, an important contribution of this particular project is the study of the *relationship* between what happens online and what happens through other media and face-to-face interactions. This combination is essential to maintaining the anthropological commitment to a holistic study of human beings.[64] If I had never set foot in Alto Hospicio, I would have never appreciated the ways in which the history of Chile and the region, as well as the founding of Alto Hospicio itself and its current political economy, so intricately influence how social media is used. Understanding marginalised citizenship 'on the ground' was essential for understanding it 'online'. I hope this book will contribute to a better understanding of the ways in which identification, normativity, marginality and citizenship are practiced through social media, but will also challenge essentialised depictions of social media as a universally democratising technology

This book is based on 15 months of field work in Alto Hospicio, spaced between September 2013 and June 2015. As part of this ethnographic project I lived with Hospiceños, ate with them, travelled on public buses and in private cars, attended neighbourhood committee meetings, birthday parties and funerals, shared beers and even survived major earthquakes alongside them. I also watched what Hospiceños did on social networking sites, including Facebook (110 friends), Instagram (following 75 users), Tumblr (following 40 users), Twitter (following 30 accounts) and WhatsApp (25 individual contacts and 5 groups). Rather than taking the users' actions at face value, I also asked them to reflect on these practices in interviews, casual conversations and two different surveys. In conducting these surveys, the help of my research assistant Jorge Castro Gárate was invaluable.

I also spent many evenings chatting with my informants on Facebook messenger or planning weekend parties through WhatsApp. Liking and commenting on Facebook posts was essential to the job, though never insincere. And finally, during the writing of this book, I have constantly kept in touch via Facebook and WhatsApp in order to fact check and clarify details. Just like the in-person methods of ethnographic research described above, social media equally allows the ethnographer to interact with informants, to see how informants interact with others and to gain valuable insights into people's lives.

Because Alto Hospicio is such a distinct place, there was little point in anonymising the city. However, the names of people and some institutions that appear here are pseudonyms. I am lucky to have done this work in a city, rather than a small town, so that it is not obvious to a local reader that I am writing about their cousin's friend; I could be referring to any one of hundreds of miners who lives in the city with his wife and three children and enjoys riding his motorbike on weekends. Of course, when anonymising, some of the richness of individuals and their lives is inevitably lost. My hope is that by using information with care I have struck a balance between protecting informants' interests and providing the reader with details that allow understanding of those I write about as real humans, rather than two-dimensional characters or simply sources of 'data'.

Beyond Alto Hospicio, this project strives to be comparative. Few ethnographic projects use comparison explicitly, but this work is part of a global study in which nine different anthropologists have studied social media in the same ways, at the same time, in field sites around the world. The Why We Post series is not only able to provide in-depth analysis of social media practices in each particular place, but also to allow for direct comparison with the other sites.

Like the other titles in the Why We Post series this book follows a standard format, though keeping with themes of citizenship, marginality and normativity discussed in this introduction. Chapter 2 explores the different forms of social media used in Alto Hospicio and how these are at times conditioned by marginality, while at other times they may be used to contest the life conditions which Hospiceños find disagreeable. Chapter 3 gives clear examples of Hospiceños' images on social media, looking at how presenting oneself as a 'good citizen' is central to curation even in visual communications. In Chapter 4 I describe the ways in which Hospiceños use social media to create, strengthen and represent intimate relationships – those between family, friends and romantic partners, often in the service of maintaining forms of normativity within the community. Chapter 5 concentrates on tensions between presenting the self as a productive citizen rather than a consumer, and the ways in which these tendencies are conditioned by gender and sexuality. In Chapter 6 I look at how Hospiceños imagine their place within a wider world, and the ways in which concentrating on local concerns reinforces community solidarity and a general sense of marginalised identification rather than more specific subaltern forms of identification. Finally in Chapter 7 I condense the information I learned through both in-person ethnography and involvement with Hospiceños on social media, giving insight into how such usage is important in people's lives and exploring what this may tell us more broadly about marginality, citizenship and normativity in the twenty-first century. As this book demonstrates in various social spheres, from the family to politics, it is precisely the normativity of social media in Alto Hospicio that makes a seemingly ordinary medium quite extraordinary.

2
The social media landscape: Performing citizenship online

On a cloudy afternoon I met Andres, Francisca and her fiancé Franklin in the main plaza before walking to a *colación* take-away restaurant. We entered the front of the shop and paid $3,000 CLP (US$5) each to the cashier, who handed us tickets to claim our food at the counter. There we peered through the cloudy glass at the possible offerings: beef, pan-fried chicken, noodles with pesto sauce, potatoes with mayonnaise, lettuce, rice and the typical Chilean salad consisting of tomatoes, onions and coriander. I gave my order of chicken, noodles and salad at the counter, then sat next to the other three on folding chairs along the wall. As we waited for the white polystyrene boxes containing our lunches to be put into plastic bags, we all simultaneously scrolled through Facebook on our mobile phones. Francisca began giggling at her cousin's new profile picture, in which she was striking an uncharacteristically serious pose. Franklin looked over her shoulder, commenting 'It looks like a Fotolog picture' – a reference to an online photo sharing site popular in the early 2000s. 'Oh, Fotolog!' laughed Andres. 'The good old days. Remember Terra? Remember chat?'

As we walked back to the apartment with our packaged lunches, Andres reminisced:

> When I was in high school we all began using chat. We had groups, so you'd just write 'hello' and throw it out there. We did that the whole time in school, everyone chatting like that. Before that it was just on paper. You pass the paper to someone during free time in school, and then they give you an answer later. How boring right! It was like that in Alto Hospicio before internet. When internet arrived it was massive. It was 1999, maybe 1998, when it started in a basic way. And people started using chat in Terra [Networks], with that horrible sound the weeeeee-dum-dum-uuuuuuuu [imitating dial-up modem noise].

After I revealed that I had never heard of Fotolog or Terra, the three began explaining to me the different internet-based communications that had been popular in Alto Hospicio over the years. The very first web portal was Terra, which allowed for text-based communication in an open chat forum. Shortly after MSN messenger arrived. Around the same time the photo-posting site Fotolog became popular, particularly because it allowed users to receive updates about their FFs, or favourite friends. Hospiceños began using IRC chat, which offered channels for individual cities in Chile. Next Latin Chat took over as the most used network; it provided different discussion forums, based on location, but also interest (beauty, films, football) or different sexual preferences (including 'erotic', gay, lesbian and group sex). This was also the time of Sexy-o-No, a site on which one could vote on others' uploaded photographs as 'sexy' or 'not'. 'I always got "sexy"!' Andres boasted as he raised his arms in victory.

With our lunches spread out on the table, and a 3-litre bottle of Coca Cola shared among us, the three continued to recount the history of social media sites used in Alto Hospicio. Around 2005 everything seemed to change, as people moved from simpler, text-based or picture-based internet interaction to platforms that combined everything – chatting, picture sharing, videos and commentary. There was a 'big jump to MySpace in those days,' said Franklin as he took a bite of potato. 'Remember Badoo?' asked Francisca and the two men nearly squealed with excitement. 'Badoo. Badoo! Oh it was much better than MySpace,' said Andres. 'And the video boom was around then too!'

YouTube and Google video sharing had become very popular, but more importantly the site El Rellano began aggregating user-uploaded funny videos of pets doing silly things and people getting hit by sports equipment. Blogs allowed people to combine all of these aspects of the internet as well, enabling users to share videos, upload their own pictures and write short commentaries. Friends could (indeed were expected to) comment. The popularity of these early blogs eventually led to the use of Tumblr. 'Finally Facebook arrived in 2008,' said Andres as he laid down his fork and refilled his glass with soda.

'So Facebook is the most important social media today?' I asked, trying to spur on the discussion. Andres explained:

> Social media today, well it's a lot like a *colación*. You don't want all the same thing. It's better if you have a mixture. But you don't want just a tiny amount of everything. You have to choose. And some things are more important. For example, you can't have social media without Facebook. You can't have a *colación* without the meat.

'And what if you're vegetarian?' Francisca challenged him. Franklin jumped in, 'Then you have Google+! It's not Facebook, but the people who use it *think* it's just as good.'

With this colourful history, the three not only gave me a sense of how important different forms of internet-based communications had been over the last 15 years. They also revealed the ways in which new forms of communications media had been quickly taken up and normalised. Such technology is almost seamlessly integrated into daily lives, until the next big 'boom' comes along and something new is rapidly adopted. Overall their account demonstrates the ways in which new media do not significantly shift individuals' lives, but simply become new conduits for enduring practices. In particular social media constitute a new –and possibly the most important – public sphere in which notions of citizenship are performed and debated, all while reproducing the forms of normativity most prevalent in the city.

Modernity and mass communications in Chile

Andres, Francisca and Franklin's story of internet communications in Alto Hospicio was only the most recent chapter of a much longer history of mass communications in Chile. The country has always been in the vanguard of telecommunications in South America, coinciding with urban Chileans' propensity to represent their country as a forerunner of modernity on the continent. In 1852, just 15 years after the commercial electrical telegraph was invented, the first telegraph message was sent in Chile. The next year the telegraph service became public. Chileans began to use telephones in the 1880s and underwater cables were laid in the 1890s.[1]

Chile is currently one of the most engaged social media markets worldwide, averaging 9.5 hours per day per visitor to social media sites. In fact the country ranks as the third most highly penetrated market for Facebook in the world, behind the Philippines and Turkey. Florencio Utrera from the University of Chile was credited with introducing the internet to Chile in 1992. Its use spread quickly due to deregulated telecommunications, which encouraged private companies to compete over prices and services. Widespread usage began in urban areas in the north of the country by the end of the decade. Throughout the 1990s the Chilean government controlled prices, expanded internet usage in schools and offered internet training to NGOs, government officials and businesses. Today Chile has the highest rate of overall broadband connection penetration in Latin America, and government projects continue to dedicate resources. On 28 June 2013 former President Sebastián Piñera announced he would focus on increasing the national number of users to bring the internet to 80 per cent of Chilean homes. He promised to lower connection costs and expand high speed broadband, providing free Wi-Fi in every community throughout the country.[2]

Logically this high penetration of internet access places Chileans quite centrally in global media participation, but Alto Hospicio and the entire Great North of Chile continue to lag behind. While many communities have free Wi-Fi access in their central plazas, for example, there are no free Wi-Fi points in Alto Hospicio. A few internet shops offer their connected desktop computers available for hire in ten-minute intervals, but there are no restaurants or cafes with Wi-Fi available to customers. Even the small, rarely used library lacks Wi-Fi access and provides no computer terminals for patrons. Many Hospiceños also complain that data service on mobile phones is less than adequate in the North. When my neighbour Alvaro returned from a trip to visit family in Santiago he told me: 'The networks are so much better there. I could even use the internet on my phone to make video calls. And the image was clear! If I try to do the same thing here [in Alto Hospicio], the call just drops.'

Often Hospiceños are left to work out their own ways of connecting to the internet. Many people place larger antennas on their roofs to capture a better signal when their internet is very slow. Others hire their neighbours or unlicensed 'companies' to make similar modifications. Self-engineered internet access has also been popular since the early 2000s, when home internet connections first became available in Alto Hospicio. Diego, an electrician in his late thirties, explained to me how he had personally wired his house for internet in 2001. Rather than pay a company to come to the house and connect the signal, he and some neighbours ran wires from the centre of the city to their houses themselves. He described the process of climbing up on roofs to reach the wires, then stringing them in zigzag fashion from street to street for about a kilometre until they reached his neighbourhood. 'It was pretty much an expedition just to get internet to the house,' he told me. Now most people have home internet installed by company technicians, but there are still some neighbourhoods in Alto Hospicio where wired internet service is not available. Families in these areas rely on their mobile phones for service. Yet even in neighbourhoods where internet is easily installed, a significant number of people admit that they clandestinely use other people's Wi-Fi networks.

In my survey of 100 internet users[3] 67 per cent of respondents reported that they had Broadband access in their homes. Another 10 per cent tethered their mobile phone to a computer for internet service and five per cent said that they used a neighbour's Wi-Fi signal. Eighteen per cent said they had no internet access on a computer in their homes. Unlike in many other Latin American contexts, internet shops are fairly rare. Most of them are located in the centre of the city rather than dispersed throughout the neighbourhoods – surprising given that

Fig. 2.1 A small internet access shop in Alto Hospicio

the neighbourhoods still without wired internet are those furthest from the centre. Those that still operate often have very limited hours and primarily cater to groups of secondary school students.

Smartphones are much more important to the ways in which residents of Alto Hospicio use social media and the internet in general. For most it is the only electronic device that is theirs alone. In my survey of social media users, only 14 per cent of people reported using a computer or tablet of their own. For all others, these internet access points are shared with parents, siblings, spouses or children. Mobile phones remain highly personal, however, with monthly data plans starting at around $10,000 CLP ($16 US). Most Hospiceños who have a plan pay around $25,000 CLP ($40 US), which allows them enough phone minutes and text messages for average use. However, some individuals such as Diego complain that the internet allotment of 1 GB is not enough for this price. He told me:

> The companies abuse the cost of the packages because they charge you for so many call minutes that nobody uses any more, or text messages, but they don't give you enough internet. Hardly anyone uses minutes any more, but they charge you, they charge you, they charge you.

However, others consider those with a plan lucky. In order to sign a contract, a customer must have a national credit card – itself restricted to those who can prove stable employment in a registered business and a particular level of income. Because of these constraints, a limited number of Hospiceños qualify for a monthly plan. Others opt for prepaid minutes, which can be purchased at any number of small shops in Alto Hospicio. For $10,000 CLP customers receive about 1 GB of data and a limited number of text messages and call time. Usually most of the minutes and messages go unused, and the phone owner buys a new allocation when their internet quota runs out.

As Diego's complaint reveals, the costs of internet access are no small matter to residents of Alto Hospicio. While many families can afford data plans and used smartphones, at times the monthly budget does not stretch. For other families, phone-based internet is simply out of the question. Most recent Bolivian immigrants in Alto Hospicio forego social media altogether, instead buying international phone credit for their simple mobiles to call the landlines of family and friends across the border. Not only is paying for internet service (either broadband or mobile phone data) a concern for many people: their points of access – the screens on which they connect – also create tension at times.

Such unequal access to internet-based applications, along with the shared nature of many screens, further normalises what appears on public social media. Eclipsing the most marginalised sectors of society, including immigrants and the severely impoverished, has an effect of further entrenching a sense of homogenous marginality rather than supporting identity politics online. Yet the great lengths to which most people go to access social media, whether sharing a computer with the family, saving up to buy a smartphone or finding an internet shop to connect, underlines both how important they are as well as how normative they have become. Their significance goes beyond merely staying in touch. Social media offers a space to express something deeper, about the self, about personal relationships and about how one sees one's position in the world.

Defining social media

Andres, Francisca and Franklin's descriptions make clear that Hospiceños use a variety of social media in various ways. Social media platforms are used for writing public announcements, sending personal messages, sharing photographs, alerting friends to news items, conveying one's mood via music, drawing attention to videos of interest or expressing a commonly held sentiment with a meme. Social media platforms are also important for communicating agreement or disagreement, or for developing relationships through phatic communication[4] such as 'liking', 'favouriting', sharing, commenting or even tagging and mentioning people in response to others' original posts.[5]

Many platforms allow for several of these different actions, and most actions can be performed using a number of different platforms. One platform may have multiple ways of interacting with friends – sharing posts, 'liking' a friend's status, chatting and tagging photographs. At the same time a single form of communication, such as writing messages, can be accomplished on various different sites and platforms. Even beyond online media, communication happens through a mixture of speaking in person, using more 'traditional' technology, such as the telephone or text messaging, and through internet-based social media. In Alto Hospicio, as across the world, social media is not opposed to, but is integrated with, communications in everyday life.

Early studies of the internet often conceptualised a 'virtual world' as separate from 'real life'. Yet Hospiceños understand that their online interactions are just as real and important as their offline lives. Just as a telephone conversation or email does not constitute a separate realm, social media are simply part of a more expansive communication landscape. Because these categories merge into one another and daily life, it is useful to define exactly what we mean by social media.

As used in this book, social media refers to platforms such as Facebook, WhatsApp, Twitter, Instagram and interactive blogs. However, defining social media based only on platforms that presently exist is limiting. As Miller et al suggest, social media are those forms of communication that provide a middle ground between public broadcasting and private communication. Before this technology, each communication medium was often either unidirectional and aimed at a large audience, as in television, radio and newspapers, or was interactive but private in nature, such as telephone conversations or letters. With the development of social media, individuals can choose the size of their audience (ranging from one to billions) and level of interaction they wish. This 'scalable sociality'[6] gives individuals more control over their self-representations to different audiences.

For example, on Facebook an individual may choose to make a photograph visible only to their 'close friends', but to share a meme with an unlimited public. Twenty-two year old Lisette, for example, is somewhat private about her new romantic relationship with Isadora. When Lisette posts pictures of the two making funny faces together or sharing a meal, she allows them to be publicly visible. When she posts pictures of the two kissing or holding hands, however, she restricts their visibility to only her closest friends. She is fairly open about her sexuality with her family and close friends, but does not always trust a much wider social media audience with what she considers a sensitive subject.

Facebook, sometimes called just *Face*, is the most popular social media platform.[7] This is because, as many Hospiceños explain, it combines the ability to post visual materials with text status updates and interactive features such as 'liking' posts, commenting and private messaging. For many people in northern Chile, it is central to their daily communications. Because of its widespread use, Facebook is the sphere in which people maintain relationships, as well as express their individual personalities and participate as citizens of the community.[8]

Alvaro, who moved with his brother and mother to Alto Hospicio from Santiago in 2005, uses Facebook to keep in touch with family and particularly with his ten-year-old son Daniel, who remains in Santiago with Alvaro's ex-girlfriend. When Daniel turned eight Alvaro helped him set up his own Facebook account so they can share pictures and chat almost daily. This private communication is important, but Alvaro also uses Facebook to express his interests, posting his own short reviews of the latest movies, as well as memes highlighting what he sees as unjustifiable policies that extend social services to new immigrants. He also takes advantage of his position as a manager of a small electronics store in the Zofri mall to publicly share pictures of sale prices on computers, speakers, televisions, video game systems and even alcohol that he sees around the mall. His friends often thank him in the comments for his 'public service' in advertising special deals to a broader public. Facebook thus allows Alvaro different levels of broadcasting, from privately conversing with Daniel to sharing pictures publicly. However, these levels only exist because Facebook provides the possibility of a seemingly unlimited public.

The public nature of Facebook provides a 'public sphere'[9] not only for individuals, but also for businesses, politicians and community groups. Official social groups and businesses take advantage of Facebook for various forms of publicity or to stay connected to the community. The volunteer leaders of 'La Escuelita' [The Little School] – an after-school programme operating in one of the poorest neighbourhoods of Alto Hospicio – began a Facebook page that they fill with announcements and pictures of special events they organise for the children, including breakdancing lessons, special crafts days and trips to the beach. They also use Facebook to promote their fundraising efforts such as selling home-made veggie burgers. The programme is run by several social work students from a university in Iquique, many of whom grew up or currently live in Alto Hospicio. They see Facebook as integral to the aims of La Escuelita, and make all posts on the page as public as possible. This is in part because their mission involves giving the neighbourhood's children a better chance at a positive future, but it also serves to promote a sense of community founded in collectively making the most of their marginalised conditions.

Raquel, a local social worker and community activist in her late twenties, ran for an office in the *Consejo Regional* [Regional Council] in the 2013 election cycle. In addition to the posters she and her friends hung up all over Alto Hospicio and Iquique, Raquel opened a separate Facebook account where she displayed her slogan and logo, explained her platform – which consisted mostly of improving community services – and linked to news articles relating to her campaign and the election in general. Even after losing the election, Raquel keeps this account open to share public, politically related news and maintains her personal Facebook account full of pictures with family and friends. Keeping the two accounts separate allows her to separate her personal life from her political and professional life, and cater her posts to two different audiences.

Facebook is important for businesses based in Alto Hospicio as well. Gonz, who began a sushi[10] delivery business with his brother Victor, explained that Facebook allows them to publish menus, advertise on other pages and even take orders. They began the business after a major earthquake when the highway to Iquique was impassable, 'providing an opportunity' for Hospiceños to get sushi when their access to restaurants in Iquique was cut off. Gonz works all day preparing sushi at home. Then, from 7pm onwards, the two brothers are ready to take orders on their mobile phones and laptops. When someone sends a Facebook or WhatsApp message with an order, the brothers put sushi rolls into plastic boxes and send them with Gonz's son to be delivered. Facebook has proved especially useful for advertising specials or even giving special offers to regular customers. 'It only gets complicated when my friends write during the shift and I don't know if they want to order or just want to say hi!' Gonz told me. He now says he regrets combining his personal and business pages, but it certainly has not negatively affected the business. Over the course of my 15 months of field work the two brothers started in Gonz's kitchen, then moved to their parents' much larger kitchen. After recruiting several family members to help out, they were still overwhelmed with orders and had to hire two additional people, making the business an eight-person operation that continues to grow.

For individuals, politicians, businesses and community groups, Facebook is a way to express citizenship – by publicly voicing allegiance to certain local political issues and by helping the community, even if only alerting them to special deals in Zofri. Facebook, then, is a key public sphere in which Hospiceños perform a normative style of marginalised citizenship.

Individuals also use WhatsApp to parse out different sizes and levels of intimacy in their intended audience. WhatsApp is used much like 'traditional' text messaging, but has added benefits of sending photographs, video and voice messages, managing groups and using emojis, as well as using mobile data rather than a messaging bundle. When I began field work in 2013 WhatsApp was just taking hold; by the time I finished in 2015 Hospiceños considered it almost as important as Facebook.[11] When I met new people, including police officers, internet installation technicians and neighbours, they almost always asked if I had WhatsApp rather than wanting to connect through email, Facebook or telephone.

WhatsApp has become especially important for families in which at least one member works in the mining industry. The mining operations are about 300 km (four hours by bus) away from Alto Hospicio, so the overwhelmingly male mining employees work one week at the mine with one week off. Vicky's husband Jorge, for instance, has worked in a copper mine doing maintenance on large machinery for over 20 years. Every other Monday night he takes a bus to the mine. Until the following Sunday he sleeps in a dormitory room that he shares with three other miners and eats his meals in the company cafeteria. He works from 8am to 8pm each day, then showers, eats dinner and usually watches videos on his computer before sleeping. His son Alex and son-in-law José both work in the same mine. Their schedules overlap, so Jorge is able to spend some evenings joking and playing cards with them. In order to stay in contact with his wife Vicky, daughter Gabriela and his grandson Samuel, however, WhatsApp is ideal. Jorge has a Facebook account, but rarely uses it. Instead he passes the night sending messages to his family in Alto Hospicio on WhatsApp, and receiving replies from his wife and daughter, often with pictures of Samuel.

Jorge's son Alex uses Facebook more than his father, but told me that WhatsApp is especially important for chatting with his girlfriend Carmela. He also uses WhatsApp to stay in contact with friends in Alto Hospicio, creating groups in order to stay a part of their daily, usually joking conversations. Alex appreciates this most on really boring days at work, because his friends send him funny videos or memes through WhatsApp to keep him entertained. He also uses WhatsApp to plan activities with Carmela, his friends and his family for his weeks off.

WhatsApp is also useful for actually doing work. Alex, who works in motor maintenance like his father, explained to me that living quarters and the offices at the mine are located far from the work sites; workers sometimes have to travel long distances between sites for specific projects. When he first started at the mine in the late 1990s, things were very inefficient because of the distances workers needed to travel. He explained:

> WhatsApp is perfect, because supervisors can just send you a message. Before you'd start out in the office and they'd tell you to go fix a motor that's a 10 or 20-minute drive. So you'd get there and discover that you're missing a part, or the motor is different than you thought so you need different tools. Well, there was no way to call, so you had to drive all the way back to get what you needed. And sometimes you had to do that two or three times. Now you just send a WhatsApp to your friend and they bring it out to you.

As noted above, businesses such as Gonz and Victor's sushi delivery company also use WhatsApp to take orders. Other business owners see an invaluable asset in the potential of privacy that WhatsApp offers. When I arrived in Alto Hospicio in 2013 there was only one bar in the city, open only on Thursday, Friday and Saturday nights. By the time I finished field work in 2015 Carlos had opened two bars near the centre of the city, both serving customers six nights a week. He often gives away specials in the bars, enticing customers to take selfies at the bar and post them on the business's Facebook page. 'But the most interesting things happen on WhatsApp,' he told me mysteriously.

In addition to the two bars Carlos also owns a strip club, which women are prohibited from entering. The club has a Facebook page, but many clients thought it was too public, so he now uses Facebook less and WhatsApp more, creating a private group where he advertises special events such as dancers from Arica or Antofagasta. The group has over 200 members who also use WhatsApp to post funny and sexually explicit memes and rowdy teasing conversations anonymously, turning the app into a virtual boys' club. 'It's just nice to have some privacy, and while Facebook is good for most things, WhatsApp lets the men be men without worrying,' he observed.

Though less public than Facebook, WhatsApp also provides a means through which individuals express certain ways of identifying, whether as a part of a family or work-related identification. Of course it also provides a more covert way of engaging with others, for matters that may be considered contrary to 'good' heteronormative citizenship.[12] Thus the ways in which Carlos uses social media for his businesses demonstrates how a combination of different media options further allows for maintaining an image of good citizenship in the public eye.

As Carlos's story reveals, group functions of WhatsApp are particularly useful to limiting the reach of certain kinds of communication. However, other platforms are well-suited for making broadcasts as public as possible. Though Instagram and Twitter are less popular in Alto Hospicio, individuals still take advantage of these platforms when hoping to gain a wide audience for their messages.

Twitter, the third most popular platform in Alto Hospicio,[13] is used to share links, photographs, text limited to 140 characters or simply to 're-tweet' another user's original post. Twitter also allows users to add hashtags to note the important topics of their post and make it searchable, but Hospiceños rarely use this feature. Hospiceños generally use Twitter as another way of writing status messages or perhaps linking to photographs, much as they use Facebook. Though the Iquique newspaper (Alto Hospicio has no newspaper of its own), local radio stations, members of local government and a few individuals regularly post news items relevant to the region, not many Hospiceños follow these Twitter accounts, reflecting the fact that news is simply not an important use of social media in general. Rather people tend to get plenty of news from televisions and radios that seem to play constantly in almost every house, restaurant, public bus, collective and private taxi in the city.

Twitter use also seems to suffer from the fact that Hospiceños say the page view itself is boring. On Facebook and other visually centred platforms images such as personal photographs and memes are central to the application's appearance. On Twitter the page is dominated by text on a white background; many users say their eyes become fatigued quickly just looking at the page. Twitter does not offer the entertainment and distraction value equal to platforms with more image-centric layouts, thus earning it the title of the most *fome* [boring] social media option. So even those Hospiceños that use Twitter see it as secondary to other social networking sites where they concentrate more energy.

Yesenia, a mother of three who works for Alto Hospicio's municipal government, often uses Twitter as part of her job. Though she tweets only occasionally, she keeps the application on her phone and follows all the local news outlets, regional and national government and several businesses in Alto Hospicio. She is very involved with senior citizens in Alto Hospicio, and always tweets announcements about activities she organises for older members of the community. Yet pictures of the 'Advanced Adult Beauty Pageant', as well as celebrations for various holidays, are always reserved for Facebook. For Yesenia Twitter is a tool for organising, while Facebook is the space in which she reflects on the activities as part of enjoyment of life.

Yesenia's son Cristian also uses Twitter regularly, but in a very different way. He is among the teens who often replicate their Facebook status updates on Twitter. On Twitter he expresses feelings including happiness, excitement, disappointment or frustration with the normal events of life; he cheers on his favourite football team, Colo Colo, or just whiles away time to avoid boredom, as many young people do on social media. Cristian connects with friends by following them on Twitter and occasionally mentioning them in his tweets, but rarely uses hashtags. Instead of using Twitter to access wider networks, it is simply one more space much like Facebook where he can interact with his school friends online. For both Yesenia and Cristian, Twitter acts as a way to place themselves within the community – yet they also realise that Twitter is not a primary public sphere in which that community is present.

They thus give minimal emphasis to the application, leaving time and energy for those that are more central to the performance of citizenship in Alto Hospicio.

Instagram is also primarily used by younger people[14] and is exclusively image-focused. Users can post photographs that are modified through cropping and changing lighting and colour tones. Unlike Twitter, however, Hospiceños use hashtags (#) extensively on Instagram, often giving the location such as #InstaHospicio or #InstaChile, in addition to other photo descriptors such as #beach, #work, #school or #family. One popular use of Instagram is family photographs and specifically pictures of children. Tamara, originally from Southern Chile, is particularly fond of posting selfies with her four-year-old daughter Angela, and occasionally with her husband Luis. She also posts pictures of Iquique's main beach when she has the chance to go, but more often the pictures depict her daily life: grocery shopping, her job selling clothing in the large Agro-market of Alto Hospicio or relaxing at home watching television.

Other Instagram users focus their posts on particular themes. When Jhony, a member of the *Zorros Rojos* [Red Foxes] Motor Club, bought a large Samsung tablet phone, he took it to an *asado* barbeque with his fellow motor club members. Over Escudo beers and smoke from the grill, everyone gave Jhony suggestions for applications to download. After creating a WhatsApp group to organise events with the club, Miguel suggested he install Instagram. 'What's Instagram for?' asked Jhony. Miguel explained, 'You upload pictures and the whole world says "I like it!" It's good for self-esteem.' Paul, another member of the group added, 'You take pictures of ugly people like us and we come out looking good. It works like magic.' Jhony downloaded Instagram and took a few pictures at the *asado*. Later, however, he started exclusively to post pictures of his motorcycle and truck. While Facebook remains his main form of social media communication, where he posts funny memes, photos from parties and comments on friends' posts, Instagram is reserved for showing off his vehicles.

For Hospiceños, Instagram is less about interpersonal communication and more about expression and performance. It becomes a place to express normative aesthetics, lifestyles and hobbies – in many ways reflecting the normativity of Alto Hospicio, without opening up conversations about that normativity.

Because functions of different kinds of social media overlap, and many of the platforms offer more than one function, it is hard to conceive of one social media platform in isolation. Rather each is understood as part of the *colación* that Andres described. His description acknowledges that with a variety of communication technologies at one's disposal, each media is defined and used in relation to other available media, a point encompassed in the term 'polymedia'.[15] Most people use a combination of several to achieve various communication aims. Some messages are aimed at a wide local audience (such as public Facebook posts) and others at anonymous, possibly international viewers (such as Instagram pictures and Twitter messages), while still others are intended for a very specific, small, known audience (Facebook messages only visible to certain friends, or WhatsApp messages to individuals or small groups). It is the ability to combine these different sizes of audience, along with different genres – such as photographs, videos, shared memes, original text and copied, shared text – that give social media its flexible qualities.[16]

Alejandra is a leader of a folkloric group, which performs a dance called Caporales. The dance itself has its origins in Bolivia, and there is even an official organisation which coordinates costumes and specific dance moves in the Bolivian capital of La Paz. Social networking sites in general become indispensable for Alejandra and her group – for communicating with the central organisation on Facebook, ordering costumes and planning trips to perform through WhatsApp and publicising their group by posting photographs on Instagram. YouTube is also important for groups outside of La Paz to learn the official dance steps that change slightly year to year. Alejandra explained that the central organisation makes a video of the group in La Paz teaching the step, and then uploads it as a private video to YouTube. They share the link through posts on their Facebook page only visible to affiliated groups in other cities, so that when those groups travel to other places any dancer affiliated to the central organisation will know the same steps and be able to dance together.

However, social media is important for other, more personal touches as well. One morning while getting ready for a performance, all the women in the group gathered at Cecelia's house to do their hair and makeup and to put on costumes. Cecelia connected her laptop to the flat screen television facing the large table in the main room of her house in order to show the crowd of 12 women a style of eyeshadow application she had found on Facebook, which had been republished from a make-up blog. At the same time Alejandra called her mother to ask a question about how to make a flourish in the traditional dancer's hairstyle of two long braids. Using the speakerphone, all the women heard her mother's garbled voice respond, 'I don't remember, just search for *trenzas* on YouTube!'

The Caporales dance group is only one instance of the ways that individuals bring different forms of social media together. Yet this example also illustrates the ways in which content from other online sources, such as blogs and YouTube, becomes reinscribed within other social media platforms.

YouTube, unlike many social media sites, does not require individuals to register in order to view videos on the site. Those who do register can post videos or comment on those posted by others, but most Hospiceños simply watch widely shared ones – usually instructional, funny web series episodes and music videos.[17] However, they do re-post these videos on social media such as Facebook, giving YouTube a 'social' aspect, though not within the website itself. The frequency with which they re-post YouTube-based content makes the site key to understanding the polymedia landscape in Alto Hospicio.

Nicole was one of the few YouTube users I met in Alto Hospicio who actually posts videos regularly. They are usually videos she records on her GoPro camera of weekend trips with her family or with her boyfriend Martin. The videos are usually edited with an added soundtrack and sometimes intercut with subtitle cards. In one video of a trip she took with friends to celebrate Carnaval in a small town in the interior of Chile, she begins by announcing to the camera 'We are starting our adventure!' Set to a club remix of a pop song, the five-minute video resembles a road trip montage sequence from a coming-of-age movie. Desert mountains cruise by as the camera faces out of the passenger window of Nicole's car. Images of the passengers getting out to stretch shows more of the landscape. The festival is similarly caught on video, particularly emphasising the crowd throwing coloured powder, confetti and water on each other – a practice common in Carnaval celebrations in the Andes. The video fades out as the song ends and the crowd continues to dance. This video sits on her YouTube page, along with silly videos she made during her university course in early childhood education and other trips she captured with her GoPro camera. Most importantly, however, she posted it on Facebook to share with those who had gone on the trip as well as her other friends.

Hospiceño musicians also use YouTube to distribute their latest songs across different social media. One local reggae group, headed by a husband and wife who go by their stage names Sista Ebony and Klandestino, spent a great deal of time and energy composing and working with a friend to make a video of their latest song. 'Miseria en la Periferia' [Misery in the Periphery] describes life in Alto Hospicio, using the idea of the periphery as a tool for political mobilisation. Sista

Ebony and Klandestino celebrated completing the song by throwing an *asado* barbeque where they showed the video for the first time. The next day they shared it with all their friends on Facebook. As Klandestino explained, the group does not have the connections to get their videos played on television or their songs on national radio programmes. By using social media, however, they have been able both to find new fans and to spread their message of social justice.

Both Nicole and the reggae musicians use YouTube as more of a repository than a separate social media site. The videos that they post are very personal, but even when others post instructional, comedy or popular music videos to their Facebook pages, these forms of media become part of their own repertoires. Similarly a number of public Tumblr blog sites take on the same function, primarily used by younger Hospiceños to supplement their social media presence.[18] Tumblr allows users to write original text, but Hospiceños most often use it to curate collections of photographs, .gifs (Graphic Interchange Format, or animated image files), videos, links and audio. Though Tumblr offers the option to viewers to 'ask a question of the blogger', it seems that this mechanism is rarely used by Hospiceños because, unlike a Facebook message, Tumblr messages do not have the potential to develop into a chat. Many users choose to eliminate this option from their page so that interactions are limited to 'liking' and re-blogging.

Hospiceños creatively rework the functions of Tumblr in order to transform sites into collaborative repositories that take on an interactive aspect. This is particularly true with Tumblr accounts dedicated to humour. Miguel and Jhony, both in their early thirties and members of the Red Foxes Motor Club, often spend afternoons in Alto Hospicio sitting on Miguel's sofa. They laugh for hours at images and videos shared on one such site, Jaidefinichon (pronounced 'High Definition'). Here site administrators post pictures, videos and links that might be described as 'raunchy': related to drunkenness, sex, drugs and bodily humour. One morning, for example, the five most recent posts to Jaidefinichon were: a video of a bull ramming a person, a meme playing on similar syllables in 'Ebola' and 'Bolivia', a .gif of a woman shaking her behind unbelievably quickly, a video of a man falling of a skateboard and a meme about marijuana using stills from the television cartoon *The Simpsons*. Jhony and Miguel both started following Jaidefinichon around 2009. Miguel explained:

> At first it was like a virus. One person telling all their friends, and that's how everyone found out about it. A lot of people sent the

link on Facebook in 2009 or 2010. Others just mentioned it to their friends [in person].

Jhony chimed in:

> And the commentary is funny too. There are memes about the president, videos of dogs walking on two legs and images of weed. And it's a different conversation in the comments about each one. But all funny. Though sometimes I don't understand. Maybe I'm too old now.

As Jhony and Miguel explained, users can submit photos, videos or other sorts of media to the owners of the blog. Those who find the posts especially funny will click to a direct link to the picture or video, to share on their own Tumblr or Facebook. Occasionally such memes are also shared on Instagram as well, or sent via WhatsApp, as Jhony observed.

> People republish things because they want to make their friends laugh. They also try to write a funny caption for Facebook to show that they don't just share funny things; they're actually funny too. That's why funny comments are so important. You have to show your own creativity.

Miguel also noted:

> Everybody sees the same thing and everybody can talk about it when they get together for a party. It's not just about seeing it, or even writing comments online, but you can laugh about it with your friends when you see them too.

So, as in the case of Jaidefinichon, Tumblr may actually become a very social form of media in which expressions are shared, contributing to a sense of commonality and belonging. While these particular Tumblr pages are a bit raunchy and foster forms of citizenship based in cultural belonging rather than community engagement, they normativise through their shared nature. However, the true value of these Tumblr sites to social media, like YouTube videos, is the way in which the content becomes translated through its context on other social media sites such as Facebook.

Reworking self-expression on social media

Linguists use the term 'intertextuality' to refer to the way in which placing a piece of text in a new context changes its meaning.[19] In traditional literary terms intertextuality includes allusion, quotation, translation, pastische and parody, and many of these genres become apparent when social media users embed other forms of media within their own and others' Facebook walls. Creating an interrelationship between texts, social media users may transform the meaning of the original text to fit their own style in a creative re-working. In the process of 'entextualisation',[20] social media users create texts for circulation by extracting them from their original contexts, so that the content references the intentions of the sharer rather than the creator.

Even when social media users do not post original text or photographs, seeing their recycled posts as a form of entextualisation reveals the creativity associated with this type of social media use. By placing videos, photos, memes, text and sometimes audio into a common space, individuals actively curate the media that appears on their own and their friends' Facebook walls as if they were museum collections that act as a form of self-expression.

Mixing media components into a bricolage creates an active recirculation of materials that draw on multiple modes of communication (text, image, audio, video etc.), aimed at re-appropriating meanings.[21] In essence social media users take discourses already in circulation and make them part of their own new forms of discourse. When Instagram photographers use filters to stylise a photograph that they then upload as a new Facebook profile picture, they use Instagram as a means to an end, rather than as a primary form of social media in itself. In doing so such users demonstrate their creativity in assembling aspects of the various media available in order to make it individual. When that same user puts a YouTube clip of a funny moment from a television programme on a friend's wall, the meaning transforms from the original plot of the television episode to something far more personal shared between two friends.

Rather than seeing this type of sharing as derivative or unoriginal, Hospiceños understand it as a type of creative reworking of the content into a new style of discourse that displays the creativity and humour of the individual who shares the content. As the creativity displayed in these strategies makes clear, social media is not deterministic. Using existing media to make new discursive play allows users to retro-fit the media they wish to use into existing platforms.

During the time of my field work Instagram required all photographs to be square, but an Insta-photographer could use applications to create square pictures from landscape or portrait aspect ratios, without cropping anything out. Facebook has no application for adding sound bites to one's own Timeline, but, by posting the YouTube video of the song a person is currently listening to, he or she allows friends to share in the sonic experience as well. Unlike with older unidirectional media such as television, film and radio, Hospiceños actively rework social media in order to craft their own forms of curation, rather than passively consume them. So, even though YouTube may look like older media, and indeed often draws on radio, film and television for content, Hospiceños appropriate it in ways that are simply not possible with previous media. The ability to embed these clips in other social media allows people to exert more impact on media than previously, and the ability to remix media profoundly changes the context in which the content is newly embedded. When Instagram photos are shared through Twitter, or Facebook users tell their friends what songs they are listening to by posting a YouTube video of the tune, these individuals actively expand the possibilities of these media platforms.

'Meme' is now a household word in most of the world. It refers to a piece of meaningful communication that spreads, often using mimicry, from person to person on the internet, including images, hyperlinks, videos, pictures, websites or hashtags. In Alto Hospicio the most common form of meme, and that to which I use the word to refer, was of visual images overlaid with text (see Chapter 3 for examples). Yet these internet memes take their name from a term coined by Richard Dawkins in the 1970s, referring to 'an idea, behaviour or style that spreads from person to person within a culture'; these are cultural analogues to genes in that they self-replicate, mutate and respond to selective pressures.[22] Dawkins' concept of the meme has been criticised, however, as lacking room for agency, change and creativity. Instead understanding media that is re-shared as part of this intertextuality, curation and even a mode of performance allows us to understand creativity and change as essential to this form of reproduction.

From a wide variety of available material, social media users choose particular things in order to communicate something. They may share the most flattering images on Instagram or publish childhood photographs on Facebook. They may write accounts of the most interesting bits of their day or chronicle the things that annoy them most. They may search for the most heartfelt meme or the funniest videos to post on a friend's wall. And while individuals do not necessarily consciously think of these acts as performance, they are always acts of choice – the public spaces of social media allow individuals to present themselves as they would like to be seen.

Understanding what people do on social media as performing does not necessarily mean that these are conscious acts, but they are nonetheless meaningful. And seeing them as performance draws attention to the fact that they are intended for an audience. The semi-public nature of social media creates a space in which information is expressed with a possibility, if not expectation, of interaction. Of course the user may never know if anyone has read it. An Instagram photograph, Tumblr blog post or Tweet may be sent out into the ether of the internet, and if no one 'likes' or comments upon it, the creator will never know if anyone saw it at all. Yet the *potential* for interaction makes social media social, because the person posting the photograph, text or video has created and shared the item with the intent that someone will see it, and hopefully respond to it.

One factor that underscores the importance of the audience on social media to Hospiceños is their desire for feedback. While few people explicitly mention that feedback is important, the extent to which they prefer media that involves extensive interaction, and concentrate on the visibility of those interactions, makes clear that Hospiceños, if only unconsciously, are drawn to social media in which they are aware of the audience and (at least some of) their responses. Though some scholarship suggests that the internet is a force that makes people more solitary,[23] this is not true for most users in Alto Hospicio. The social media sites they choose, and the ways in which they choose to use them, overwhelmingly focus on social interaction that is based in their local community and bleeds over into their face-to-face social life with friends, family and local organisations. The social media platforms that allow for the most feedback and conversation are popular because they are reliable for facilitating an audience.

There is nothing about platforms such as Twitter or Instagram that keeps people from engaging with others through comments and responses. However, people use Facebook most frequently because they are most likely to get a response on that platform. This forms a sort of feedback loop in which people perceive that others use Facebook more, so when they want feedback they use Facebook to express something, which in turn keeps others coming back as well. As this cycle continues, people know that if they want their friends, family, colleagues, acquaintances and even enemies to see something, Facebook is the place to express it. In essence Facebook is the most truly social of the social media for people living in Alto Hospicio.

Because social media provides a semi-public stage for these performances of the self, it also helps to establish and redefine what is normative, and what a 'good citizen' looks like. The photographs that people post give a sense of what one should aspire to in terms of one's own looks as well as that of their surroundings (see Chapter 3). The ways in which individuals identify themselves as part of familial relationships help to shape what people understand as a normative family (see Chapter 4), while the ways in which people express pride in certain activities as part of what it means to be a man or woman shape people's understanding and expectation of gender (see Chapter 5).[24] Even in discussing local or national politics, individuals demonstrate what sorts of belonging and solidarity are important in the community (see Chapter 6). Not only do users give their actions meaning through adhering to normative standards;[25] in their public performance on social media, these very actions help to shape what most Hospiceños consider normative.[26]

Of course not all Hospiceños would say that they hope to fit in to the normative standards of the city, either online or in daily life. Instead they follow the norms implicitly, producing 'conformity in the absence of the intention to conform'.[27] Their knowledge of local social norms is built up through experience, rather than explicitly taught. They act in accordance with normative behaviours, not through some means of rational calculation but simply because those behaviours seem natural. In fact for most Hospiceños the normative social expectations around them and in which they participate remain invisible.[28] Learned behaviours, naturalised through repetition,[29] become mental schemata of common sense.[30]

These unwritten but well known rules for social behaviour make up what might be considered 'social scripts'[31] that express what is taken for granted[32] or seems natural to individuals within the group. Most people, without even thinking about it, reproduce these social scripts in their mundane acts and the way they present themselves in everyday life.[33] From the way they dress to the food they prepare, from the way they greet neighbours to their topics of conversation – whether online or offline – people behave according to unwritten rules.

Even within these social scripts, however, Hospiceños often express individual preferences, styles and opinions. While some approach local politics with gravity, others complain about the national government with lighthearted humour. In their lives offline some prepare food using an old family recipe, while others simply mix ingredients according to their own taste. Social media provides a space for making these expressions publicly visible. Posting pictures, memes, status messages and even private messages to friends is as much about self-expression as about personal communication. While individuals do not necessarily consciously think of these acts as presentations, they are actively making choices about how they want to present themselves. In essence social media provides a stage for performing the self.[34] Performing in this sense is not 'acting', but 'enacting'; not a false representation of a 'true self', but the production of oneself as a culturally recognisable subject.[35] These users characterise themselves, categorise themselves, locate themselves in relationships to others and situate themselves within the narrative that they want to tell of their life.[36]

Building a balanced social media diet

As Francisca, Franklin, Andres and I finished up our colación lunches, I looked down at my polystyrene container. 'OK, so if Facebook is the chicken, what is Instagram?' With the three interrupting each other, it was decided as follows: Instagram is the pesto pasta – totally unnecessary, but it has good flavour and it adds some colour to the plate. WhatsApp, on the other hand, is the salad – just as necessary as the chicken, but easy to forget – but when you do, you almost immediately notice its absence. 'Twitter is my rice,' Franklin said, 'really boring, but it's good for filling up. And YouTube is the ají [hot sauce]. I wouldn't eat it alone, but if you put it on top of the other stuff, it makes it even better.' 'And look,' said Andres, with a fork full of a bit of everything, 'This is how you make a Tumblr page', as the overflowing utensil disappeared into his mouth.

My lunch companions understand that, for social media to be enjoyable, a combination of different forms is ideal. It is in the creative use of multiple forms, not just in complimentary ways but in combination, that social media gains its popularity in Alto Hospicio. Most importantly of all, however, the meal must be shared. Whether with family, friends or acquaintances, social media is useful, enjoyable and even addictive because it allows people to share common experiences, often related to their marginalised subjectivity, and to construct a collective sense of belonging through normativity. Having access to multiple modes of media in order to do so allows for more possibilities and more resources in this creative work.

Hospiceños use social media to stay in contact with family, advocate for local reform, buy and sell items, build friendships, sort out work logistics, express individual interests and almost always make people laugh. Yet all of this is done within the social scripts of normativity, performed for the audience of other Hospiceños looking on through their computer or smartphone screens. It is clear not only how social media is understood as a normative mode of communication, but also how it becomes a tool for social negotiation about what is normative and what exceeds the boundaries. Social media is at once a private communication medium, mode of mass broadcast and method of aligning oneself with various relationships, identities and ideologies, particularly for expressing identification as marginalised as well as performing as a 'good citizen'.

3
Visual posting: The aesthetics of Alto Hospicio

In Alto Hospicio there is a homogeneity that pervades the visual land-scape. People, each with their individual differences, still fit neatly into the setting. Their T-shirts and jeans, often purchased used from the Agro market, are rarely meant to attract attention. There are few big build-ings and very little advertising. Houses all seem to look the same, like giant Lego blocks stacked one or two high on each narrow street. One street looks just like the next, with a row of houses flanked by corner shops; the cars that pass by the main plaza seem to be all of the same few makes and models. Even looking at the Facebook pages and Instagram feeds of Hospiceños, it is hard to distinguish one from another.

The repetition of architecture, inconspicuous corner shops, run of the mill clothing styles and even stray dogs lounging in the plazas seems to reject the existence of anything out of the ordinary. Even on social media, normativity calls no attention to itself. There is something so normative about all of these aesthetic aspects in Alto Hospicio that they seem to reject difference passively. Indeed, normativity often seems to be the absence of doing anything different or special. Yet Alto Hospicio provides an example of the ways in which doing something ordinary is no less active than doing something extraordinary. It is a choice, though at times an unconscious one, that manifests in various ways, many of which are visual. Such normativity is closely connected to a sense of being a good local citizen, of fitting in and accepting marginality as part of belonging in the community.

Aesthetics may seem to be something wholly divorced from notions of citizenship. However, aesthetics are a key mode through which citizenship may be expressed or contested. Understanding this normative aesthetic as actively (though at times unconsciously) created allows us to see the ways in which it also produces a certain form of citizenship. Aesthetics are grounds on which dominant (often capitalist) ideologies are reproduced[1] or contested.[2] In looking at visual elements of Hospiceños' social media, it becomes clear precisely how aesthetics becomes a key way in which individuals present themselves as 'good' marginalised citizens, reworking dominant ideals and promoting their own sense of collective normativity.

Instagramming the uninteresting

The aesthetic normativity of social media in Alto Hospicio is particularly apparent in visual representations of the self, often considered the sites at which performance and identification are most evident on social media. Typical selfies[3] in Alto Hospicio, even for young people, are usually taken at work, in their own home or that of a friend, or during a brief outing to the centre of Alto Hospicio or Iquique. These photographers rarely seem to aim at conveying a sense of glamour.

While both of the examples of selfies in Figs 3.1 and 3.2 are clearly posed, and we might assume the subjects hope to look their best, it is clear that the amount of effort and staging put into the photographs is minimal. The man in Fig. 3.1 is posed on a street corner on a typical neighbourhood street in Alto Hospicio. He turns to look at the camera and flashes a 'peace sign' – perhaps a now-universal worldwide casual pose for photos. The woman in the photograph in Fig. 3.2 has positioned her hair so that it appears in the frame of the photo, yet she chooses a background of a blank wall. Neither individual shows off particularly nice clothing in the photographs, nor does either choose an especially noteworthy background. Perhaps most revealing, however, is the fact that when these Hospiceños uploaded their selfies both photos received several 'likes' and comments focusing on the subject being good-looking, using the words 'guapo' [handsome], 'hermosa' [beautiful], 'te ves bien' [you look good] and 'preciosa' [pretty].

Pictures in which the subject intends to present a 'good-looking' pose, like those below, are one common form of selfies that Hospiceños upload to social media, but plenty of other pictures portray a more playful and casual look. These photographs tend to talk back humorously to the well-known stereotype of the selfie as narcissistic. In essence, when the subjects of the photos know that they might not pass as 'good-looking' because they are not well-dressed or posed, they reject this framing by 'pulling a face'. Such photos are popular among Hospiceños, both

Figs. 3.1 and 3.2 Two typical selfies of young Hospiceños

Fig. 3.3 Two young Hospiceños take a selfie with silly faces

young and old, perhaps precisely because expending energy (whether mental or physical) to compose a good-looking photo is simply not within the common repertoire. Yet such a manner of being informal and spontaneous is just as standardised as the formal poses with which they contrast.

The ways in which individuals talk back to the formality of the posed selfie are abundant. One inventive way popular among young Hospiceños is the foot photo, or 'footie'. These photographers are almost always in a lounging position while watching television or playing a video game, giving the viewer a sense of the mundane life that the photographer wishes to capture. The 'footie' is so casual that the photographer does not even have to move from a resting position to pose. The picture can be taken with minimal movement simply by angling the smartphone, already in hand, and snapping a photo without even pausing the television show or video game. It is the ultimate post portraying relaxation.

Figs. 3.4 and 3.5 'Footies'

Figs. 3.6 and 3.7 Work photographs

Teens and young adults are those who most often post several pictures a day,[4] usually of mundane items such as new gym shoes, breakfast, their freshly washed car, 'selfies' taken at school or work and photo collages made with another app. These images give a sense of the monotony of everyday life. Taking and posting photographs often seem to be strategies for passing time while bored; indeed the photos themselves often include hashtags such as #bored, #aburrido or #fome. Young people pass time by photographing their workspaces (whether at their job or school), snapping pictures of their surroundings while relaxing at home (often watching television or listening to music) and taking selfies in sites around Alto Hospicio. Some photos even express the ultimate boredom: waiting in a queue while running errands. Figure 3.8 depicts the queue to pay bills at the Movistar mobile phone company.

These mundane photos suggest that the very purpose of photography for these young people in Alto Hospicio is not the same as for previous generations. There are few Hospiceños who do not possess a mobile phone with a camera or a separate digital camera. Cameras, film and the developing process were once relatively expensive, giving

Fig. 3.8 'Waiting in line to pay my bill #instabored #instafome'

photographs an aura of significance. But the ease with which Hospiceños now take endless digital photos evidences a changing relationship with the medium. The purpose of the photograph was previously to record the experience, whereas now, for many people, the photograph serves to enhance the experience.[5] Often young people snap photos with no intention of displaying them in their homes or on social media.[6] And, given the low quality of many that Hospiceños post, it seems that image quality, composition and subject are not so much the point of the exercise: rather the meaning is in the action. Photography is a way to pass the time, while posting the image on social media also opens up the possibility of discussion and praise from peers. Such discussions further help to ease periods of boredom. The photograph then works to pass time in a double sense – first in the instant of taking the picture and second in the time (hopefully) spent discussing the picture itself, along with whatever conversations might emerge on social media in the comments section or in private messages as a result of the photograph.

Of course Hospiceños also consider it important to capture entertaining moments with photography, and even use the act to frame an event as 'fun'. They commonly post photographs that feature the moments of life meant to be enjoyed, often consisting of food, drink and friends. These photographs work to frame moments – many of which are relatively mundane – as worthy of documentation and thus fun, special or noteworthy.

Again these pictures are taken with minimal effort and staging, suggesting that in Alto Hospicio the product of photography has become less consequential as the act becomes more important. People do not appear to pay much attention to their appearances, aside from the now almost universally understood symbolic modes of demonstrating 'a good time' – tongues out, burlesqued smiles and hand signs. They do not arrange their clothing or their bodies in particular ways, other than to make sure their faces are visible and fit within the frame. People often do not even appear in the photograph. Simply depicting the food or drink serves to symbolise a good time, allowing the human enjoyment to be implied through the material objects.

It is also worth noting that each of the pictures shown here were first posted to Instagram, associated in many places with overt curation of images. Curation here is used similarly to in an art museum, where different aesthetic objects are placed in relation to one another to create a narrative or simply an ambiance. Media coverage of Instagram usually focuses on the application's affordances for visually enhancing photos, allowing users to crop them into squares and choose 'filters'

Figs. 3.9 and 3.10   Photographs of food

Fig. 3.11   Photograph of friends

which change the contrast, colour tone, saturation and focus of the photos. What results is often something that looks like an over- or under-exposed Polaroid picture.

For many users worldwide, this is the appeal of Instagram – turning the ordinary into the nostalgically beautiful. It allows for the curation of a set of photographs that displays the artistic sensibilities of the user, the beautiful places they have visited, their stylised selfies and their clever eye for finding interesting compositions among the ordinary moments of life. For contrast I display here (Figs 3.13 and 3.14) two Instagram photos by users from Santiago. Both present subjects that are widely considered 'beautiful' for art[7] and use filters to enhance their appearance.

For these users Instagram reflects a more explicit concentration on the result of photography rather than the action of taking a picture. In many contexts the measure of a good Instagram photo is not simply its display of a moment in life, but its ability to combine a keen

Fig. 3.12 Photograph of leisure

photographer's eye, interesting composition and skilful use of filters to create an aesthetically pleasing final product.[8]

The Instagram photos here from Alto Hospicio contrast with these ideals in almost every possible way. They do not feature subjects such as artistic works, well-presented restaurant food, beautifully decorated spaces or stylish fashion. Yet the contrasts are apparent even when Instagram users from Santiago portray the 'mundane' subjects of feet, work, their breakfast at home or the neighbourhood. Rather than the picture simply portraying the mundane subject, these users often compose the photographs and use filters to give them an artistic feel in an effort to elevate the mundane.

My point here is not that photographers in Santiago are qualitatively better than those in Alto Hospicio, but that their aims are different. For many Instagram users in Santiago, there is a sense that rather than capturing the mundane, Instagram and social media in general should be used to present the extraordinary moments of life: the

Figs. 3.13 and 3.14 Instagram photographs from users in Santiago

Figs. 3.15 and 3.16 'Mundane' items as subjects of Santiago users' Instagram photographs

beautiful vistas, delicious food and special moments with friends. These users in Santiago follow common ideals of curation more closely, while Instagram and Facebook users in Alto Hospicio present visual materials that corresponded more closely to an unedited view of daily life. In the context of other Hospiceño users doing the same, these pictures seem perfectly normal and 'natural' images to post on social media. These are pictures of 'normal' life.

It is clear that these photographs on social media are consistent with the way Hospiceños see offline life. In homes, clothing and these photographs, Hospiceños privilege an aesthetic that corresponds to the normativity of their everyday existence. Portraying this normativity constitutes its own form of aesthetics. These collections of photographs are not devoid of aesthetics. Rather, along with the spaces and material goods common in Alto Hospicio, they constitute a particular, unassuming aesthetic.[9]

Selfies, like most other forms of Hospiceños' social media photographs, simply provide a view into their daily lives. Yet to say that they are without aesthetics misinterprets the photographers' intentions. These photographs are precise examples of the aesthetic that corresponds to the particular form of normativity most prevalent in Alto Hospicio. As Hariman suggests, 'Because the camera records the décor of everyday life, the photographic image is capable of . . . aesthetic mediations of political identity.' These mundane selfies allow Hospiceños to perform their normativity and, along with other forms of social media postings, to place themselves squarely within the dominant conception of a 'good citizen' in the city'.

Daily life and social class on social media

The representation of daily life in social media photography works as a compliment to the social media presentation of social and economic class. Most Hospiceños present themselves as within the bounds of normative wealth and economic means of the city. And while most residents identify as marginalised, some families are of comfortable means – they have several wage earners to support the family and are able to afford such luxuries as the latest electronics, private vehicles, at least one mobile phone for each family member, and are able to spend extra earnings on entertainment activities. Yet they would consider it distasteful to present themselves as 'wealthy' (or what might appear middle class to those in Iquique). Instead, maintaining an appearance of conforming to Alto Hospicio's marginalised position on social media allows for perpetuation of the social scripts of normativity.

While in many contexts people often use visual representation to make claims to higher status and wealth, Hospiceños actively choose to emphasise what they have in common with their neighbours and social media contacts. This is not to say that they are insincere about their wealth, but most people feel it is inappropriate to use social media to show off wealth and class position that departs from the norm. Instead, highlighting certain kinds of economic problems with a humorous twist allows them to contribute to collective discourses on the marginality of Alto Hospicio and its residents.

Hospiceños rarely perceive a stigma associated with lapses in their ability to afford certain luxuries – internet access among them. They quite readily admit to their material shortcomings, often approaching the subject in a joking manner. For example Eduardo, a 40-year-old man who had recently lost his job with a mining company, quipped one afternoon, 'People with money are always connected. Those with less money are only connected sometimes. And those with no money have to look for free Wi-Fi.' And because free Wi-Fi in Alto Hospicio is difficult to come by, those with 'no money' usually remain disconnected.

Because of these constraints, it is also not unusual to see public notices on Facebook that announce 'Friends, I will not have internet for the next two weeks. If you need me call my sister's mobile phone or come see me at work'. A smartphone plan or pre-paid credit is often the only internet access for many Hospiceños. Connections in Alto Hospicio in general are tenuous, depending on the strength of mobile signals (notoriously slow in Alto Hospicio), neighbours paying their own bills or friends' willingness to pass on credit.

Yet being without money has wider implications for social media. As Eduardo explained:

> Social media are very different if you have money. For instance, now when I'm poor I have two options. Before my internet is shut off [from my mobile phone] I can say to the world that I'm poor and hope that someone I have invited out before will invite me out and buy me a drink. If I'm poor without internet I'm just disconnected and have to find something else for entertainment. But when I have money I go out, I go to parties, I take pictures and put them online. I can be like Tony Stark [from the Iron Man movie franchise] – rich, eccentric and post pictures that prove it all on Facebook.

He then showed me the meme he had posted previously featuring Tony Stark; it represented the character's wealth and lifestyle, labelled 'payday', in contrast with a photograph of an impoverished-looking man crouching, labelled 'the rest of the month'. 'That just pretty much sums it up. Sometimes you have money, sometimes you don't,' Eduardo said with a sigh.

Rather than being stigmatised, these lapses in internet access fit seamlessly into other forms of expressing identification with a marginalised economic and social class. Poverty is even its own genre of humour on social media. When the iPhone 6 became available many Hospiceños circulated popular memes reflecting on its unobtainability. One joke lamented the feeling of the new iPhone bend while in the front

Fig. 3.17 Meme featuring Tony Stark, Iron Man character
Line 1: 'Payday' Line 2: 'The rest of the month'

pocket, only to remember that it is not an iPhone but a Pop Tart. Another expressed excitement: 'I am so happy the iPhone 6 has come out! Now I can afford to buy an iPhone 4 second-hand!'

iPhones, like Xboxes, are often used as symbols of luxury goods in a way that large-screen televisions, cars and cameras are not. This humour works because Hospiceños have a common understanding that iPhones are out of reach, as well as a shared experience of some form of feeling poor. Thus through this shared form of self-mockery, they build a sense of belonging in the community which takes as its base the normative experience of being marginalised.

Those who pushed the boundaries of class presentation on social media at times became a topic of gossip. Much as Vicky resented her ostentatious neighbours, other women complained about their acquaintances who showed off too much of their wealth on Facebook. Lilia, a mother of five in her fifties, told me:

> I have known plenty of people that are always talking about how poor they are. But then on Facebook I see they have a new car, they went on a trip, they buy accessories. Personally, these people bother me. Facebook tells the truth. They're stingy, they don't want to share.

For Lilia, social media works as a window that allows her to check up on neighbours and acquaintances in an effort to patrol the boundaries of normativity.

The joys of mediocrity

Hospiceños usually represent their wealth as normative on Facebook, but performing normativity extends beyond their current economic situation to the ways they present their aspirations (or lack thereof). A common genre of meme shared on Facebook represents success or a luxury lifestyle framed through humorous exaggeration. The meme picturing Tony Stark provides one example of this exaggeration, in which payday is presented as a moment of luxury in an otherwise meagre existence. Through this and other funny memes Hospiceños contrast themselves with representations of success, thereby actively aligning themselves with normativity.

One funny example of this style uses self-deprecation to position the individual as mediocre. The meme, which Jhony and Miguel originally found on Jaidefinichon, then shared on Facebook, features several sperm racing for an egg. The meme presents the self, even before

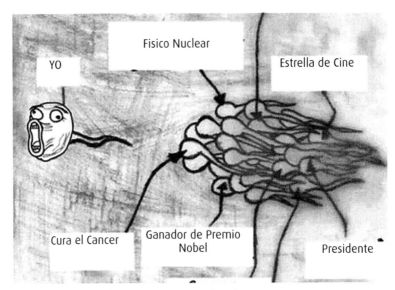

Fisico Nuclear

YO

Estrella de Cine

Cura el Cancer

Ganador de Premio Nobel

Presidente

Fig. 3.18 Meme depicting sperm racing for an egg
Me   Nuclear Physicist   Movie Star
Cure for Cancer   Nobel Prize Winner   President

conception, as the disappointing result of almost random chance. Of all the possible sperm with extraordinary potential for brilliance, good looks and leadership qualities, the one that succeeds is mediocre. This form of humorous exaggeration places the self in contrast to greatness, claiming solidarity with the average individuals of Alto Hospicio. The frame of humour indicates a joking acceptance of such fate.

Another meme declares the advantages of physical mediocrity, claiming, 'Being ugly and poor has its advantages. When someone falls in love with you, they do it from the heart.' Again, individuals who post this meme portray themselves as mediocre or even below average in looks and wealth, but highlight the positive side of their situation – the knowledge that their relationships are sincere. At the same time they subtly suggest a correspondence between above average (good looking and rich) individuals and insincerity. They present normativity as a positive characteristic and devalue that which is usually idealised, reinforcing the sorts of social sanctioning created by women such as Vicky and Lilia in their gossip about neighbours and friends who show off too much.

Acceptance or even pride in a mundane life is especially apparent from a certain style of meme that overwhelmed Facebook toward the end of 2014. These *Rana René* (Kermit the Frog, in English) memes express a sense of abandoned aspirations. In these memes the frog expresses

Fig. 3.19 Rana René meme

Translation: 'Sometimes I want to quit working. Later I remember that I don't have anyone to support me and I get over it'

Fig. 3.20 Rana René meme

Translation: 'Sometimes I think about modifying my motor. Later I remember that I only have enough [money] for an oil change and I get over it'

A veces me dan ganas de
romper la dieta...

luego me acuerdo q no la he
empezado y se me pasa.

Fig. 3.21 Rana René meme Translation: 'Sometimes I get the urge to break my diet. Later I remember that I never started and I get over it'

desire for something – a better physique, nicer material goods, a better family or love life—but concludes that it is unlikely to happen and that therefore '*se me pasa*' [I get over it].

Similarly, during June and July of 2013 a common form of meme served to contrast the expected or idealised with reality. The example in Fig. 3.22 demonstrates the 'expected' image of a man at the beach – one who looks like a model, with a fit body and tanned skin set against a picturesque background. The 'reality' shows a man who is out of shape, lighter skinned and on a busy urban beach populated by other people and structures. It does not portray the sort of serene, dreamlike setting of the 'expected'. In others, the 'expected' portrays equally 'ideal' settings, people, clothing, parties, architecture or romantic situations. The reality always humorously demonstrates something more mundane, or even disastrous. These memes became so ubiquitous that they were even used as inspiration for advertising Toddy cookies.

Health and body image are often commented upon in posts that demonstrate how normativity is more highly valued than excellence.

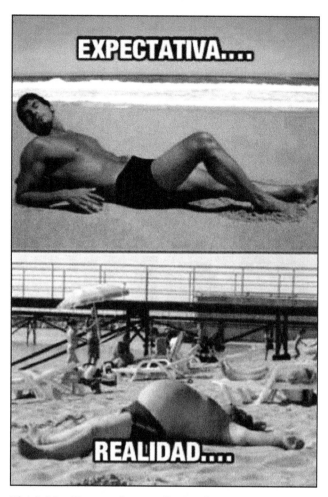

Fig. 3.22 'Expected vs. Reality' style meme

Unlike in many contexts where fit bodies are idealised, in Alto Hospicio it is precisely the imperfect body that is widely praised. One common meme suggested, 'A man without a belly is like a sky without stars'. Overall, discourses alluding to the acceptance of different body shapes manifest in the use of nicknames as well. Many parents or older relatives refer to their children (no matter their age) lovingly as 'mi gordo/a' [my little fatty]. Many people also called their siblings, cousins or friends Gorda or Gordo. In a sense, these are reactions to the more general idea promoted by mass media, including global television and movies, national or international magazines and even local celebrities that thin or fit is the most sexy and desirable body shape. Whether consciously or

Clic aquí para participar

Tus vacaciones soñadas están a un meme de distancia ¡Crea el tuyo y participa!

Fig. 3.23 A Toddy advertisement modelled after the 'Expected vs. Reality'-style memes

Fig. 3.24 Meme depicting a tombstone inscribed with 'Here rests my desire to study'

unconsciously, Hospiceños communally valorise a positive body image that acknowledges the ways that most people look – something quite distinct from the forms that mass media implicitly suggests are the most desirable for both men and women.

Education is another theme that emerges in posts where Hospiceños identify with limited ambition. Most young people in Alto Hospicio finish high school (*segondaria*) and many begin studies at local universities, but only a few complete a university degree. When a young person (or an older adult) finishes university the whole family is very proud, but, given work options in the region, it is also understood as an achievement reserved for only the brightest and most dedicated students. More often people train for technical degrees in electrical, mechanic or other skilled trades related to mining or work at the Zofri dock. Others eschew advanced education and go directly into the workforce, so that they can begin contributing to the family income or support their own young families immediately. These local norms and expectations endow university education with a sense of distinction that many Hospiceños equally admire and see as superfluous. Because this treatment of education is almost universal within the community and reflects the limited ambitions of Hospiceño normativity, it becomes excellent fodder for humour on social media.

Humorous memes are important to Hospiceños because they allow for play. Yet the jokes are only comfortable for most audience members if they experience the humour as non-threatening to the core values at stake.[10] In the context of normativity in Alto Hospicio, joking is a safe and obviously popular way for people to express their comfort with the normative lives they have chosen. Rather than expressing disappointment or regret that they have not aspired to more, they reaffirm to themselves, and to those like them, that their decision to remain within the bounds of normativity is acceptable or valued within the community.

Humour often revolves around self-deprecation or forms of heightening emotion, only quickly to diffuse the situation.[11] The 'I get over it' memes featuring Kermit the Frog work in this way to excite the audience, but then quickly diffuse the expectations. This functions as a form of self-deprecation associated with low income and/or ambition. While the joke would work in any context, the Hospiceños who choose these memes as part of their social media performances communicate that they not only understand the joke, but also see a correspondence with their own feelings and ambitions. Within socially accepted ideals of normativity, joking becomes a perfect way of expressing normativity, even while articulating desires to go beyond the norm. Humour allows individuals to express desires that are, under the circumstances, probably unobtainable, while simultaneously assuring others that they realise such ambition lies beyond the expected social scripts. This reinforces the sense of normativity, regardless of whether the individual feels constrained or comforted by it.

Furthermore, the visual elements of these types of humour reinforce normativity by relying on recirculated images that are almost by definition accessible to everyone. Memes do not express the originality of the individual who posts them. They are rather expressions of creativity, in that by aggregating various humorous memes on certain topics social media users actively curate funny Facebook walls, Instagram feeds, WhatsApp groups and Tumblr feeds. This means that even when memes express desires that seemingly go beyond the norm, they are still tied to some sort of collective desire, as the product of someone else's making. Images then both work as shorthand and as a further normalising aspect of social media usage.

Rethinking normative aesthetics

The unassuming form of normativity that Hospiceños present online seems at first glance to have little to do with curation. Material culture scholars suggest that individuals create social identities in part through material forms in their homes, workplaces, places of consumption, personal belongings and the styling of their bodies. Social media is just one more place where such self-styling may occur. This ability to display collections of aesthetic forms was never possible in such a public way for the grand majority of people before the internet became ubiquitous.[12] Yet it was often precisely the absence of particularly styled clothing, architecture and photography which characterised the normativity of Alto Hospicio. In expanding our ideas about what curation and aesthetics might entail, we see that the identities and lifestyles Hospiceños presented on Facebook and Instagram are both consciously constructed and corresponded to a certain, communally sanctioned social script. The aesthetic forms presented online bear a visual resemblance to the aesthetics of daily life in Alto Hospicio.

Of course, not everything an individual does – either online or offline – is an act of conscious curation. Yet when social scripts are deeply rooted, acts of curation that correspond to these forms of normativity do emerge unconsciously. Any time individuals represent themselves, they are constructing stories about themselves for others to interpret.

Again this happens both on the street and through social media, yet social media is particularly important because it provides wider access to resources. One does not need to be able to afford a Tommy Hilfiger wardrobe to represent the brand as part of their aesthetic online.

Social media also broadens the audiences for whom individuals can perform, with the possibility of a global public. Yet when Hospiceños do not take advantage of these broadened scopes, it becomes even clearer how deeply rooted the social script of local normativity is. To eschew aesthetics associated with 'good taste' because they are out of an individual's reach is one thing: to do so as a choice is another. Directing one's self-presentation to others in the same community, in a context where a global audience is possible, again reinforces the importance of local identifications and normativities, rather than positioning the self within a wider sphere. This exploration of Hospiceños and the visual materials that they post on social media then reinforces the notions of unassuming normativity that is visible simply on the streets of Alto Hospicio. In that sense social media is an extension of daily life, rather than a contrast. Hospiceños' ways of identifying represented therein further work to support community values of interconnection, social support, hard work and distinction from contexts understood as inherently different.

Hospiceños' conceptions of good citizenship become inscribed in their use of visuals in social media. The aesthetics produced in daily life are reproduced on social media, and there become a claim to authenticity as marginalised subjects. As Geertz notes, art and aesthetics may constitute elaborate mechanisms for 'defining social relationships, sustaining social rules, and strengthening social values'.[13] And when made public for a wide local audience through social media, aesthetics and visuality become central to their identifications, always intertwined with normativity and citizenship.

4
Relationships: Creating authenticity on social media

I am something of a suspicious character in Alto Hospicio. To begin with, I visibly stand out. As a very light-skinned person of Polish, German and English ancestry, I simply look very different from most of the residents of Alto Hospicio, whose ancestry is some combination of Spanish, Aymara, Quechua, Mapuche, Afro-Caribbean and Chinese. During my first week in Alto Hospicio a woman stopped me as we passed on the street near the commercial centre of the city. 'You look North American!' she stated matter-of-factly, then walked away without waiting for a response.

Beyond the simple surprise that my physical appearance evokes at times, I am untrustworthy as a single woman. As I began to develop relationships with people in Alto Hospicio they were often confounded that I had no male partner or children. Even though many people leave family behind in other countries or regions of Chile when migrating to the area, they usually move with a least one family member. The fact that I lived alone aroused suspicion. As my conversations with new acquaintances developed they would often quiz me on my social relations, as if searching for a relationship with someone in the community that might give me some legitimacy.

I of course found this frustrating – not only because as an anthropologist my job depends on developing relationships with people in the community, but also because I knew I would be living in Alto Hospicio for 15 months and I desperately hoped to make friends. Yet without some sort of evident social relationship, people were wary of befriending me.

After frustrating attempts to make friends in person, I joined a Facebook group called 'Everything Going On – Alto Hospicio'. I wrote a public message:

> Hello, I'm an anthropologist studying social media in Alto Hospicio. If anyone would like to participate in my study, or even offer advice to a newcomer in Alto Hospicio, please write me a message or respond in the comments.

Miguel, the administrator for the group, quickly sent me a friend request and offered to help. He connected me to other Hospiceños on Facebook and regularly sent me announcements for events. After two months of online communication, he invited me to see a film with his group of friends. I happily accepted, eventually becoming a regular part of the group. Miguel later told me that when he first saw my post on the Facebook group site, he was suspicious of it. He clicked on my Facebook profile and thought, 'What is a gringa like this doing in Alto Hospicio?' His curiosity prevailed, however, and he engaged me in conversation.

> I was nervous about meeting you [in person] the first time, because I didn't know what to expect. I was pretty sure you were a real person, but I was not sure. I thought maybe you weren't real. Maybe it was a fake profile. But then I saw you walking toward me and I just remember being really relieved.

Because I did not fit into the assumptions about who lives in Alto Hospicio, I experienced social barriers at first. While most other individuals there have extensive social networks, those outside of their social circles still often regard them as objects of suspicion. As in my case, social media at times provides ways to confirm a person's authenticity. For more recent migrants to Alto Hospicio, social media may be an important inroad to getting a foothold in the community. Similarly absence from social media, particularly among the most impoverished Hospiceños, acts as yet another barrier to their integration in social life. All of this is true because in Alto Hospicio, as in many other contexts,[1] the relationships that individuals maintain with other members of the community are precisely what make them part of that community. And the visibility of these relationships, whether in daily life or on social media, is essential. Without visible ties one remains an outsider.

The visibility of relationships on social media – primarily Facebook – functions as a mode of authentication in which community members recognise each other as similar to themselves, trustworthy and legitimately part of the community. In essence relationships are central to the notions of belonging that allow individuals to identify themselves and others as good local citizens. In making visible different forms of relationships, Hospiceños highlight family and friendship, in effect solidifying and expanding these relationships. By performing these relationships visibly through social media, Hospiceños both claim belonging and publicly negotiate what it means to perform as 'good citizens' online.

Suspicion, authenticity and visibility

Suspicion was a common theme in Alto Hospicio. Padre Mateo, a local Catholic priest, explained his perspective to me. I had gone to meet him at his small home in *Autoconstrucción*, one of the poorer neighbourhoods. As he served me tea I explained my project about social media. He thought for a moment, then responded, 'Well, I suppose it's good people are being social, even if it is online anyway. People don't talk to their neighbours here. There's no trust.'

Most people use their smartphones while in the home or at work. It is rare to see someone using their phone while walking down the street or sitting in a plaza. Even in restaurants and in shops, people seldom look down at their phones. This is equally true when travelling on public transport. The bus ride from Alto Hospicio to central Iquique takes about 45 minutes, which always seems to me the perfect time to catch up on social media. However, most other passengers listen to music, fall asleep, eat snacks or talk to their companions rather than using their phones.

One day in the central market I talked with a group of vendors about smartphones. I asked specifically why so few people use them in public spaces, and they responded that people are always afraid someone will snatch their phone. 'Sometimes right out of your hands,' said a woman who sells jackets on her stall. 'Oh, the pickpockets are all around in Alto Hospicio,' added her friend, who sells children's school supplies. 'I think close to 75 per cent of people have something stolen from them every year.' This saleswoman's estimation is inaccurate according to official crime reports,[2] yet there is a widely held perception that one is never safe from pickpockets in Alto Hospicio. At least once a week I see a friend post on Facebook that they have been assaulted and had a mobile phone stolen. Even Padre Mateo mentioned this to me, lamenting how much more common petty theft is in Alto Hospicio than in other Chilean communities where he has worked. However true or untrue, this perception certainly has a profound effect on local discourses and behaviour.

Even when I first posted a message on the 'Everything Going On – Alto Hospicio' Facebook page, the responses revealed the ways in which

Fig. 4.1 Cartoon meme depicting the stereotype of *flaites* in Alto Hospicio. Translation: 'How I am in reality/How people see me when I say that I am from [Alto] Hospicio'

residents conceptualise danger in the city. Several people told me to be careful, posting advice about which blocks were dangerous to walk alone (even during the day) or which neighbourhoods were filled with drug dealers and *flaites*. Others offered warnings such as 'never go into anyone's house', 'don't eat or drink anything anyone gives you' or 'only use regulated radio taxis. The ones you hail might rob you'.

Many people are constantly worried about having things stolen from their cars – even such seemingly valueless items as half-full plastic water bottles – as well as having the car itself stolen. Car security systems are so ubiquitous in Alto Hospicio that one must learn quickly to sleep through the beeping and honking of car alarms. Jhony, a member of the Red Foxes Motor Club, was especially worried about having his Jeep stolen by Bolivians. 'It's 4-wheel drive, so if they steal it they can just drive it over the border, in the middle of the desert to avoid check points, and then it's gone,' he explained to me.

Local suspicion was also heavily influenced by the still recounted story of the 'Psychopath of Alto Hospicio', who kidnapped, raped and murdered 14 young women in 1999 and 2000, throwing their bodies into an abandoned well in the desert. When their parents reported the teenagers missing, the police force refused to investigate. Because the girls were from very poor families, the police believed they had more likely run away to become prostitutes or joined the narco-trafficking trade as 'mules' in Peru. Using the stigmas of illegal activity associated with poverty, the police shirked their responsibility to investigate and the disappearances continued. Even when families of the young women tried to involve investigators at the national level, the investigative police force ignored their requests. Only after the final potential victim escaped from her assailant did law enforcement officers begin to search for a suspect. When police eventually caught 'the Psychopath' they discovered that he was a relatively recent migrant from the central region of Chile: a newcomer who had few connections in the community.

What was especially significant about both stories was that the suspicious character was an outsider. These discourses relied on stereotypes of distrust. Bolivians are likely to steal cars; newcomers may potentially kidnap children. The residents of Alto Hospicio, still a place with a sizeable migrant population, are often suspicious of those they do not know. The suspicion that I aroused when I first arrived in Alto Hospicio was simply another example of how locals view unknown individuals as untrustworthy and possibly dangerous until they have a better sense of who they are, their motives and, most importantly, their connections in the community.

The ways in which individuals describe their social media use reflects this mentality. Strangers are not to be trusted. Yet mutual friends have the ability to transform someone from a stranger into a potential friend. When Miguel made 'friend suggestions' on Facebook so that I could add his friends to my account, few people declined my request. However, when I requested people without mutual friends I was almost always rejected.

Older Hospiceños in particular are quite suspicious of fake profiles and criminals searching for victims online. While many teen users create fake profiles to play pranks on friends, older Hospiceños stigmatise these types of profiles. They are particularly suspicious of online relationships, often retelling stories they have heard about con-artists using fake profiles to lure unsuspecting individuals into relationships in order to scam them. Rodrigo and Gabriel, two middle-aged men who work at the port in Iquique, had a conversation about social media one afternoon as they paused to eat lunch in the company dining facility. 'There are lots of people, they speak beautifully, but when they are in person they change their way of being. There are criminals like that. Rapists and extortionists. They look for victims online. That's why this technology is no good,' Rodrigo warned.

The truth was that, in all of my interviews and surveys, I did not meet anyone who had been taken advantage of online. The only example of online dishonesty I encountered came from Jhony. He explained to me how he had once developed a romantic relationship online with a Brazilian woman whom he later discovered had lied to him; she had sent him pictures of another woman that she had taken from a website. However, even this level of subterfuge actually seems to be a rare experience among Hospiceños. Yet suspicion and discourses of danger online proliferate. This suspicion is one reason that the authenticity of others online becomes a primary concern for Hospiceños.

'Authenticity' is a term, much like normativity, that can be defined in various ways, depending on its context and the aims of the person using the word.[3] The concept of authenticity does not indicate an 'inherent essence', but is relational; it relies on contrast with what individuals in the context consider false or deceptive. Authenticity can be established by the ways in which people represent themselves through various communication methods,[4] including spoken and written language, self-styling and the visual modes of representation I discussed in Chapter 3.

For Hospiceños, social media is a space for representing themselves authentically – as they are in daily life. This does not necessarily mean that they divulge their deepest secrets in order to be genuinely themselves, but rather that they employ certain tactics to distinguish between realness and artifice. I am not suggesting that on social media all Hospiceños always tell the truth, nor that they never engage with notions of fantasy nor express themselves outside of the bounds of local normativity. Rather, performing a sense of authenticity as a Hospiceño is the mode of social media use that predominates. In visual terms this means curating profiles that corresponded to local expectations of visuality, for example photographs recognisably taken in Alto Hospicio and Iquique, sharing memes and almost always commenting with humour.

Following such norms serves to mark an individual as belonging, but for Hospiceños demonstrating relationships is an even more direct way to present themselves as familiar rather than strange. In many contexts friending strangers may lead to increased status, and is at times central to the reasons why people use social media.[5] In Alto Hospicio, however, evaluating someone as a stranger is likely to result in social exclusion – refusal of friending, deletion or at least ignoring the 'non-authentic' user. Strangers are objects of suspicion: only those who may be authenticated through some aspect of their online profiles are to be trusted enough to accept friendship or interact.

Authenticity relies heavily on the visibility of relationships with others in the community, and social media is central to the ways that Hospiceños make these relationships visible. As Pappacharissi suggests, Facebook is 'the architectural equivalent of a glass house'.[6] Knowing that social media postings can be seen by members of the community, users perform their social ties to and for others.[7] However, these performances of authenticity are not simply a product of social media; anthropologists have documented the importance of visibility in relationships long before the internet, or even computers, were invented.[8] Social media does not revolutionise these relationships; its importance lies in providing a new medium in which labelling and visibility can occur. Particularly in the context of suspicion related to the community's marginalised position, social media is key to the ways in which authenticity is produced, as part of creating a sense of belonging and broader concepts of citizenship.

Family relationships on social media

In Alto Hospicio social life is centred on private spaces such as the home. Rather than meeting friends at the local bar on a Friday night, Hospiceños invite a few people over to their houses. They celebrate important events with an *asado* barbeque with the extended family at home rather than an elaborate meal in a restaurant. Hospiceños watch important football matches in the kitchen, drinking cans of Escudo beer with family and friends. Even marriages are often quiet family affairs rather than large community celebrations.

This intimacy of events means that often Facebook is one of the most publicly visible ways in which people interact, particularly for non-school age children. Relationships, whether between family members, romantic partners or friends, remain out of the public eye. For this reason it is often important to demonstrate these relationships actively on social media.

The family is usually the most important institution in Hospiceños' lives. A majority of families have three or four generations living together, often encompassing one or both parents, their adult children, their significant others and young grandchildren all in the same modest house. Families eat meals together and combine financial resources. They are generally all expected to help with the physical and emotional labour of the group, whether that involves caring for children or helping out with home construction projects. Families watch films together, go on outings to the beach or events in Iquique and simply pass time chatting after meals. Parents and children are usually emotionally close, and there seems to be little resentment towards parents other than the usual teen complaints of not being allowed to stay out late or do recreational activities before finishing schoolwork. While some parents and grandparents feel that social media has become a barrier to the types of intimacy that families once shared, most proudly embrace social media as a way to connect further with their families and to express familial love.

On average, survey respondents said that about 30 per cent of their Facebook friends were family members.[9] Almost everyone under the age of 50 had at least one parent as a friend on Facebook, and 80 per cent of respondents were friends with their brothers and sisters. Of course, being Facebook friends does not necessarily constitute meaningful interaction. Yet by looking at the actual Facebook timelines of family members, it is clear that most do interact frequently. Mothers and fathers both post copious amounts of pictures of their children (and grandparents of their grandchildren), often using these images as their profile and cover photos on Facebook. Children in their twenties and thirties post photographs and messages on their mothers' timelines, and tag their parents in photos, memes and shared bits of text.

Facebook allows users to elect 'family members' among their friends, and for Hospiceños this often was a way of demonstrating not only familial ties, but close friendships as well. In general the line between close friendship and familial relation is often blurred, a situation reflected on social media. The category of 'family', both on social media and in daily life, includes not only several generations of sanguine relatives (those related through blood),[10] but also individuals or other families of 'fictive kin' who have been close for a long time.[11] Most people choose to list their parents, siblings and children as family members on the information page of their Facebook account, but it is clear that these lists also include brothers, sisters, cousins, aunts and uncles who do not share any formal kinship ties. A young man's best friends will often be listed as brothers. The younger sister of a good friend could be listed as a cousin. And god-parents or other family friends of older generations are listed as aunts and uncles. These lists, of course, reflect the titles that Hospiceños use face to face, particularly for *tias* and *tios* [aunts and uncles], showing the importance of the family as the primary organising unit of social life. Extending these fictive kin designations to social media, however, also serves to make these relationships more visible. Listing someone as a family member, as well as visible interactions such as posting on their timeline, signal the strength of the relationship to a wider audience.

In Alto Hospicio many children (of all ages) feel that it is important to show affection by explicitly thanking their mothers on Facebook. In doing so, they not only engage with their mother, but also perform for a wider audience the role of being a good child. They post photographs of the family doing activities together, such as celebrating a birthday, cooking meals together or simply spending time at home. The reverence a mother receives from her child serves as a form of authenticating the child as a respectful and respectable person.

Like the posts discussed in the previous chapter, memes are an easy way in which children can connect with their mothers. Many acknowledge the sacrifices mothers made for their children. One meme of simple pink and black text on a white background declares: 'My mother . . . traded her beautiful figure for a huge belly; traded her purse for a diaper bag; traded her calm nights for long sleeplessness; traded her makeup for big circles under her eyes. I believe that the perfect woman exists and she's called Mom.' Sometimes mothers respond with a similar meme almost word for word (See Fig. 4.2).

While mothers and their adult children share these kinds of memes, parents of younger children perform parental satisfaction on social media by documenting their children's growth in photographs and status updates. And while clearly these posts express sincere affection, they serve a dual purpose of marking life stages related to normativity and senses of good citizenship in Alto Hospicio. Young people here often become parents in their late teens or early twenties, and social media use reflects this timing of life stages. Hospiceños comment that it is very unusual for young people to reach 25 without having had a child. Twenty-four-year-old Nicole often complained that her own parents and her boyfriend Martin's parents pressured them to get married and have children quickly. When I asked Martin about this he told me, 'Well, people usually have children when they're

Fig. 4.2

Motherly love meme. Translation: Sometimes I have changed an eyeliner for dark circles . . .

Straightened hair for a ponytail

Crazy nights of parties for staying up all night taking care of my sick child

Stylish purses for a diaper bag

I'm mom . . . and it doesn't matter at all to me what I've left behind for the LOVE AND SATISFACTION of a 'MOM, I LOVE YOU SO MUCH'

13 here! No, the usual age is 20. By 25 the train has left the station, at 30 it must be that you're really professional. By 35 you're getting really worried. Well, at least that's what people say!' My survey results seemed to confirm these expectations. Of people between the ages of 30 and 39, 100 per cent of men and 86 per cent of women had at least one child.

Expecting a baby is an important life stage in Alto Hospicio – but also serves to perform to Facebook and other social media audiences the act of entering into adult life, settling down and accepting responsibilities. Even when people speak about stereotypical *flaites*, they note that often after having children they settle down to become a 'family man'.[12] Performing the role of parent on Facebook communicates a certain level of maturity. Both expectant fathers and mothers anticipate their baby's birth by posting pictures of material goods associated with a baby, sonograms, monthly updates of the size of the future mother's belly and even humorous memes and cartoons relating to children.

In many countries pictures of expecting parents on social media anticipate the arrival of a new member of the family with much love and excitement. They express a period of time that carries with it a social significance. The pictures are not so much about the precise subject of the photograph – just how big the belly may be or the exact shape of the foetus in the sonogram – but what they represent: less the enjoyment of pregnancy than the excitement of preparing for a future child. In Alto Hospicio these photographs also communicate to the public their social positioning as parents (or soon-to-be parents), again with the aim of legitimating their status as trustworthy or not subject to suspicion.

As children are born and grow up, both mothers and fathers continue to post photographs of them. Often, as noted above, they include their children in their own profile pictures or cover images on Facebook. Young girls are often referred to as 'mis princesas' [my princesses] and young boys as 'mis gordos' [my fatties], always with a sense of pride. Indeed, in many families in Alto Hospicio a sense that young children can do no wrong exists in tension with the value placed on being 'bien educado' [well educated]. Rather than applying specifically to formal education, being 'well educated' is better demonstrated through good manners, using the formal 'usted' [you] instead of informal 'tú' when speaking with adults and in general using good grammar. While minor threats are often given, such as 'no television while eating the meal if you won't finish your dish', these are usually empty, and children who come to appreciate this often ignore them. Yet young children are without a doubt expected to behave well outside of the home: They are expected to thank adults for meals or gifts and to play quietly in public. Children are valued as gifts,[13] but their conduct, even when they have become adults, reflects on their parents. On social media mothers create posts expressing pride that their children are 'good kids' who respect and love their parents, while children express pride that their parents are a part of their lives.[14] Such representations reflect positively on parents as capable of raising good children and thus portray them as good citizens themselves.

Portraying oneself in a positive light on social media is especially important in Alto Hospicio because the small number of public spaces limits the visibility of relationships. Both parents and adult children are able to represent their identification with a family-based lifestyle, and thus further authenticate themselves in the valued social scripts common in

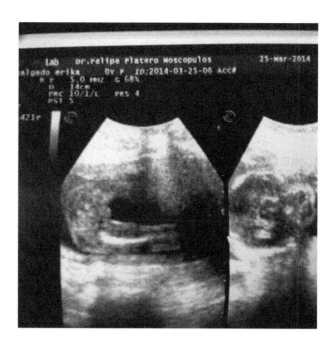

Figs. 4.3 and 4.4   Photographs of pregnancy

Fig. 4.5 New baby meme. Translation: Why hire a professional photographer if we can take [photos] ourselves. . .

Alto Hospicio, through social media posts that demonstrate their familial connections clearly. Visible family connections work to strip away suspicion, as there is an underlying assumption that parents are more trustworthy than individuals without children. Similarly, portraying oneself as a devoted child, a devoted parent or a parent who has raised well-educated and respectful children reinforces perceptions of individuals as valued community members and 'good citizens'. And while all families have their own quarrels and internal family secrets, in Alto Hospicio the emphasis on family online truly seems to reflect the closeness and importance of family in daily life and behind closed doors.[15]

Social media sites of visibility

The centrality of private spaces to social life in Alto Hospicio means that in addition to familial relationships, romantic relationships and friendships also gain visibility most prominently on social media. Padre Mateo explained to me that formal marriage is somewhat uncommon. Young people often remain unmarried because they perceive that tax benefits and government assistance to buy a home are actually accessed more easily when single. However, it is common for couples to cohabitate, even if in the home of one of their parents, and to have children together. While these arrangements are certainly public, at times changing their Facebook status from 'pololo/a'[boyfriend/girlfriend] to 'novio/a' [fiancé(e)] or 'esposo/a' [husband/wife] may be the most public expression of commitment.[16] For example, when 22-year-old Giovanna became hospitalised a week before her planned marriage to Cristobal, they cancelled the wedding ceremony. More than two years later they still have not rescheduled, and their Facebook relationship statuses remain 'engaged'. For Giovanna and Cristobal, formal marriage is not as important as community recognition of their relationship. After having a child together and both moving in with Cristobal's parents, there is little question about the seriousness of the relationship. With the visibility of other aspects of their relationship, formal marriage is simply unnecessary.

Nicole and Martin have been a couple since high school; when I met them the relationship had lasted about six years. In 2013 both still lived with their respective parents and siblings, though they spent most nights together. Martin's mother was quite critical of this arrangement and often chastised them, saying that they should not be spending the night before making a decision to get married. 'That's why we always stay at my house,' Nicole told me. Eventually Martin's mother began to wear them down; one evening in August, when they invited me for a dinner of home-made pizza, they told me they had started discussing marriage. Just a week later I saw Nicole's post on Facebook: 'Without signing a document, without giving a previous announcement and without vows, we have made a promise.' She uploaded a picture of the two wedding bands the couple had bought.

The two then began looking for an apartment, eventually finding one in the same complex as Nicole's family. They adopted a dog together

Fig. 4.6 The picture of rings that Nicole and Martin posted on their Facebook pages

and bought a car within the next year. They had a small 'housewarming party' in their apartment, with plenty of snacks and mixed rum and coke drinks, but that was the only official celebration of their new life together. Facebook was the most public announcement of their new commitment.

The importance of visibility is perhaps best illustrated by the moments in which its absence creates a rift. Iliana and Guillermo, both in their thirties, had been dating for a year and had become quite serious, moving in together in their own apartment only a few months after they began the relationship. However, for their one-year anniversary Guillermo was working at the mine, so they celebrated with a long video conversation using Skype. Around 11pm Guillermo told Iliana that he loved her and hung up in order to shower before his early bedtime. Iliana then decided to write a special message about him on her Facebook wall. 'One year ago my life changed. I have smiled, laughed, and spent so many wonderful days hand in hand with the person I love. Thank you for changing everything, honey.' Still early in the evening, she hoped Guillermo would see it and write a comment with a sweet message for her before going to sleep. Hours later, however, he had not even 'liked' the message.

> I kept seeing our mutual friends like it and comment on it, and I kept thinking, why hasn't he? Did he fall asleep so early? So I waited until the next day and he still hadn't even liked my message! I had to wait until he got off work at 8:00 at night to talk to him again, and I felt a little silly but I asked him about it. He told me 'Oh, I didn't know it was about me.' I thought – how could it not be about you? Who else am I holding hands with? Who else do I call 'honey'? So maybe it was silly, but I erased it and wrote a new message that said 'It's so sad when you write something from the heart and the person it is meant for doesn't understand.' Within two minutes he commented 'If you tag the person they will know.' I thought that was so stupid! Obviously, it's about you, but you want me to tag you anyway. Fine.

Iliana went on to tell me that since this incident she has tried to tag him in more posts, but it does not always occur to her naturally. She recounted another incident that occurred a few weeks after their anniversary.

> I told him I was going to a party with some friends, and he asked if my ex would be there. I said yes, but that he has a new girlfriend too. I asked if he would feel more comfortable if I told my ex explicitly that I was in love with my new boyfriend, and he said, 'Well, maybe if you put it on Facebook. And tag me.'

Clearly Guillermo abides by the 'Facebook official' rule, often espoused by friends of new couples, those who get engaged or even those announcing a pregnancy. Nothing counts as 'official' until it is entered into the public record, as evidenced by its announcement on Facebook.

Fig. 4.7 This cartoon, shared by Giovanna while planning her wedding, illustrates the 'Facebook official' mentality: 'I now declare you husband and wife. You may now update your Facebook statuses.'

Other couples seem to express their relationship more naturally on Facebook. Nicole and Martin, for example, regularly post pictures of themselves together, sometimes in matching clothing, other times kissing for the camera. Almost daily they post messages on each other's walls expressing something along the lines of 'I love you, my little piggy'

Fig. 4.8 A photo collage that Nicole shared featuring herself and Martin

or 'Just a few hours without the love of my life and I miss you'. Not only does using common nicknames such as '*chanchi*' [little piggy] communicate a sense of intimacy directly to the other person, but the use of these terms of endearment also performs the intimacy of the relationship for a broader audience of social media users, serving to authenticate the relationship further in a public fashion.[17]

The story of Carlita and Alex (and his ex) demonstrates the other side of public visibility – a case in which unwanted visibility caused tension and jealousy. Alex and Carlita had been dating for several months when Carlita told me she was upset that Alex still kept in close contact with his ex-partner. She told me she trusted Alex, but was suspicious of his ex because she wrote to him 'too much' on social media.

> A few times she would call, and I could tell he felt like he had to keep the conversation short, because he knew I was watching and listening. But she would also click 'like' for every picture he put on

Facebook. She would comment and call him 'sweetie'. And I could see she was sending him voice messages on WhatsApp all the time. I mean, I couldn't say anything really, but it annoyed me. I just thought, this woman that I don't even know, she's disrespecting me, right in front of me. But if I say anything I'm the crazy jealous girlfriend. But lately she hasn't written anything, so it's getting better.

For Carlita, part of the insult was that some of these messages were public. While phone calls and WhatsApp messages were private, she would also comment in affectionate ways on Facebook. It was this other woman's presumption that it was acceptable to acknowledge publicly lingering affection that was the most offensive to Carlita.

For Carlita, like most Hospiceños, the visibility of relationships is what legitimises them within the community. In fact, making relationships visible on social media not only communicates something to the public of social media, it sometimes also has the ability to transform a more insecure type of relationship into an enduring one. In Carlita's case, the visibility of Alex's ex posting publicly gave an apparent precariousness to her relationship. Guillermo, on the other hand, hoped to solidify his relationship with Iliana through public posting, leaving no doubt in anyone's mind (particularly her ex-boyfriend's) that they were together. For Nicole and Martin, meanwhile, announcing their commitment on Facebook served the role of a public wedding. In each of these cases visibility served not only to authenticate the relationship, but also to confirm that these relationships fit into the kinds of social scripts that seem natural within the community.

Performing relationships in absence

While performing relationships online is important for almost all families and couples, social media becomes even more important in relationships that must endure physical distance. Given the importance of mining in the area, and the shifts, often a week in length, that mining employees work, there are many people (mostly men) who spend extended periods away from home. In these situations it is particularly important for people to maintain romantic or family relationships through social media. Direct communication, through Facebook messenger, WhatsApp and even Skype, are important for maintaining a personal level of connection during times of absence. Yet beyond personal communication of updates on family life and daily expressions of love, the act of missing a person is important to perform publicly on Facebook as well.

This often manifests in a genre of posts that publicly state that one person is missing another. Many miners post a daily tally of number of days on their shift and days remaining, together with a mention of what they miss, such as 'Today 5/7 – two more days until I see my honey and little munchkins'. Equally their partners, and at times their friends, siblings or parents, post their desire to see the absent family member again. Many memes express this as well, being shared among miners and their families. One week when Guillermo left for the mine Iliana tagged him in a meme expressing her feelings about the upcoming week. 'How I'm going to miss you my fatty . . . I hope the days pass quickly to be close to you. Have a great shift my love #ILoveYouToInfinity.'

Similarly when friendships become harder to maintain in person, they often shift to social media. When women in Alto Hospicio enter their twenties and thirties they often have young children, which means they are relatively house-bound, at least to an extent that many complain about their inability to get out more often. Yet at this age they are

Fig. 4.9 Meme shared among female friends. Translation: 'Me!!! I'm crazy, difficult to understand, cold, loud and sometimes intolerant, and much more. But if you don't accept the worst of my character, surely you don't deserve the best of me. Unfortunately, not all women will copy this on their walls because they think they're angels. Let's see how many of my crazy friends will share it.'

still more socially aligned with female friends. These younger women often post photo montages from months or even years past, depicting activities with friends, for instance a night out, cooking dinner together or going to the cinema. They tag their friends and write messages such as 'I have known my best friends for so long. They are always there for me, and they know I always have their backs. Thanks ladies!' Others share memes expressing similar sentiment such as the one above (Fig. 4.9).

When 32-year-old Nina shared this particular meme, she accompanied it with the comment 'That's how we are!' and tagged seven of her female friends. Each of the tagged friends, as well as a few other women who knew the group, commented on the status with lighthearted agreement. This visibility among friends served to cement the group, and to express pride in the similarities of each other's personalities.

In many ways the visibility of friendship and even romantic relationships online creates some obligations based on assumptions of reciprocity. Hospiceños feel that it is important to reciprocate visibility in a relationship, whether a friendship or a romantic association, in order to maintain good relations. If a friend takes the initiative publicly to acknowledge the friendship online by posting a meme or photograph, writing on a friend's wall or tagging friends in a post, they usually expect that those with whom they engage will equally acknowledge the relationship publicly. Different levels of obligation and visibility exist. In casual friendships, for instance, a mere 'like' of a status is sufficient, whereas for closer friends tagging, posting further memes or engaging in conversation in comments is expected.

Friendships between male peers involve their own types of reciprocal obligations, usually based around mocking humour rather than more frank expressions of solidarity. While it is rare for men to tag groups of friends in a single post that explicitly highlights their friendship, men do tag their friends or share links on their Facebook walls pertaining to their particular interests. These are usually accompanied by a sarcastic comment, which invites the recipient as well as mutual friends to continue commenting with sarcasm or other types of offensive but witty banter.[18]

For both men and women, friends demand attention offline and online. I witnessed or was told about quarrels due to neglect among both female and male friends. One member of the Red Foxes Motor Club was chastised by the whole group following his absence from several outings after starting to date a new girlfriend. 'It was fine when the group bothered me about it, but later my best friend wouldn't return my calls.

I thought he was being a child, but he was really upset that I hadn't seen him in weeks,' he explained.

Other friends use social media subtly to express their disappointment in friends they perceive to be less than loyal. One woman told me that one of her best friends had recently become Facebook friends with her ex-boyfriend's new girlfriend.

> I was a little hurt. She was supposed to be my friend. I know she still sees my ex sometimes because they were friends even before we started dating. But it seemed funny she added this new girl. The next time I saw a meme about friendship, I made a point to share it and tag her. Not only to remind her how close we are, but also to show that girl, maybe she had my ex-boyfriend, but my girlfriends stay with me!

For groups of friends, interactions such as tagging, commenting and particularly joking through Facebook both strengthen the friendship, especially in times of absence, and also make visible these friendships – and thus how the friends are positioned in the community. Even when individuals are not able to see their romantic partner or friend in person, the relationship can be maintained and made visible for purposes of authenticity through interactions on social media. This suggests that Hospiceños experience anxiety, jealousy and expectation, as well as comfort and trust in friendships, in much the same ways online as they do offline. For them online interaction is not just a pale reflection or a less authentic means of expressing relationships as compared to face-to-face interaction. Their emotional involvement demonstrates that there is little value in trying to separate offline and online aspects of their relationships; they are intertwined, and interactions in one mode develop from their interactions in the other.

Building trust on social media

While connections to family and romantic partners are important for gaining authenticity within the community, the visibility of these relationships is particularly important when meeting new people. The visibility of other relationships can alleviate suspicion, particularly in new romantic situations. After Jhony described to me the online romance he had with the Brazilian woman, he told me that now he only pursues women whom he meets through mutual friends, though this includes using Facebook. 'It's much better meeting a friend of a friend, because you know who they are. They are nearby and have the same interests. And you know they are real.'

Though he said he would not admit it to his friends, he continues to search for love online.

> My friends do it too, even though they won't admit it. Before it was Badoo. Now people use Facebook, and that's almost as good as real life because you can find out so much about the person. If they don't have many friends you get suspicious. But if you have friends in common there's no reason to worry.

Thirty per cent of survey respondents said that they had dated someone they met online, but almost none used applications or websites specifically designed for that purpose. Miguel, who also told me he occasionally uses social media to meet women, further explained.

> People don't trust things like dating websites, or something like Tinder. You don't know who the person is. You can't see their friends, or really a profile on the application. But people trust Facebook. If you're looking at someone on Facebook, you can see your mutual friends, and you can see where they are from and maybe their hobbies. So you get a sense of the person, who they really are. You know they're not fake.

These young men feel that Facebook offers a much fuller representation of the person, and seeing an expanded profile allows the viewer to 'authenticate' the person by seeing their social network – their family, friends, colleagues and acquaintances. To encounter a mutual friend or acquaintance in the person's friend list reduces suspicion of artifice and increases confidence that the person is authentic – both 'real' in the sense that they are not using a fake profile, as well as similar in the sense that they are located in the same social sphere. On the other hand a short list of friends unknown to the user indicates a level of artifice to the profile, signalling that perhaps the person is not to be trusted.

At times social media not only makes visible social networks, but also facilitates their expansion. More important than writing statuses, or even than posting photographs, memes, videos or links to websites of interest, relationships are fostered through the commenting in which people engage. It is not unusual to find a single sentence status update that has more than 20 comments by Hospiceños. Many comments are positive and supportive. When a young woman posts a new profile picture, it usually receives comments from all of her close friends and relatives expressing essentially the same thing: 'Oh daughter/niece/friend/cousin, you look so pretty and happy!' When someone expresses a complaint, for example neighbours playing music too loudly, comments usually range from 'How annoying!' to 'Do you want to borrow my big speakers so you can show them your music is better?' These comments generally serve a function of staying in contact and supporting friends and family, simply by reminding them that their Facebook friends are paying attention and care about them.

Others comment in humorous and mocking ways – particularly male friends, as I mentioned above. Alvaro, when returning to Alto Hospicio from visiting family in Santiago, wrote a one-word status message: 'Travelling.' The first comment was purely informational, asking 'From where to where?' and Alvaro responded with an equally simple answer 'Santiago – Alto Hospicio'. But from there the conversation diverged.

> Alvaro's cousin: Did they inject you to travel?
> Alvaro: I know asking will have negative consequences, but no. What kind of injections?
> Alvaro's cousin: Haha, all the animals when they travel, they have injections to sleep. Be careful, the fines are steep for animals that don't get injected. Good luck on your trip!

After this initial exchange, 20 more comments appeared – from Alvaro's other cousins, friends and even one friend's mother. All played off the joke that he lacked certain 'civilised' attributes and should be treated like an animal while travelling.

This type of mocking language is similar to ritual insults such as 'joning' or 'signifyin' that linguists discuss for African American Vernacular English (AAVE) speech communities. When successful these language games demonstrate verbal skill (or in the case of Facebook or Twitter[19] written language skill) and social status.[20] The speakers and audience share the understanding that what is being said is open to evaluation for their skill with verbal play.[21] Unlike AAVE ritual insults, however, in the context of Hospiceños on Facebook the ability to make a witty comeback is not necessary. As Alvaro demonstrated in his reply, he understood that it was an insult – 'I know asking will have negative consequences' – but this neither detracted from his response nor did it

negate the power of the original insult. Instead the meaning is negotiated and then built upon in further comments, in a group effort that
reinforces social ties. Furthermore, these exchanges build on local common knowledge (such as Alvaro's cousin's [incorrect] assumption that
everyone would know that animals were injected to travel), which highlights the importance of community within these exchanges.[22]

It is also noteworthy that these exchanges take place in comments
rather than in private messages. Such mockery is aimed not only at the
subject of playful insult, but at a wider audience as well, playing on
shared cultural knowledge.[23] And in Alto Hospicio this humorous form
of exchange almost always makes extensive use of Chilean language
conventions, in another level of marking authenticity as a member of
the language community. The ability for others to add to the joke, or
even just respond with 'hahaha' creates a common space for people to
converse in a playful way. In effect almost all commenting, whether
explicitly positive or joking, serves to form cohesion, not just between
the post writer and the commenter but among all those who comment.
In the case of Alvaro, many of the people who commented did not know
each other personally. Yet all played off one another to create a complex
running joke among a wider social group.

This type of cohesion has impacts that extend beyond social media
as well. Community is created not only by supporting friends, but also
in the instances in which friends of friends begin to engage directly with
one another. Several people told me that they first 'met' a friend by seeing their comments on a mutual friend's Facebook posts. At times they
might jokingly spar or build on one another's mocking jokes within the
space of Facebook comments. As Miguel put it:

> If you have a friend and they write something funny, then you
> might comment. And then friends of friends – people you don't
> know – may see that comment, and then maybe you get into a dis-
> cussion with that person. Eventually you see that you keep com-
> menting on the same posts, and you'll become Facebook friends.
> A few times this has happened to me, and then I end up at a party
> with that person, and it's almost like we already are friends. After
> that we might do activities together, like really become friends.

Creating a semi-public dialogue, visible to friends of friends who often
join in these joking exchanges, these individuals become first potential and then sometimes actual friends. In turn becoming Facebook
friends leads them to engage in activities face to face, whether sharing

meals, playing sports, going out or any other number of leisure activities. Having more local acquaintances also helped in finding a new job, buying and selling used items online, or even in searching for potential partners.

Authentic citizenship online

Interactions on Facebook actively maintain relationships, communication and social ties in Alto Hospicio. Yet they also build community through creating new relationships. Social media posts serve as visual markers of these relationships, which then authenticate the relationship to others in the community. In a marginalised community, where suspicion often acts as a barrier to senses of citizenship connected to community belonging, this visibility is vital. It provides a way of ensuring an individual's authenticity in order to develop trust.

When I asked Hospiceños to send me 'selfies' to include in this book, not a single person sent me a picture alone without prompting. Men sent me photographs of themselves with friends, women with their children or nieces and nephews, and teens with their classmates. The message was clear: individuals see relationships as more definitive of 'who they are' than any form of individual self-expression. Even the selfie – often thought of as the ultimate example of self-centred performance on social media – is in Alto Hospicio a way to represent the self as enmeshed in relationships with others. Each person may not consciously decide to make their relationships visible in order to appear as an authentic character on social media, but they do actively judge others on these criteria, perpetuating the social script.

In family relationships (whether sanguine or fictive), romantic partnerships and friendships, Hospiceños publicly perform reciprocal interactions on social media. The importance they place on the visibility of each kind of these relationships online reflects the ways in which connections to other people in Alto Hospicio are a key part of what it means to be part of this community. Because relationships are important to maintaining the prevailing normativity of Alto Hospicio, these social scripts tend to reinforce the discourses of homogeneity that are clear in discussions of race and class (as discussed in Chapter 1), as well as gender (which Chapter 5 will explore). Thus the visibility of relationships online becomes a key component of the normativity of Alto Hospicio – not because there is any inherent connection between relationships and normativity, but because in this context both constitute a performance of being an integrated member of the community and a 'good citizen'. Furthermore, as the practice of becoming friends with a mutual acquaintance makes clear, once an individual is authenticated as a member of the community he or she is trusted to be included in new social circles much more readily. In essence, social media acts as a conduit for building and sustaining relationships as a mode of reinforcing local norms, citizenship and the idea of community itself.

5
Work and gender: Producing normativity and gendered selves

One day while scrolling through postings I noticed a controversy brewing on 31-year-old Omar's Facebook wall. He had posted some text – meant to evoke a mixture of sincerity and humour – about his vision for the future.

> Searching: for a woman who wants me to cook her lunch and clean the house. She is required to work, buy the food and treat me to drinks occasionally. Also maybe buy me an Xbox. Send me a message!

Several men posted supportive comments or 'liked' the post, but a few of Omar's female friends and acquaintances wrote comments which accused him of being *flaite*, or scummy, for such a post. One complained about men in general: 'Why do men think they can just be lazy and someone will take care of them? You're perfectly capable of working. Time to go look for a job!' To this other men responded that women were perfectly capable of working as well, yet no one complained when a woman moved in with a man and let him support her.

While this argument was not resolved in the comments on Omar's Facebook wall, it does reveal some of the deep cultural assumptions that circulate in Alto Hospicio. These assumptions maintain that there is something of a symbiotic relationship between men and women. Men almost always work outside the home and women often maintain the daily functioning of the house. They clean, cook for the family, take kids to school, care for younger children, go to the utility offices to pay water, electricity, cable and telephone bills, and otherwise organise the daily life of the family. Men work long hours to ensure that there is sufficient income to keep the home running. Women at times work outside the home as well, but when they are with a male partner these jobs are usually considered supplementary income.[1] The daily lives of individuals, and thus their self-understandings, are deeply affected by this gendered division of labour.

Omar had recently quit his job at the mine due to chronic health problems aggravated by the high altitude of the mining operation and was considering other work options. I ate lunch with him and his mother Ximena one day, and over a bowl of rice and lentils she asked him, 'Gordo, what's your plan for getting a job?' He responded with frustration, listing some possibilities. Then he changed his tune. 'Wait a minute! Constanza [his sister] has never had a job. And she has two kids. You never ask her when she's going to work. Why me?' Ximena laughed and reminded him that Constanza had a fiancé who also worked at the mine and provided for her and her children. 'And I need you to take care of me. I'm getting old!' she added.

As previous chapters have shown, social scripts in Alto Hospicio are deeply laden with expectations of homogeneity – in terms of class, race, education, access to resources and even what is acceptable to show off. Yet gendered forms of normativity are just as deeply embedded in the social and economic lives of Hospiceños. Omar's post demonstrates the ways that differences in expectations for women and men adhere to normative social scripts surrounding gender, sexuality, families and work. When Omar expressed his desire (whether sincere or ironic) to live outside of this norm, his expression was met with criticism. Most notably this criticism came primarily from women, suggesting that they did not see gendered normativity as an oppressive structure, but as something that was mutually beneficial.

These gendered expectations, which in part form notions of sexual citizenship, are closely tied to practices of work and labour, both within and outside of the home. Social media becomes a key ground on which these expectations are expressed, challenged and most importantly reinforced, regulating the boundaries of acceptable and unacceptable ways for men and women to behave. Social media provides both access to a world of examples of different gendered assumptions and an arena in which to test out other possibilities. But in Alto Hospicio social media is most often used as a stage for many individuals – both men and women, both young and old – to reinforce forms of gendered normativity and 'good citizenship' that have structured social life in Alto Hospicio and Northern Chile in recent decades.[2]

Work and industry in Northern Chile

Since the Great North was incorporated into Chile after the War of the Pacific (1879–83), its economic activity has always been defined by its natural resources: first nitrate, now copper and the Pacific Ocean ports that allow for a proliferation of international trade. Mining in particular is essential to not only the North, but to the nation as a whole, making up 60 per cent of the nation's exports and a large part of its GDP.[3] Scholarship on mining in Chile is plentiful, but almost always focuses on economic and environmental issues, particularly in relation to indigenous groups and corporate social responsibility.[4] While these are important concerns, the impact of mining and what may be called the mining lifestyle on individuals' daily lives and self-understandings should be equally important to anthropological analyses. Analysis of labourers' personhood, the conditions in which they labour and even the structure of life outside of the workplace are of equally vital importance to understanding the reorganisation of the labour process within neoliberalism.[5] The ways in which such work regimes intersect with gender and citizenship are of further importance in understanding normativity. The lens of social media allows us to appreciate how mining not only effects the environment and economic systems, but also people's daily lives, interpersonal relationships, sense of identification and notions of what makes a 'good' Northern Chilean citizen.

Hospiceños suggest that about 25 per cent of male residents work in mining, many of whom also have several family members who work in the industry. Most mining employees spend 5, 7 or 12 consecutive days working 12-hour shifts. During these work periods they live in dormitories at the mine. Social media is incredibly important for miners during these work weeks, providing key links between distant family members. Older miners use text messaging and increasingly WhatsApp to communicate with their families, while younger men keep up with their friends' latest news on Facebook and use WhatsApp to communicate with girlfriends and their parents. Many miners lament that the worst part of the job is feeling so far away from their friends and family. One miner even described life at the mine as being in an 'asylum'. Yet many also say that the highlight of the job is the fact that their schedules allow them to spend a good deal of time with their families. When working 5, 7 or 12 days at a time, miners are usually entitled to an equal number of free days, so rather than weekdays and weekends, life for mining families is often divided into weeks-on and weeks-off.

Jorge and Vicky moved from Arica to Alto Hospicio with their two young children, Alex and Gabriela, in the mid-1990s, so that Jorge would have a shorter weekly commute to his job as a mining machine mechanic. When Alex graduated from high school Jorge encouraged him to take a job at the same mine, and eventually Gabriela began dating their colleague José, also from Alto Hospicio. When I met them in 2013 Jorge, Vicky, Alex, Gabriela, José and Samuel, Gabriela's son from a previous relationship, all lived together in a large house in the centre of Alto Hospicio. The men's shifts overlapped by a few days, so the house often filled and emptied like an hourglass. Jorge would leave on Monday night, then José on Tuesday and Alex on Wednesday. At times this coincided with Samuel's father's schedule of visits, and only Vicky and Gabriela would be left in the house. Then, as the new week began, one by one the men would return to the house, and the time that Vicky and Gabriela described as lonely and boring would become busy and lively.

Both miners and their families live in a sort of waiting game for weeks off. In Vicky and Jorge's family this means that, while the men work, the women try to accomplish as much in the home as possible. Mining companies pay sufficient salaries to enable the earnings of Jorge, Alex and José to support the extended family of six people. Vicky and Gabriela spend their week cleaning, doing laundry, shopping for food and household items, going to doctor appointments and working on home renovations. In their 'down time' the women watch telenovelas or children's cartoons with Samuel. In the evenings they chat on Facebook with friends and family who live in other cities, as well as with their partners at the mine.

When the men arrive home from the mine the whole family enjoys time together, eating big meals and taking day trips to the beach in Iquique. With half of the family away half of the time, multi-generational families like this usually prefer to live all together. Vicky, in particular, likes having everyone in the same house because her parents and siblings live in Arica, about five hours away. 'If we lived in separate houses I would be lonely during the men's shifts. I'd rather have my daughter and her family here in the house, to keep it lively. If no one's around there's not even a good reason to cook for myself,' Vicky told me.

This arrangement contributes to a sense of matriarchy in the house. Because Vicky is always there and her husband often is not, there is an overwhelming sense that she is in charge. She manages the finances and is not afraid to ask Alex and José for contributions. She is often the one who makes sure that Samuel goes to school and has his homework done.

She does the cooking, but also directs conversation at the table during lunch, the biggest meal of the day. She is a kind and joking women, often calling Alex, José and Gabriela by pet names, but there is an unmistakable sense that she is a woman who should not be crossed.

Of course not all families are so structured by a mining work-schedule, but the division of labour within the other families is remarkably similar. Men most often work in manual labour industries and women care for the home. At times women also work in service industry jobs, but they generally still take the majority of the responsibility for the home, even when working in the paid labour force as well. Many people take jobs in Iquique, particularly at regional offices, at the port or in the Zofri mall. However, it is important for women in particular to work closer to home, so that they can be present for big family lunches, continue to manage day-to-day life in the house, and ensure everyone in the family is organised for their own activities.

The landscape of commerce in Iquique thus greatly impacts the types of work that both men and women take. While Alto Hospicio is a sizeable city, the physical spaces of commerce are quite limited. Those that do exist are almost all small, family-owned businesses (the supermarkets and home improvement store being the only exceptions). Indeed, the majority of commerce that takes place in Alto Hospicio happens in small family-owned *almacenes* [corner stores] or the market stalls of the *Agroferia* [outdoor market]. While the markets have official administration, vendors pay rent for their assigned stalls and there is even a small fee for customer parking, the overall feeling of the place is one of informality. Prices may be haggled, for anything from a head of lettuce to a used smartphone or sweater. One can find kitchen wares, cleaning products, children's toys, small furniture, new and used clothing, power tools, key copiers, cameras, phones, used stereos, pet merchandise and all manner of food products mixed among the stalls.

Shopping in the Agro market remains a normal task for Hospiceños, but Facebook is becoming an alternative to this type of commerce. Used products including furniture, baby-related goods, clothing and even cars are constantly being bought and sold on numerous Facebook pages with names such as 'Everything for Sale – Alto Hospicio'. With no local exchange websites such as Craigslist or Gumtree, or even the availability of eBay or Alibaba for purchasing international goods, Facebook takes their place, as well as partially encroaching on in-person commerce in the *ferias*. While most Hospiceños use these sites to sell the occasional older television or outgrown baby accessories, some entrepreneurs create Facebook profiles for their small retail businesses which function entirely through the site. These entrepreneurs are largely women who capitalise on internet commerce in order to maintain a business without neglecting their usual tasks in the home.

Even as new forms of labour emerge in Alto Hospicio, work in the city remains quite distinct for men and women. Normative social scripts often incorporate these differing forms of work; in addition, notions of normative femininity and masculinity are often deeply tied to the kinds of work in which women and men engage. As individuals post about their work, it is clear not only that men and women overwhelmingly labour in different manners, but also that they incorporate these different forms of labour into their self-understandings. The ways that representations of both work and gendered expression become visible on social media allows for further reinforcing their prevalence.

Work and masculinity

Men's work in Alto Hospicio tends to be in industries traditionally labelled 'masculine', often revolving around manual labour and skilled crafts. Other than mining, many men work at the docks in the Zofri port, in construction, as drivers of taxis or shipping vehicles, or as electricians or mechanics. These types of work are often central to men's sense of self and are shared with great pride. On Facebook men post memes declaring the value of their profession and the importance it carries in their daily lives.

These men, who dedicate long hours to manual labour, often view work not as something that takes away from other preferable activities, but as something integral to the way that they understand their lives. One cargo truck driver posted a photo that expressed his pride in being a driver – an idealised picture of a truck against a sunset overlaid with the text, 'This is not my job, this is my life.'

One miner expressed a similar sentiment through a piece of text shared as a photograph on his wall, titled 'What is a miner?' where he tagged all of his workmates. The photo seemed to be taken of text that was printed out on a white sheet of paper and posted on the wall in a work place. Of course it is hard to tell if this photograph was taken at this miner's own workplace or had been extensively passed as a meme on social media before he posted it. It could have easily been used to describe work in a number of professions. Nonetheless the miner felt it had particular salience for him and his line of work.

Fig. 5.1 Meme depicting identification at work. Translation: 'This is not my job. This is my life'

> What is a worker? A worker is that man that gives his life for his family. It is he that leaves his family and goes far in order to give them a much better future. That man that is honest and honourable, it is he that doesn't have Christmas, New Years, nor holidays, that doesn't celebrate his own birthdays nor those of his loved ones. That doesn't know summer from winter, because all the days are the same. It is he that like a national flag is washed with rain and dried in the sun. He is that man that doesn't see the birthdays of his children, but always shows their pictures proudly saying "This is my son or my daughter!" His work is anonymous, but his feat is immortal. The doctors cure sicknesses, the architects build, the teachers teach, and I as a WORKER offer the most humble that I have. A LIFE FAR FROM HOME.

It is no surprise that miners develop a strong occupational identity. Isolation and group solidarity, combined with the history of the labour movement in the area, provide a context in which identification with this particular form of work is almost essential for mental health. Miners' experience of collective socialisation, high interdependence, physical proximity, physical boundaries, isolation and danger often contribute

Fig. 5.2 Meme depicting frustration with work. Translation: 'Fucking shift, I want to go down [to home]'

to strong work subcultures.[6] While Hospiceño men's work may not be glamorous, it remains a source of pride and is central to identification and self-understanding.

While work is often integral to men's identification, part of this involves complaining about it. One of miners' biggest complaints is separation from their families and the physical distance between work and home. Many miners post a daily tally of days completed of their shift and days remaining, such as 'Today 5/7'. Others post memes that explicitly communicate a desire to go home. Almost all post Facebook messages on their partners' or family members' walls telling them that they miss and are thinking of them. One man even posted photographs of snow in the Altiplano on his girlfriend's Facebook wall, with the message 'I'm cold!' in an effort to share daily challenges. These types of posts allow the workers to share their daily lives with absent individuals.

Fig. 5.3 Photographs from the mine. 'I'm cold'

In their time away from their families, however, men also create lives at the mine that are not just centred on their labour. They make friends and entertain themselves in ways that allow them to feel something beyond simply being a worker, making their shifts not just 'time away', but an important part of their social lives as well.

Mining is perhaps the most obvious example, but many other lines of work are spaces almost exclusively made up of men. This contributes to worksites being characterised as overall masculine spaces, in which workers often incorporate a joking 'locker room' type attitude. One young man described the attitude as '*mariconeo*' or 'faggy'. He told me, 'Everyone goes around doing things really gay. Joking, touching each other's asses. Bothering each other, like playing pranks on one another. Because it's seven days without your family. You get bored. You invent ways to amuse yourself. Everyone hugs. Just jokes.'

Fig. 5.4 Photograph from the mine. 'At work with my *compañeros*, a good group!'

Fig. 5.5 Photograph from the mine. Miners working in masks for Halloween

Fig. 5.6 Photograph from the mine. Miners celebrate a colleague's birthday in the recreational restaurant at the mining site

Fig. 5.7 A meme illustrating 'the *Titanic*' position

Another young man described a common joke, which he called 'the *Titanic*'. 'If you ever find your friend at the edge of something. Like if there's a gate, or a railing that they are looking over, you just go up behind him and say "do the *Titanic*", and then spread your arms out. Like Leonardo on the boat.' He told me that most of his friends think it is funny and play along, but a few are annoyed and get angry.

This form of joking, often referred to as *weando* in Chilean Spanish, carries a connotation of immaturity and is often contrasted with a more serious life outlook. Alex told me this is even part of a common saying at the mine.

Fig. 5.8 Translation: '*Titanic,* and an unforeseen problem'

De la garita pa adentro	From inside the gate
Anadamos weando	We go around joking
De la garita pa abajo	From outside the gate
Somos personas educadas.	We are educated people[7]

'It means in the mine, we mess around with each other. But in the city, we all say hello to each other, "hello how are you?" more formal. They are two different lifestyles, and we act accordingly.' Yet, as the memes above demonstrate, social media allows for some mixing of the two lifestyles. Despite the physical distance between home and work, social media provides a conduit for workers to have a piece of home while at the mine, as well as enabling them to continue joking with friends, acting as another form of masculine space while in the city. While the spaces of home and work – particularly for miners – are mutually exclusive and circumscribed, social media allows them to mix the two, thereby mixing their different manners of formal interaction and *weando*.

While this sort of joking masculinity is primarily reserved for work, or at least work friends, men also perform specific sorts of masculinity as part of their families. Men often post explicit philosophies about being a man. These position them as being in charge, the provider of resources or the saviour of the family. One popular meme declares: 'Man is not one that abandons the ship leaving his family to drift. Man is he who takes the problems on his own and his family on his shoulders and rows so the boat doesn't go down.'

Although this meme uses a metaphor of rowing a boat, this form of manual work stands in for others forms such as mining, construction or even office employment that keeps a family 'afloat'. Most men see it as their duty to support the family financially and, as comments on Omar's post confirm, many women are complicit in, or even actively support, this conception of men's duty to work. Both men and women see work as integral to men's self-identification or the ways in which they express who they are to a larger audience. While men often complain about their long shifts at the mine, they also speak of their jobs with great pride and see their work as an important contribution to the family. Many Hospiceños confirm these men's contributions are ways of caring for a family, just as important as women's caring through emotional labour.

Women's work

While many men work in trades in which their interactions are primarily with other workers, women's work is often more geared toward inter-action with clients. In performing jobs working with children, the elderly, in Iquique's casino, supermarkets, small shops or in customer service for a local business, women also incorporate their work into notions of self-understanding. In fact, they are often just as adamant about expressing the importance of their work as men are. Michelle, a pre-school educa-tor, always becomes very offended when she is considered anything less than a trained professional. On a number of occasions when referred to as a *parvularia* [along the lines of a 'preschool worker'], she would take time to explain that she was actually an *educadora de parvulario* ['a pre-school educator'] and all that the job entails. She would even vent this frustration on Facebook at times, explaining to the potentially massive audience of social media all of the education and background training necessary for her career.

Many other women work as part of a family business. Because Alto Hospicio hosts so few chain businesses, family-owned corner shops, butcher's shops, pet shops, restaurants and various other service businesses proliferate. Women's labour in these areas is considered essential to the operation and longevity of the business. While such work is not necessarily closely connected to women's self-understanding, it is part of their family involvement which is central to their identification.

Yet the majority of women over 40, and plenty of younger women, do not identify closely with their work outside of the home. Most women who take paid employment work in jobs paid by the hour, for instance in supermarkets, small corner shops, the mall at Zofri or as cleaning professionals.[8] These jobs are usually considered as supplementary income for the family, and are often thought of as temporary. Women may work a few months at a supermarket, but if the family decides to remodel part of the house, or if a relative becomes ill, they are likely to leave their job outside the home in order to dedicate time to these other matters. When the project concludes or the relative recovers, they might begin to look for work again, perhaps taking a job as a cleaner at an Iquique hotel.

As social media gains popularity in Alto Hospicio, many women see Facebook as an opportunity for a side business. Women often sell prepared lunches from their homes, taking orders through Facebook and WhatsApp, or have online retail businesses selling everything from imported handbags to sex toys. Usually they open a separate Facebook page for these businesses, though the proprietor usually makes sure to post announcements on their personal account. While these businesswomen hope for longevity for these online stores, they are equally seen as 'supplementary' rather than essential income for the family.

In July 2014 Maritza launched a new business, Sexo Escondido [Hidden Sex]. She ordered a set of sex toys, including aphrodisiac pills, vibrators, lubricants, handcuffs and massage oil from a company in Santiago. She then created a Facebook page, posting photographs and describing the products, offering complete anonymity to customers, though the 'likes' on the Sexo Escondido Facebook page remained public. She sent invitations from the page to her friends (including her siblings, parents, aunts and uncles). She also made sure to request friendship from the bar in Alto Hospicio, as well as other local businesses, such as a pastry shop and a handbag sales outlet, that operated primarily through Facebook.

She told me that she thought there would be a lot of interest in an online sex shop. Her rationale was that the sex shop in a prominent neighbourhood in Iquique had been in business for years, but Alto Hospicio had nothing like it. She liked the fact that Facebook provides a bit of secrecy for people who may not be comfortable publicly buying sex products.

Several months later, when I asked Maritza about the business again, she told me that she had not sold many products. She remained hopeful, though, because there are not many businesses in Alto Hospicio. She knew that she had a strong base of friends, acquaintances and other community members in Alto Hospicio who would be eager to support a neighbour rather than someone unknown to them. She still had her day job, working as a cashier in a local supermarket, but the family relied primarily on her husband's income.

> I don't worry about selling things quickly, because I have another job. And David [her husband] has a good job. It's more just for fun. If it takes a while to sell, that's fine. More than anything, I just thought it would be nice for the city to have something like this. For people to be able to buy without going to Iquique, and from a community member.

Commerce such as Maritza's sex shop and other Facebook-based businesses takes place without the kinds of bureaucratic oversight to which formal shops or even stalls in the Agro market are subject. They are usually presented as hobbies or fun pursuits rather than business or 'work'. Yet they are also spoken of as vital to the community. Maritza frames her business as fulfilling a need in the community, thus it further functions as a form of service rather than simply a means of making extra money.

Her thoughts are reflected in general perceptions of local businesses. Most people do not see them as advertising to make more money, but rather as making their ability to fulfil needs visible – again conceived as something of a symbiotic relationship with their clients. As institutions (in this case corporations rather than the government) have left the city without more structured means of exchange, individuals and small groups take responsibility for creating services. Regulations are left aside, and the economic relationship is seen as mutually beneficial in Alto Hospicio.

This attitude is particularly relevant for food delivery businesses. Much like the paucity of commercial retail outlets in Alto Hospicio, the restaurant sector is small. There are dozens of small lunch restaurants, about ten Chinese or sushi restaurants, two fried chicken fast-food chain locations and one pizza delivery service. For a city of almost 100,000 people, however, this leaves quite a bit scope to sell more prepared food. Plenty of families operate fast-food type pick up services out of the front room of their home, serving *completo* hot dogs and *salchipapas* – a mixture of fried potatoes and bite-sized pieces of hot dogs. Other family businesses, usually run by women, find success creating a pre-order and delivery service through their Facebook pages. Home-made sushi delivery businesses at times seem to dominate my Facebook newsfeed. In these businesses the owner will publish the daily or weekly specials on the page, allowing customers, with several days' anticipation, to place their orders, and to specify the time that they would like the sushi delivered. On the day of operation the owner will create large batches of home-made sushi, such as rolls with tuna or salmon, avocado, cream cheese and rice, and then send a family member for delivery along with the small cups of soy sauce and sweet teriyaki.

These businesses are so closely associated with women's labour that when Gonz and his brother Victor started their sushi delivery business they listed it on Facebook as 'Ana's sushi', using Gonz's wife's name. Gonz explained:

> I thought people would trust it more with a woman's name, you know? And Ana helps with taking the orders or putting together the boxes, so it's not really wrong. But I always think it's funny when we see a customer and they talk to her like she runs everything. I just stay quiet and smile.

Gonz had the idea to start the delivery business after a major earthquake, when the highway to Iquique was cut off. He often mentions that he does not even like sushi himself, but saw that it was becoming popular in Alto Hospicio so learned how to make it by watching YouTube videos. Then he put in a Chilean spin.

> Chileans like rich food. They like hot dogs with lots of mayonnaise, so much mayonnaise it's overflowing . . . so I tried to make sushi more Chilean, with lots of cream cheese, with avocado and lots of sugar in the rice. And the panko fried rolls are the most popular, without a doubt. So now people in Alto Hospicio can get exactly the kind of sushi they like, without having to go to Iquique. I make it easier for everyone.

Customers enjoy the convenience of delivery, but also see it as a way to support local businesses. For local entrepreneurs such as Gonz or Maritza, these Facebook businesses allow them to supplement other income by

Sushiland Alto Hospicio agregó 2 fotos nuevas.
13 de enero a la(s) 14:05 · ⚌

No sabes que preparar para el almuerzo??? No t preocupes en Sushiland Alto Hospicio tenemos la solución, pide tu rico sushi y sorpre a tu familia!! Tenemos 20 piezas calientes fritas en panko, 10 piezas envueltas en cibuolette, 10 piezas envueltas en sésamo!! Con diferentes rellenos, como camarón, pollo, kanikama, cebollin, albahaca, queso philadelphia. Haz tu reserva x inbox o al número ▮▮▮▮▮▮▮▮▮

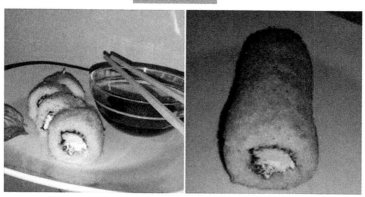

Me gusta · Comentar · Compartir

Fig. 5.9 A sushi advertisement. Translation: 'Don't know what to make for lunch??? Don't worry, at Sushiland Alto Hospicio we have the solution. Order your delicious sushi and surprise your family!! We have 20 pieces hot fried in panko, 10 pieces wrapped in scallion, 10 pieces with sesame!! With different fillings like shrimp, chicken, onion, basil and cream cheese. Make your reservation by inbox or call!!'

opening food businesses informally; thus avoiding the bureaucracy associated with having an official restaurant licence. The ability to set their own hours or only open sporadically also allows families to maintain primary jobs, travel or devote time to other pursuits, attending to the business only when they want or need to, depending on demand. In such a way these entrepreneurs, usually women, positioned themselves not only as caretakers of the family, but also as caretakers of the community.

While women often say that they enjoy administering these types of businesses, it is clear that they are not central to their self-understanding – despite the labour they put into these operations, they continue to report their occupations as homemaker or nonworking. Yesenia, who works part-time for the municipality and often volunteers even more time to organise community events, told me several times that she was 'unemployed'. Her Facebook page, like those of many middle-aged women, focuses on her family and community involvement. These women position themselves as mothers, grandmothers, cooks, organisers and managers. Most women's postings revolve around family and friends, or creative activities that contribute to the home.

Family is very important to most Hospiceños. It often acts as a source of validation (see Chapter 4), as well as acting as a group with whom resources are shared and which is the centre of social life. Many young women, shortly after completing high school, begin their adult lives as mothers, and their Facebook posts proudly show off the latest pictures of their children. However, identifying as a mother involves more. It is often the creative work involved in being a *good* mother, and thus a 'good citizen' that becomes a focus of attention on social media. Pictures of activities with children and craft projects often dominate young mothers' Facebook walls. At times they upload dozens of photos

Fig. 5.10 Photographs of party decorations. 'Decorating a party for my little princess'

Fig. 5.11 Instagram of shopping trolley. 'Today, in the supermarket'

showing off not only their child's birthday party, but also the lengths to which they have gone to decorate, organise and hold the party. Of course birthday parties are not everyday occurrences, and the mundane details of life, such as taking care of the home, are also displayed on social media.

As children grow up, some women feel their primary purpose in life has changed and begin directing their energies towards business pursuits, as discussed above, or more involvement in the community. Such women often post status updates announcing community events, expressing their pleasure at events' success or share pictures of their own involvement. Yesenia often posted photos of events she helped to organise for elderly people in the community, such as the beauty pageant for older women shown below.

While these posts in some ways serve to demonstrate normative notions of interacting in a strong community, they also serve as a form of identification for the women who post them. Though their children

Fig. 5.12 Photographs of community activities. 'They are our queens! Congratulations to all of the older adults of our city . . . And thanks! They don't know how they give me energy!'

may be grown, these activities keep the women active and, as Yesenia suggests, give them energy.

Of course not all women are able to rely on income from men's wages, whether that of their father, brother, husband or son. Although formal marriage is uncommon, separating from a partner with whom an individual shares a child often completely rearranges the daily lives of both women and men.[9] If young people leave the family home to establish their own house with their partner, they often return after a break up. Local priest Padre Mateo confirmed this trend, suggesting that in part young people do not like to get married because they do not see their relationships as permanent, even when they have children with their partner. Instead, women in particular think of their natal family as the keystone of their family life.

For single mothers, support from the natal family is not always sufficient to maintain their own families. While some women get by working at a supermarket or cleaning homes, with financial assistance from their parents or siblings, others need to seek employment considered more serious and permanent. Many of these women work in office settings in Iquique, leaving their children alone or with family after schooltime; others even work in food service or cleaning in the mining industry. Though working at a mine provides the best source of income by far, it requires week-long shifts away from the family – something many Hospiceños considered much harder for a woman than a man. 'Because it's one thing for a man to be out of the house all the time, but for a woman it's harder,' one male heavy machine operator told me. Many women also complain about sexual harassment in the mining operations, because they only make up about 10 per cent of the workers.

Many male miners seem to feel a certain sense of pity about women who work at the mine. Their sympathy reflects both the women's own alienation from life at the mine as well as the perception others have of the life circumstances that compel women to work in the mining industry. One male mine electrician told me, 'Generally, if [women] are working up here, they need a good salary. Most of the women I know, if they go to work cleaning, it's not that they like it; it's that they live alone, or they have kids and need to support them. So they take advantage of the opportunity for a good salary.' For these women, as for many men, salary is more important than lifestyle and enjoyment of work. It is viewed as a noble sacrifice to make for the family.

While, on one hand, the ways that men and women treat work differently suggests gendered imbalances in the community, most people value work within the home as a legitimate form of labour.[10] Such a belief contributes to the sense of how men and women work symbiotically to balance different types of necessary labour, rather than one relying on the other completely. The normativities associated with types of gendered labour are strong, but many women still often feel empowered and exercise this social power within both the family and the community. While social scripts about gender thus prescribe particular ways for men and women to labour, relate to their families and friends and even express themselves in public, social media reveals how these scripts are usually met without contention.

Gender, work, pleasure

Because work is usually naturalised as either feminine or masculine, labour and gender tend to reinforce one another in individuals' self-understandings. A miner who sees himself as masculine will highlight the masculine aspects of his work, thus reinforcing both pride in his job and using work-related behaviours to reinforce his sense of masculinity. A woman who enjoys working with young children will emphasise the emotional aspects of interactions as the highlight of her job, thus calling upon a typically 'feminine' characteristic of the work – emotional labour[11] – as the reason she identifies deeply with the job. This is, of course, mutually reinforcing. What is always already assumed to be masculine or feminine makes the person who performs the act *feel* more masculine or feminine, and becomes reinscribed in discourse as precisely that which constitutes femininity or masculinity. This is because, as most contemporary theory on gender emphasises, gender is not something inherent in a person, but a socially determined concept. Gender is actively created through various forms of self-expression, behaviours and even unconscious actions that are slowly learned throughout a lifetime along the lines of dominant social scripts.[12] These aspects and actions of individuals, taken together and in the context of other individuals' self-expression, create the impression that gender differences in personality, interests, character, appearance, manner and competence are 'natural'. The gendering of work that is apparent in Alto Hospicio reinforces this appearance of naturalness.[13] As most jobs are primarily held by either men or women, and these divisions by and large fall along the lines of historical gendered division of labour, it is easy to see the boundaries as natural – even though in other situations or contexts, work may be divided differently.[14] Gender is not simply an aspect of work, but is constructed through the work itself.[15]

Work then contributes to a broader sense of gendered normativity, in which the aspects of labour – usually wage earning manual labour for men, and supplementary emotional labour for women – correspond to overall typifications of men and women. Workers of both genders are more likely to accept, or even to be proud of, their labour identity when it allows them to enact gender in a way that is satisfying.[16] Thus it is not surprising that social media expressions about work often reinforce the aspects of work that men and women find most satisfying or worthy of pride. Men portray their work as requiring a tough exterior ('it's cold') and elements of sacrifice ('A worker is that man that gives his life for his family'), but also is made tolerable through the sort of camaraderie typified by the immature laddish humour among friends of *weando*. Women portray their work as forms of emotional care, often using creativity for the benefit and enjoyment of others (particularly young children or the elderly), and through their work strengthen the bonds of family and community.

The economy of Alto Hospicio and workplace relations have created something of a 'separate but equal' mentality about gendered labour. Yet the implications for these gendered expectations have effects that reach far beyond the workplace (whether that is away from or within the home). These divisions in many ways structure a kind of gendered citizenship in which being a trusted member of the community relies on following gendered social scripts related to labour. Though these self-understandings may not be entirely conscious or explicitly articulated, they inform actions. Because these expressions are usually implicit rather than explicit, simply asking often does not elicit clear explanations of these gendered identifications. However, social media is one visible way in which they became manifested.

The types of gendered expression apparent in the division of work also become manifested in men's and women's general styles of expression on social media. As evident in the previous chapter, the ways in which men and women relate to their friends of the same gender is often different: men assume joking, sarcastic tones, while women post emotionally charged memes aimed at their female friends or children. Similarly, when men and women post about the types of activities that give them pleasure, they continue to follow the dichotomy of manual and emotional labour.

Many men spend a great deal of time posting memes, pictures and status updates related to vehicles. Motorcycles, cars, trucks and jeeps are relatively cheap, either purchased new from Zofri or used from other traders in the area, so they are well within most families' means. Yet rather than presenting vehicles as consumer goods, they are usually portrayed as a site of (pleasureful) work. Gelber writes that at the turn of the twentieth century in the United States, the typical middle-class man began taking over home chores previously done by professionals. This shift happened without cultural resistance because 'household construction, repair and maintenance were free from any hint of gender role compromise.'[17] Particularly in Northern Chile these realms correspond to the types of manual labour the majority of men do for wages,

Figs. 5.13 and 5.14   Photographs of work or modifications on vehicles

thus their theoretical market value gives them masculine legitimacy. Framing these activities as being performed for the family's benefit reasserts this already strong conception of masculinity. Photographs of vehicles on Facebook rarely simply show off the car; they usually portray a modification, such as special lighting, or the process of work, such as engine maintenance.

While some women are part of this 'car culture', and are usually welcomed by men, it remains clear that they are women participating in something masculine, rather than their presence serving to make the cultural form more feminine. The meme below, which suggests, 'Just because she loves cars doesn't mean she is less feminine', seemingly complicates the gendered association between cars and masculinity. Yet it only posits jeopardy for femininity, suggesting that the overwhelming masculinity of cars could be powerful enough to de-feminise a woman. Though it rejects this postulation, the meme (and thus we might assume those who share it) never question the association between masculinity and vehicles, as might a phrase such as 'Just because men like cars doesn't mean they are any less masculine'. Instead, because the activities associated with cars corresponded to the types of manual labour that are part of jobs heavily populated by men, the association with masculinity remains unchallenged.

Similarly, men's enactment of family-related tasks is often framed as a welcome helpful hand. One meme, depicting a man decorating a cake, suggests, 'Just because you help your woman in her work does not make you less of a man. On the contrary, it makes you a unique and great man' (see Fig. 5.16). This meme, similarly, does not question 'woman's work' as being based in the home and taking care of a family. Instead it reassures men that 'helping' is not enough to erase their masculinity; rather their masculinity is so deeply instilled that doing something deemed feminine simply reaffirms one's status as a 'great man'.

These memes, which reference forms of labour associated with another gender, further suggest that, while types of work for men and women are naturally different, there is no shame in doing work that pertains to the other. Yet in reaffirming individuals' ability to cross gendered work lines, these memes reinforce the idea that this line indeed exists. That which is naturally 'feminine' about women and 'masculine' about men cannot be erased through their individual behaviours or hobbies.

Fig. 5.15 Meme depicting gender assumptions. Translation: 'Just because she loves cars doesn't make her less feminine'

Fig. 5.16 Meme depicting gender assumptions. Translation: 'Because you help your woman in her work doesn't make you less of a man. On the contrary, it makes you a unique and great man'

Normativity and sex(uality)

Memes that depict a man doing 'women's work' or a woman pursuing 'men's interests' actually serve to strengthen gendered assumptions. In many ways expressions of sexuality on social media also strengthened the connections between manual labour for men and emotional labour for women. This appears most explicitly in reference to men's work, as again they identify more closely with their paid labour than women. This was especially true for men working in the mines, because expression of their sexuality is constrained while at work. Given the 90/10 per cent gender division, and rules that prohibit women from entering men's dormitories and vice versa, the miners I spoke with described heterosexual activity at the mine as a complicated feat. They suggested homosexual relations could be slightly easier, but public bathrooms and shared dormitories did not make it particularly easy. Instead pornography was widely thought of as a substitute for sexual intercourse. As one male mining mechanic jokingly put it, 'There's a microtraffic in porn at the mine, and it's shameful on a world scale.' Social media is key to these exchanges, with individuals trading short videos via their mobile phones. Another young man who drives large vehicles carrying mining extract explained that 'for every worker, they have 20 friends in the city who send them stuff too', whether music, amusing videos or pornography. 'And no one is ashamed', he concluded. Though the mechanic described the prevalence of pornography as shameful, he did so in a sarcastic way, actually reinforcing the driver's point that no one is ashamed of it. While in other situations the prevalence of pornography might be considered inappropriate, within the mining context it was accepted as a natural alternative to actual sexual relations.

Indeed there is little shame for men who express sexual desires and frustration about their inability to fulfil them while at the mine, whether they are in a relationship or not. Such enforced abstinence is often portrayed as one more form of sacrifice that miners make in order to support their families, and thus is part of their pride in their work. This manifests in a genre of somewhat self-deprecating memes that miners post about the perils of infrequent sexual activity.

These memes are passed around as part of the humorous and immature *weando* social relationships between men, strengthening homo-social bonds but also reaffirming masculinity through connections between sexuality and their labour. Not only does their work make them more masculine because it supports their families and relies on skills associated with masculinity: it is also a sign of their sexual virility. To express frustration with weekly abstinence confirms the sexual desire assumed to be part of manliness. The following meme, though seemingly from a woman's point of view, is often posted by men on the last days of their shifts. 'Today he comes home from his shift. He has seven days in the mine. He comes home like a Bolivian truck.' This meme is particularly locally suited, relying on knowledge that a Bolivian truck – frequently seen travelling from the port up through the Altiplano to the Bolivian border – is usually overloaded with goods to be delivered in Bolivia. The metaphor suggests men coming home from the mine are 'overloaded' with sexual frustration, while playing on local stereotypes that subtly denigrate Bolivians.

Fig. 5.17 Meme posted by a miner about pent-up sexual energy after a week at the mine.
Translation: 'Today he comes home from his shift. He has seven days at the mine and comes home like a Bolivian truck'

Women are far less likely to post explicit references to sexuality, though their desires are referenced in more subtle ways. At times they post sexual memes depicting nude or scantily clad bodies, obscured by a foggy camera lens and overlaid with text expressing sentiments such as 'being with you one night is worth the wait' or 'what I want with you I don't want with anyone else'. When women do post memes with explicitly sexual messages they often portray sexuality as simply a substitute when more romantic forms of connection are unavailable.

While not all social media users post content related to sexuality, it is certainly not uncommon and is rarely commented upon in negative ways. In fact sexual content only seems to cause a stir when it involves overly graphic visuals. The fact that references to sexuality are quite common and tolerated suggests that sexuality is considered to be a natural part of individuals' self-expression. The connections drawn between men's work and their sexuality serve further to cement the naturalisation between masculine forms of labour, men's gender expression and heterosexual sexuality.

The fact that women are less likely to post explicitly sexual content reflects two interrelated factors of gender and sexuality.[18] First, in the context of Alto Hospicio, femininity is more likely to be understood as something that women 'naturally' possess, whereas men's masculinity is an achievement, attained in part through heterosexual sex, or at least representations of sex online. As something of an achievement,

Fig. 5.18 Meme depicting sexuality. Translation: 'If you're going to play, play with my clitoris, not with my heart. It feels better and it doesn't break'

masculinity is also expected to be more performative than femininity,[19] requiring men to affirm their manliness through self-expression (particularly on social media); women's femininity is called into question far less often. Often, both in daily life and on social media, men who fail to perform in ways that their peers regard as sufficiently masculine are chastised. 'Insufficient masculinity' is evidenced by anything from a man not finishing his beer to not supporting his family. While some popular memes refer to 'a real man' as someone who goes to great lengths to maintain his family economically, others chastise men whose girlfriends are more masculine than themselves. This may be evidenced by pressuring her male partner to finish his alcoholic drink by shouting 'al seco maricón culiao' [drink it all, fucking fag].

While 'maricón' is often used as a homophobic slur,[20] it also at times indicates other forms of failed masculinity,[21] much as 'fag' does in American English.[22] However, the liberal usage of maricón I noted both in daily speech as well as in social media posts does not necessarily indicate homophobia, but rather suspicion over non-normative gender performance. It is not uncommon for people to identify themselves as lesbian or gay on social media, either posting romantic messages on their partner's Facebook page or explicitly using hashtags such as #gaychile or #iquiquelesbiana on Instagram. In the public eye, however, these individuals usually follow normative gendered expectations. Many gay men upload selfies of themselves at manual labour jobs next to pictures of their partner, and women describe how pretty and sweet their girlfriends are. Though gay men are granted a bit more leeway in terms of expressing music tastes (such as Britney Spears) or types of conspicuous consumption (posting Instagram photos of Dolce and Gabbana cologne advertisements) than straight men are, overly camp expressions are absent. Alex gave me a clue to this absence when he compared his gay uncle to a gay neighbour he had in his old neighbourhood.

> My uncle, he's calm. He has a male partner, but he's not like showing it all the time. He's just like any other guy. He works at a hotel, and is really close to his family. The contrary example is my old neighbour who is always going around, talking like a woman, wearing flashy clothes. He calls attention to himself. That's why he has problems. The neighbourhood kids mess with him. I don't think it's safe for him. But my uncle, he is always fine. Because he is a *normal* guy. Most people will say 'I have no problem with gay people, I just don't want them showing it off.' So when they're calm, like my uncle, no one really cares. It's totally fine.

This reflects drag performer Pablito's fear of his family finding out about his night job, while they are perfectly content knowing that he is gay (see Chapter 1). Maintaining separate Facebook pages allows him to perform publicly as a gender normative individual, while keeping his activities that go beyond these norms more private. As Alex's narrative makes clear, these normativities are closely connected to work. Alex did not emphasise his uncle's employment, but he did highlight that he provides a source of income, thus connecting his normativity to the fact that he holds a 'normal' job. He also mentioned his uncle's connection to his family, as well as the fact that his outward appearance corresponds to normative expectations of Alto Hospicio.

As in most other facets of daily life, normativity is a deciding factor in whether social media posts or other forms of expression are acceptable. Gay men and lesbians in part disrupt what many Hospiceños assume to be a natural universal order of complementary polarity (male/female; heterosexual/homosexual; masculine/feminine) in which gendered behaviour, desire and expression relate in a congruent and coherent manner. However, most individuals' adherence to other forms of normativity, and particularly those associated with work and family involvement, are sufficient to grant them 'good citizen' status.[23] Thus for both men and women of any sexual preference, adherence to social scripts related to gendered work functions as a form of authentication. The expression of labour, gender and sexuality on social media is often intertwined, representing the conjunction of the three that serves to reinforce and maintain the others.

The point here is not that all Hospiceños fall into polarised, binary gender categories. In fact, as many of the examples in this chapter demonstrate, people deviate from these ideals all the time. While labour in part creates the structure on which these gendered ideals rest, it is also labour that acts as the conduit through which they are at times challenged. Despite the fact that Maritza's Facebook sex shop was not terribly successful, her expectations that female customers wish to purchase sex toys clearly evidences that adherence to social scripts which equate masculinity with sexuality and femininity with romance are not universal among Hospiceños. And the ways in which miners joke with each other, doing 'the *Titanic*' or other 'faggy' pranks, demonstrates the ways in which their notions of masculinity are actually quite flexible. Of course, self-understandings include aspects of sexual desire and behaviour. However, as the treatment of gay men's and lesbians' gender expression makes clear, in the context of Alto Hospicio gender normativity supersedes non-heteronormative sexuality.[24] Adhering to gendered normativity allows leeway in terms of sexuality because individuals are still perceived as following the appropriate social scripts, particularly when they are legitimised by their economic activity.[25]

However, the ways in which gender is performed and policed on social media reveal the normative ideals of gender in Alto Hospicio. Certainly representations of non-normative gender and sexual expression appear on social media. Yet they are usually framed in ways that support social scripts of complementary masculinity and femininity, rather than challenging this binary. Most Hospiceños do not see these forms of normativity as oppressive, but instead understand them as natural preferences. Yet what is perhaps most revealing is the fact that rather than providing a space for discussion and debate about such assumptions, social media is a visible public space for reaffirming and reinforcing these normativities. Those who disagree or have non-normative preferences do not seem to feel empowered to speak out through these media. Indeed, questions of who is empowered to speak, and about what topics, reveal the extent to which certain forms of normativity are embedded and actively maintained within the community.

Productive gendered citizenship

While scholarship on gender normativity (and non-normativity) is abundant, understanding how these norms are constituted and why they prevail is always context dependent.[26] In the case of Alto Hospicio, adherence to normative social scripts in many diverse areas of social life, as well a strong division of labour, provides the context in which gender normativity is highly pervasive. While in some contexts work, gender and sexuality are not closely linked,[27] in Alto Hospicio there is a tight relationship between the three. The prevalence of either men or women in a form of work becomes evidence that the job demands specifically masculine or feminine qualities, and consequently that individuals of a particular gender might be best suited for the work.[28] These assumed predispositions toward manual or emotional labour are also thought to reflect gendered preferences for types of labour as well as leisure activities. As these ideas become embedded within individuals' self-understandings, they further entrench binary conceptions of gender. While there is considerable flexibility in notions of proper gender performance, this does not undermine the appearance of inevitability and naturalness that continues to support the division of labour by gender.

The close connection between acceptability, gender normativity and work emerges from the importance of labour to marginalised identification in Alto Hospicio. Marginality is associated with the extraction of resources, including labour. T. H. Marshall defines citizenship as 'a claim to be accepted as full members of the society', yet questions whether the inherent inequalities of market economies can be reconciled with notions of full membership.[29] While in many instances neoliberal citizenship is defined through consumption,[30] Hospiceños' marginalised citizenship is defined through productive labour. Participation in the labour market – and thus the ability to pay taxes, participate in local schools, raise families and engage in other activities that make people an integral part of their local communities and institutions – can be understood as a form of participatory citizenship that allows those often excluded from citizenship to make citizenship-like claims.[31] The centrality of work to this claim to citizenship therefore means labour is also central to notions of normativity.

Given the importance of wage labour in contemporary economies, it comes as no surprise that work is central to the ways in which individuals understand their lives in Alto Hospicio. In structuring family relationships as well as those within the community, work is a mediating factor in almost all of the relationships that Hospiceños think of as important.[32] While work may be important on some levels for individuals in any context, it is particularly important in Alto Hospicio because it provides another level of authentication, demonstrating the individual's position in the community and marking them as a 'good citizen'. Salient social roles allow individuals to understand themselves as well as present themselves positively to the community[33] through reference to their occupations, forms of unpaid labour and other ways of gaining income that resemble a hobby rather than a career.

When Omar expressed a desire to not work outside of the home, therefore, he not only expressed something contrary to the normative gender divisions in Alto Hospicio – he also expressed something understood as contrary to identifying with marginality. To not want to work, in many ways, framed him as a 'bad citizen' who, rather than contributing to his family and community, hoped for an 'alternative lifestyle'.

By providing space for gendered expression, as well as identification with particularly gendered activities or aspirations, social media is also central to expressions that meld gender, work and citizenship.

To be a 'man' is to provide for the family; to be a mother involves emotional and creative work. These gendered prescriptions for identification do not necessarily correspond to the lived experience of all Hospiceños, but they do highly structure the ways in which they express their self-understanding online. In so doing they reveal the ideals of good, gendered citizenship that are central to Hospiceños' focus on normativity.

6
The wider world: Imagining community in Alto Hospicio

On 1 April 2014, around 8:30 pm, an earthquake measuring 8.2 on the Richter[1] scale struck 50 km from Alto Hospicio. The buildings shook violently for three minutes and the electricity went out. In complete darkness people began to evacuate the apartment complexes and houses as another earthquake, this time measuring 7.8, trembled a few minutes later. These earthquakes caused seven deaths, but the real disaster unfolded over the coming days, weeks and months.

For almost two weeks there was no electricity or running water in the city. The highway that connects Alto Hospicio with Iquique suffered giant fissures, leaving many stranded below or forced to walk 13 km uphill in order to arrive home. Service stations were closed to all except emergency vehicles, so very few people were even able to leave the city. Thousands of families had severely damaged homes and tent cities popped up in every neighbourhood of Alto Hospicio. The national emergency service team organised water tanks that made rounds through the city, and provided toothbrushes and blankets to those in need, but to many people's anger only allotted one of each per family. Those whose homes were beyond repair often waited more than a year to gain access to more stable, temporary, trailer-like housing. Hospiceños deemed these measures an inadequate governmental response.

The perception that government assistance during this time was both insufficient and slow to arrive only exacerbated Hospiceños' feelings of disenfranchisement. While citizen groups from nearby Arica and Antofagasta (each about five hours by car) organised volunteer brigades equipped with water, nappies and other essentials, Hospiceños were outraged at the slow response of the national government. They complained to neighbours in their tents, in central plazas, in the market as it reopened and, of course, on social media. There was no electricity, but people charged phones on emergency service generators stationed throughout the neighborhoods, or even on car batteries. With everything else at a standstill, social media use was one of the only ways to pass the day, waiting for things to return to normal, and it remained widespread in the post-earthquake atmosphere.

Whereas Alto Hospicio residents rarely take great interest in sharing news articles, in the post-earthquake atmosphere they popped up all over Facebook feeds. Those with dormant Twitter accounts began to tweet again and photographs of the destruction filled Hospiceños' Instagram accounts. Tomas, who had graduated from high school a few months previously, posted a photograph on Instagram showing his family in a tent in the plaza in front of their apartment complex. He wrote the caption, 'En el refugio esperando cuanto temblor venga . . . saludos desde #altohospicio #palaspeliculas #palasnoticias #palmundo' [In the shelter waiting out so many aftershocks. . . hello from #altohospicio #forthemovies #forthenews #fortheworld]. Though young Instagram users often wrote hashtags such as #altohospicio or #chile as a way to represent the local, Tomas's hashtags departed from this usual behaviour in explicitly announcing that the representation of Alto Hospicio and what happened there were 'for the movies, the news and the world'. Though he did not actually expect that the movies or world would pay attention, these hashtags expressed hope.

Hospiceños' photographs included the fractured highway, falling roofs and homes with residents' belongings strewn all over the floor after being shaken from the walls, shelves and drawers. Others posted photos of makeshift camps, depicting the new living arrangements of those whose homes were destroyed or were still too unstable to be inhabited during continuing aftershocks, ranging from 6 to 6.5 on the Richter scale. Photos of people waiting in queues for water, petrol and vaccinations were popular, as were images of empty grocery store shelves. The captions and hashtags for these photos seemed to ask for recognition not only of the destruction that occurred, but also of the continuing hardships people were facing, living in a city that had essentially lost its entire infrastructure.

These photographs give insight into the ways people may imagine themselves as part of, or at least worthy of attention from, the nation from which they normally feel excluded. While some neighbours wrote their claims to being part of the nation on cardboard signs, these young Instagram users claimed a place in the nation simply through using hashtags such as #porlasnoticias and even more commonly #chile.

Fig. 6.1 Author's own Instagram photograph of a sign near a large apartment complex declaring '[Alto] Hospicio is also Chile'

Hospiceños' use of outwardly focused hashtags during this time suggests that these users saw the internet and social media as an outlet for their voices. Though they usually assume no one is paying much attention to heir mundane selfies and footies, in a time of crisis they attempted to seize new media to reaffirm their place within the nation – if only as a claim to necessary relief and resources, as well as provide witness to the world of what was happening.

Social media use after the earthquake, of course, represents an anomaly which sharply contrasts with the usually locally focused ways in which Hospiceños used social media. Yet particularly in declarations that Alto Hospicio must not be forgotten as part of the nation-state, it is clear that Hospiceños, despite their feelings of disenfranchisement, still feel a claim to being part of the Chilean 'community'.

Hospiceños often experience their positioning in contrast to 'the wider world' and the Chilean nation-state, rather seeing self-sufficiency and commitment to the community as more important than wider affiliations. Yet their affiliations at all levels serve to shape and reinforce the forms of normativity that prevail, thus contributing significantly to the social scripts by which their daily lives are often affected. While the internet, and social media in particular, have been considered phenomena that unite the world, increase communication and possibly even homogenise people from diverse backgrounds, in Alto Hospicio, social media has overwhelmingly reinforced a focus on the local 'community'.

Imagining community in Alto Hospicio

Hospiceños understand themselves as a group that is politically unimportant because politicians do not need their support or vote. However, marginality is about much more than simple political representation. To be marginalised is partially about disenfranchisement, but also about living without basic needs being met. It is about being a producer rather than consumer. Hospiceños lack both political power and spending power, and within a neoliberal political economy they are then left out by both centralised politics and the consumerist system.

Hospiceños often see their commitment to the community as more important than wider affiliations. In recent years anthropologists have admitted that the 'communities' they study are rarely as cohesive as early anthropologists once took them to be.[2] Whether communities are rooted in a geographic location or are conceptualised around a shared interest, activity or worldview, they are not natural formations, but are actively produced by the people who consider themselves to belong to the particular community, through actions and discourse.[3] In essence community only exists when it is imagined to exist by those who want to belong to it.

Identification with community in Alto Hospicio works on different levels, much as Nicole's proclamation, 'I am Hospiceña, I am Nortina and then I am Chilena' demonstrated. Hospiceños see themselves as disenfranchised, but as deserving of a place in the Chilean nation. Though they lack 'horizontal comradeship', or the sense that they are on an equal footing with the cosmopolitan Others of Santiago, their claims that 'Hospicio is also Chile' represent a reconception of what being Chilean means.

Alto Hospicio is a small enough city that inhabitants do indeed meet face to face, but as their anxieties and suspicions about strangers (discussed in Chapter 4) demonstrate, people do not immediately, automatically or naturally become part of the community simply as a result of their presence there. Without sufficient social connections, unknown individuals are still strangers; they are considered to be the type of people who might put on airs or even steal mobile phones in the plaza. Instead normativity is a powerful discourse through which an idea of community cohesion is imagined. Rather than their physical proximity being sufficient, most Hospiceños feel that the basis of their sense of community comes from their shared social values and feelings of disenfranchisement. Belonging, for Hospiceños, takes the form of shared exclusion from institutions of power and collective responses that include resource sharing, dissent and ideological distancing from the people and places that they associate with this institutional power.

Frazier suggests that the northern region of Chile has been 'only partially incorporated into the nation'.[4] Nation-building, as a political project, relies on individuals' investment in that project and, as we have seen in Alto Hospicio, investment in the nation-state is minimal. But Hospiceños do not necessarily reject notions of nationalism and citizenship. Within the context of two centuries of explicit "Chileanisation," Hospiceños instead reconfigure what they understand the nation to be, framing their own marginalised experiences as those which are authentically Chilean and the experiences of more centralised urban cosmopolitan citizens as Other. Through social media Hospiceños highlight certain aspects of Chilean identity that correspond to their own experiences. Just as many young people used Facebook and Instagram to provide witness during the earthquake, residents take to social media both to make visible the aspects of Chileanness with which they identify and to represent the local area in ways that correspond to certain ideals of homogenisation.

Disenfranchisement from national politics

I started field work in Alto Hospicio just two months before a national presidential election, yet there were hardly any visible advertisements for presidential candidates in Alto Hospicio. Instead almost all political posters advertised local *Consejo Regional* [Regional Council] candidates.

My neighbour Sarita, a single mother of four in her forties, explained her views on politics, echoing those of many other Hospiceños.

> [Politicians] are all corrupt, nothing changes, and it's just like choosing the least terrible candidate. Everyone says they're from the *pueblo* [people], but once they're in government they only help themselves, or businesses that pay them off. Everything's run

by the businesses here, and the rich get richer and the poor get poorer. The middle class get a little poorer all the time too. Soon we middle class people won't exist!

Sarita's exasperation reflected the apathy expressed by many other Hospiceños. The weekend before the election I was talking with a group of young miners who would be on their week-long work shift during the election. I asked if they had to vote early or if the company gave them a leave to come back to Alto Hospicio to vote. 'Oh, well, I'm not going to vote. I don't know how it works with the mine,' one of them told me. The others agreed, saying they thought the company would give people time off without pay to vote, but none of them saw much point in voting. 'The candidates are all the same anyway. And they never do anything for the North. They just take our money for the benefit of Santiago.' This was the first presidential election in the country under a new law that repealed mandatory voting, and many people suggested that the population was relieved that they no longer had to participate in a system they perceived as corrupt and useless.

Indeed, in the whole of Chile, 5.7 million out of a possible 13.5 million (42.2 per cent) voted in this first presidential election in which voting was voluntary. The northern region of Tarapacá, with a turnout rate of less than 39 per cent, had the lowest voting rate.[5] As the newly elected (for the second time) Michelle Bachelet said in her victory speech from

Fig. 6.2   Graffiti that reads 'Don't vote . . . yes to the popular struggle'

Santiago, 'Today a lot of Chileans did not vote. We must persuade them to believe again, not in me, not in a party, not in a political group. We have to make them believe again in democracy.' With this Bachelet acknowledged a wider sense of exasperation with politics, of which Hospiceños were only a part but were also the most extreme example.

Exasperation with the political system was quite clear, looking at Facebook postings. Humorous memes disparaging the leading candidates flooded my news feed. Many played on the theme of 'If your mother is going to vote for Michelle [Bachelet], steal her identity card.' In fact almost all political postings were humorous memes, shared countless times. While a few links to newspaper articles appeared, originally composed messages proclaiming one's personal reasons for voting a particular way, or even reasons why a particular candidate was a poor choice, were practically non-existent.

As in many Latin American countries, Chile has a plethora of political parties and in the election of 2013 there were 17 candidates. This necessitated a run-off election after the initial vote on 17 November 2013. In the weeks leading up to the second election on 15 December memes intensified, particularly comparing the two remaining candidates. Both Michelle Bachelet and her adversary Evelyn Matthei are blonde, middle-aged women who actually grew up together. They represent the Socialist Party and the Independent Democratic Union, respectively, both of which are considered mainstream and centrist.[6] Many memes played on the fact that the women are very similar, yet at the same time very different from the average citizen of Alto Hospicio or Iquique.

One meme makes light of Matthei and Bachelet, playing on their bright coloured clothing. With Matthei in yellow and Bachelet in red, the meme refers to them as Bilz and Pap, a popular Chilean soda brand that features a red soda and a yellow, papaya-flavoured drink. The brand's marketing scheme declares 'Yo quiero otro mundo' [I want another world], promoting themes of creativity and imagination. Yet the meme suggests these women 'viven en otro mundo' [live in another world], separating their lives from the marginalised experiences of Hospiceños.

Memes such as these are the primary way through which Hospiceños express political positioning on social media. They are not shy about communicating their criticism or distrust of politicians on Facebook, but the amount of original content is very limited. Individuals usually post memes without comment and, unlike most other Facebook activity, they garner very few comments from friends, though often receive dozens of 'likes'. Overall people simply express disdain or annoyance at national politics, seeing it as very far removed

Fig. 6.3 Meme depicting Matthei and Bachelet corresponding to popular soda brand Bilz y Pap

from their concerns and having little impact on their daily lives. As Alex told me some time after the election, 'I'm not very political. I only know that I don't feel any benefits from the government.' This did not surprise me. Alex had previously declined joining me to watch the movie *NO*, which depicts the 1988 referendum to decide Pinochet's permanence in power. It follows the opposition – the 'No' vote – and their advertising campaign that eventually wins the people's right to elect a president democratically. The film, directed by Chilean Pablo Larraín, was nominated for a foreign-language Oscar and was considered an international success. But Alex said he had no interest in seeing it because he didn't really understand politics. 'People of my parents' and grandparents' age, they lived through it. But I don't really know the history, so movies like this . . . well, I'd rather watch *The Walking Dead* or something.'

Juan, a local activist and former student movement leader, helped to explain the apathy I sensed among many Hospiceños.

> There is a lost generation on the left in Chile. The [Pinochet] dictatorship did an excellent job of getting rid of the opposition. They killed or 'disappeared' everyone. There was no one left at the end. No one to lead a resurgence. So we're starting over.

Fig. 6.4 Meme depicting 2013 presidential candidates
Bachelet (on the left): My father was in the Chilean Air Force
Matthei: My father was also in the Chilean Air Force and he gave me
the moon and the sun
Bachelet: But my father gave me cake with Colun (brand) caramel,
he gave me pancakes with Colun caramel and he gave me powdered
pastries with Colun caramel
Matthei: It shows, fatty

The violent political atrocities experienced a generation ago, along with
the enduring political separation that Hospiceños perceive between the
North and Santiago, in large part explain the fact that people feel alienated by national politics. Most Hospiceños reserved the label 'politics' for
national issues from which they usually express distance. Though they
very strongly identify with particular aspects of Chilean culture, they
see their citizenship as Chileans through a frame of disenfranchisement
and disinterest. Yet for many their sense of community requires a certain
level of participation in local politics. By framing this type of activity
as 'community involvement', they separate what they see as necessary
concentration on local issues from what are usually considered corrupt
political dealings on the national level. Such demarcation allows them

to denounce 'Politics', while remaining involved in the local dynamics of the municipality.

Local P/politics

Juan and his *compañeros* [comrades or political associates] see themselves as part of the rebuilding of the Chilean left.[7] They run for city office, organise art exhibitions and performances, stage protests against neoliberal multinational capitalism, arrange observances promoting environmental responsibility and have even founded their own political party. These former classmates from Universidad Arturo Pratt in Iquique see local change as the means through which large-scale change is possible. Juan, who acted as the de facto campaign manager for Raquel's *Consejo Regional* campaign, told me the night before the preliminary election, he would 'obviously' vote for Raquel, but had not yet decided which presidential candidate to vote for. For him the local election was far more important.

The primacy of the local was visible from both Juan and Raquel's Facebook posts about elections as well. On a daily basis both posted articles from local newspapers about local candidates. One evening, while I was drinking tea with both of them, Raquel explained her platform, which focused on greater access to public services and reversing the massive waves of privatisation that have happened in Chile since the 1980s. At the end of the conversation Juan mentioned a YouTube video that I should watch for more background on Raquel's campaign. The next day he sent me a link to the video saying, 'This should explain some of what I was talking about last night. Let me know if you understand'. The campaign video,[8] for presidential candidate Roxana Miranda of the *Partido Igualidad* [the left-wing Equality Party], gave a brief overview of the process of privatisation in Chile and promoted Miranda's platform of re-nationalisation for certain sectors. With the video Juan connected Raquel's campaign to a larger one, yet he framed it not as Raquel being part of a national movement, but rather as the national candidate's platform serving to explain further Raquel's local platform.

Even outside of election season, the memes these *compañeros* post on Facebook correspond to local or regional concerns, such as the borders with Peru and Bolivia, rather than national issues. They often post memes simply as remembrances of important events in local history, such as actions by the Pinochet regime or Nitrate Era labour organisation. These memes at times call for participation in protests or events, and other times simply provide a visual reminder of the past.

Each year, as mid-December approaches, the Facebook pages of Hospiceños are filled with Christmas-inspired posts. Pictures of the family wandering through the forest of lighted trees that overlooks the city of Iquique from Alto Hospicio appear alongside funny memes about a Santa Claus too lazy to deliver presents after smoking marijuana. As in much of the world December is a time of celebration, with friends and family sending each other seasonal greetings messages through social media. Most Hospiceños post pictures of their homes decorated with artificial trees and lights or showing children participating in Christmas-themed activities at school.

But mid-December in Northern Chile is for some a time of remembrance of the Santa Maria School Massacre. On 21 December 1907 thousands of striking miners from nitrate fields in the area were gunned down under General Roberto Silva Renard, after they refused to disband. They had been camping for a week in Iquique to appeal for government intervention to improve their living and working conditions. It is estimated that about 2,000 people were killed. For many decades the government suppressed information about the massacre. However, in 2007 the government conducted a highly publicised commemoration of its centenary, including an official national day of mourning and the re-interment of the victims' remains.

The festive photos and messages shared on Facebook in the days leading up to Christmas are interspersed with forms of remembrance for this historic tragedy. These posts often call for participation in remembrance ceremonies and protest marches. Though most often posted by people in their twenties and thirties, these events are constructed for all generations. As the flyer below attests, a protest march is often accompanied by live bands with political messages and activities and toys for children, including balloon animals.

While in other parts of the country much more importance is given to remembering events such as the Pinochet coup (11 September, 1973)[9], in the north, even when remembering the past, local concerns supersede national issues. In particular it is important to acknowledge events that highlight class and labour solidarity across other kinds of borders and differences. For young activists local politics are indeed Politics, connected to larger issues and histories, but with their own distinctive local foci.

Young activists such as Raquel and Juan both use social media to espouse their own political views as well as to demonstrate the

Fig. 6.5 Meme posted by several young Hospiceños calling for participation in an event commemorating the Santa Maria School Massacre. Translation:

Torturous Work during the Nitrate Era

The workers arriving to strike in Iquique

Live music, silk-screening, balloon animals and more. . .

Commemorative Act – Santa Massacre of Iquique

Walking with memory we create history

21 December – Cemetery no. 1–16:00

relationships between their forms of politics and those of larger movements. But in Alto Hospicio only a small minority engage in this type of political awareness. Only 11 per cent of survey respondents said that they felt social media had facilitated or influenced their participation in politics. Yet interpretation of the word 'politics' is key here.[10] I did not strictly define the scope of politics. In interviews and daily conversations it was clear that most people defined politics as operating on a national level, while local matters were framed as community issues. Facebook groups promoting the building of a hospital in Alto Hospicio, opposing high parking fees in Iquique or simply organising neighbours to advocate for more resources for their neighbourhood are popular, but not considered to be 'Politics'. Thus people contribute to the community in other ways, often using social media as a conduit, and in so doing they perform their contextually normative visions of what the community should be. Posts often envision the kind of community citizens desire for Alto Hospicio. Middle-aged adults, and particularly women, often use social media to promote the types of community programming that they see as important to a close-knit community.

Yesenia, who works part time for the municipal government, is one of the most visible examples of this social media usage. At least once a week she posts pictures and a short written recap of a community event she has attended or helped to organise. These include family-oriented celebrations at Carnaval time and a travelling telescope and astronomy programme, as well as events she and her colleague Paula organise monthly with senior citizens. Her commentaries on the senior citizen events are often very indicative of her ambitions to make the community safer and more civically oriented.

Near Halloween in 2014 Yesenia posted a series of photographs taken during a costume party with older adults in Alto Hospicio, accompanied by the caption, 'Enjoying myself with the older adults of our city . . . We have to care for them and protect them as we would like for ourselves.' Especially in her observation 'we have to care for them and protect them as we would like for ourselves', Yesenia performs her own community involvement, aiming to set an example for those who view her profile. She is not merely demonstrating what she has done, but also calling on others in Alto Hospicio to participate in imagining a particular type of community with her. These posts usually precipitate comments from other women who have participated in the programmes, as well as dozens of 'likes' from participants, neighbours, colleagues in the municipal government and other acquaintances. Not only is Yesenia performing what she promotes as positive community engagement; she is offering a vision that is supported by others in the community as well.

In these types of posts residents such as Yesenia actively construct a vision for community horizontality, treating others as one would like to be treated, caring for those less fortunate and sharing community resources. In the context of a nation-state perceived to be absent, posts like those of Yesenia, Juan and Raquel carry a subtext of self-sufficiency, acknowledging that community members must create their own social support or methods of change. Yet such posts also promote normativity, in that they depict no individual aspiration to rise above a struggling community. Instead they call for collective aspiration in which each individual should help to improve the community together.

Fig. 6.6 Photographs of community activities. 'Enjoying myself with the older adults of our city. . ..We have to care for them and protect them as we would like for ourselves'

Being culturally Chilean

While Hospiceños often distance themselves from Santiago and national politics, their sense of being culturally Chilean is strong. Memes demonstrating their Chileanness are common on Facebook as well as platforms such as WhatsApp, Tumblr and Instagram. Yet what one calls Chilean culture is highly context-dependent, and proximity to cosmopolitan centres, as well as class, education and racial identification, impact significantly on what individuals consider to be the hallmarks of Chilean society.

Much of what Hospiceños are redefining is the sense of social class that is representative of 'true Chileans'. Mendez[11] argues that class boundaries in Chile play a critical role in social life, and 'middle-classness' is considered central to Chilean authenticity in Santiago.

Yet Hospiceños use Santiago as a foil for what they see as authentically Chilean, positioning this urban, middle-class identity as an exception. Instead they perceive their own marginalised experiences to be more representative of true 'Chileanness'.[12] Hospiceños are quick to distinguish their lived experiences from those in the cosmopolitan capital, and in doing so they render important their own sense of normativity. Postings on social media then are an important clue to the ways in which Hospiceños envision the nation.

Hospiceños often use the name 'Santiago' to stand in for people whose lives are defined by class-consciousness, consumerism and international connections, the politicians who funnel resources away from the region and, most importantly, the national politics from which Hospiceños feel disenfranchised. Rather than seeing themselves outside of the nation that Santiago represents, however, they envision Santiago as the anomaly, the cosmopolitan city in a nation of otherwise

Fig. 6.7 Meme depicting distance from Santiago. Translation: 'He's going to Santiago. He's going abroad'

working-class normative people. In essence they reverse the logic of marginality, positioning marginalised people at the centre and those wielding the power to marginalise as Other. This sentiment is particularly well represented with the meme shown in Fig. 6.7, shared by several people in their late teens and early twenties in November 2014.

One young man in his early twenties who shared this meme wrote as a caption: 'It's really far from everything.' By this he means that the distance between Santiago and 'everything' is more than just physical: the capital represents a different kind of mentality and lifestyle as well. It is home to politicians, cosmopolitan types and rich people – particularly those who profit from mining in the northern region.

While Santiago may appear to foreigners and those living in the Metropolitan Region as 'Chile proper', it is not the 'Chile' with which people in the North identify, as evidenced by their frequent use of the hashtag #SantiagonoesChile ['Santiago is not Chile']. They see the North as being more normatively Chilean in many ways. In July 2014 many Hospiceños circulated the meme 'Ten reasons to confirm that Jesus was Chilean' (see Fig. 6.8). The meme was shared by both those who regularly attended Catholic, Methodist or Evangelical church services and those who considered themselves agnostic, atheist, questioning of religion or otherwise non-religious. In essence the humour of the post made it fair game for any Chilean.

Each of these reasons reflects something considered 'Chilean' that is not associated with exceptionalism or a certain class affiliation, but that spans these divisions. To elaborate: (1) Chile is a major wine-producing country, which means that wine is quite cheap and enjoyed by people all over the country and of all economic means, as (4) indicates. Of course nothing goes with drinking like parties, for all occasions, as illustrated by number (9). Hospiceños also perceive an essential part of their 'Chileanness' to be the loyalty expected from their friends and other parts of their social networks; betrayal is considered the worst sort of treatment, thus (2) and (3) correspond to their conception of friendship (in addition the English words 'brother' and 'bro' are used widely to substitute for 'amigo' [friend], particularly among young men). Number (5) is particularly salient in the North where fishing is a major industry, after mining and importation; and though prostitution is not particularly common or visible in Alto Hospicio, the sentiment corresponds to the idea that one should be friends with all types of people, rather than feeling superior. Familial constructions often dictate that children live with their parents until marriage (and often for quite some time after), thus allowing many under the age of 40 to get by without working,

10 razones que confirman que Jesús era chileno!!

1. Weno pa'l vino
2. Chascón, apatotao y trataba a todos de "hermano"
3. Se lo cagó uno de sus compadres
4. No tenía plata, pero nunca faltó el copete
5. Tenía amigos pescadores y putas
6. Vivió con la mamita hasta los 33
7. Nunca trabajó
8. Se hacía el gracioso.. caminando sobre el agua.
9. Cuando supo que se iba a morir, lo primero que organizó fue un carrete
10. Era seco pa'l verso, y si no tení[a] cómo explicarlo, inventaba cuentos.

Fig. 6.8   Translation: Ten reasons that confirm that Jesus was Chilean.
1. He was good with wine.
2. Long hair, an entourage, and he treated all as 'brothers'
3. One of his crew betrayed him
4. He never had money, but never lacked booze
5. He was friends with fishermen and prostitutes
6. He lived with his mother until he was 33
7. He never worked
8. He did tricks . . . walking on water
9. When he knew he was going to die, the first thing he did was organise a party
10. He was good with words, and if he didn't have a way of explaining he invented stories

corresponding to numbers (6) and (7). This meme thus reframes seemingly mundane aspects of a normal Chilean life, playing on common knowledge of religion.

Indeed many of the posts identifying with a conception of Chileanness highlight mundane forms of social life. Some post pictures of typically Chilean foods such as *completo* hot dogs or *pichangas* [a dish of French fries covered in onion, beef, sausage, and fried egg]. Others show the flag as displayed for the *fiestas patrias* on 18 September or a game played by the national football team. On other occasions the language used is sufficient to indicate an association with Chileanness.

In fact language is probably the most commonly used way of expressing national identity on social media, even when used only unconsciously, for example in writing daily status updates on Facebook. Chileans are known for distinctive pronunciation that involves dropping letters, slurring words together, heavy use of slang and adding the practically meaningless 'poh' to almost every expression. They also conjugate the second person informal as *vos* rather than *tú* so that one should

Fig. 6.9 Meme depicting Chilean language conventions. With slang spelled out [with standard Spanish]:
Papi weon [tipo] culiao [jodido] fome [aburrido] kasikasik [jajajaja] la wea [cosa] Wat [qué]?
La wea [cosa] cuatica [loca] weon [tipo] culiao [jodido] kisaikias [jajajaja] fome [aburrido] Habla bien hija de puta
Approximate English translation:
Dad fucking dude the bullshit is boring.
What?
The crazy shit fucking dude it's boring
Speak correctly bitch

ask a friend '¿como estai?' rather than '¿como estás?'. This conjugation also creates the common phrase 'cachai?', from cachar, to catch – used just as commonly as a phrase-ending insertion similar to 'you know?' in English. Hospiceños, like other Chileans, also frequently employ the word 'weon'; somewhat equivalent to 'dude', which can mean either friend or asshole. Chileans realise this language use is unique and view their ability to distinguish themselves so thoroughly by linguistic means as a point of pride.

So while users may unconsciously embed language in social media posts, they also take a self-conscious approach to language usage and often highlight its rarity, particularly in funny memes. Though first created and shared by a Bolivian with Chilean friends, the meme in Fig. 6.9 was widely shared by Hospiceños, exhibiting a sense of pride in their humorous (but difficult to follow) style of Spanish.

While this example is perhaps exaggerated (though not necessarily more exaggerated than some people naturally become with a few Cristal beers) and intended to be funny, it also portrays a form of national pride associated with the use of Chileanisms. The distinctive form of speaking marks one as unequivocally Chilean, and thus included within a nation they imagine as horizontal (with the exception of Santiago) – in terms of being working class, racially homogenous and otherwise normative.

De-politicising indigeneity

Hospiceños represent the Chilean nation on social media in certain ways, in order to include their own community within that imagining, but they also imagine their own city in certain ways to promote the sort of solidarity that creates a sense of belonging. Class normativity often takes the form of acceptance of the economic instability that is part of a working-class lifestyle. Yet perhaps more importantly, particularly because Alto Hospicio is a city of migrants, Hospiceños promote national and racial homogenisations in ways that erase specific subaltern identifications in favour of a broader sense of marginality.

While census and survey results suggest about 10 per cent of Hospiceños identify as indigenous, these identifications are not overly visible in daily life. Just as Nicole and her family never mentioned the fact that they have Quechua origins, most indigenous people may identify as such on a survey without seeing this form of identification as central to their daily lives. As such, indigeneity remains for the most part hidden in Alto Hospicio. Much like other forms of Hospiceño social life, parties, meetings and other gatherings are usually private affairs held in the home, and equally those organised by indigenous people are not publicly visible. I met several Bolivian migrants in Alto Hospicio: young women from La Paz selling plastic kitchen goods in the Agro market; two brothers and their wives, all from Cochabamba, who own a car-wash near the central business district; and several families who live in the poor neighbourhood where 'La Escuelita' afterschool programme operates. Yet these people do not participate publicly in Bolivian cultural activities or celebrations of Bolivian national holidays. Nor do they fly the Bolivian flag in front of their homes, as many Hospiceños do with the Chilean flag. Instead their parties are private, usually held in pueblos in the Altiplano rather than in Alto Hospicio. Their nationality is only made visible by their use of certain distinctive language such as '*pues*' (in contrast to the Chilean "*poh*" – simple filler words) and '*no ve?*' (in contrast to the Chilean "'*cachai?*'—meaning 'you know?' or 'you understand?').

In Alto Hospicio, for the majority of residents, indigeneity is not an important category with which to identify because the sense of marginality in disenfranchisement from national politics supersedes more specific identifications of marginality. Even the *Consejo Nacional Aymara* offers a library and consultation resources for indigenous people seeking to access government benefits, but does not sponsor public events. Their Facebook page is primarily used to advertise such services or general forms of good citizenship, for instance promoting biodiversity and the creation of national parks. Because of the privacy of most personal gatherings, social media is one of the most visible social spaces of Alto Hospicio. Yet in this space indigeneity usually remains either invisible or subsumed within a more general marginality.

When themes of indigeneity and international migrants are visible on social media they almost always represent a non-indigenous Chilean perspective. Chileans by birth complain that migrants are taking resources that rightfully belong to Chileans – for example preferential housing access, greater healthcare coverage or the bonuses awarded to mothers to cover childcare costs. During certain times of the year when these issues become more prevalent, numerous complaints surface on Facebook. Though certainly there are Hospiceños who are sensitive to the migrants' plight, no public condemnations of these types of messages appear. Instead the messages are supported with 'likes' and positive comments or left to stand without response. While indigeneity is officially a category considered 'vulnerable' in state rhetoric, most Hospiceños feel that the financial and political marginality of all residents should be treated equally. In many ways they resent the extra affordances given to indigenous peoples in such areas as healthcare and housing.

As other scholars[13] of indigeneity have found, discourses of class solidarity related to proletarian ideals contrast with discourses of indigeneity,[14] which distinguish certain people as *more* marginalised, *more* disenfranchised and thus *more* deserving of special treatment. Both kinds of discourses involve notions of marginality, but incorporate the concept in different ways. Given the modes of normativity prevalent in Alto Hospicio, it comes as no surprise that indigeneity is usually discursively erased, while community solidarity is highlighted. Particularly in the context of economic migration based on a mining industry,[15] indigeneity – with its associations with ecological stewardship – presents an imagined threat to the livelihood of the community. Instead downplaying indigeneity marks an individual as part of Alto Hospicio's community, contributing as a citizen to the common good. So, even for Alto Hospicio's indigenous people and migrants, identifications based on economic marginality and desires for belonging are more salient.

However, indigeneity does serve as a form of cultural expression in de-politicised ways, and is often transformed into a shared expression of 'northern culture' which allows all Hospiceños equal participation and enjoyment. Altiplano dances associated with Bolivia are popular in Alto Hospicio, but are transformed from 'indigenous culture' into 'northern culture'. Indeed, many Bolivians denounce the performing of Altiplano dances by Chilean groups, particularly in the context of continuing animosity over land lost in the War of the Pacific. Yet this is a rich part of the North's cultural life; almost every religious feast holiday is celebrated with dances such as the Morenada, Caporales, Tinku and Diablada, along with La Cueca (equally associated with Chile and Bolivia) and dances from Chile's Polynesian territory on Easter Island (Rapa Nui). While debates over whether the dances may be properly considered 'northern culture' or are strictly Bolivian continue outside of this context, no one in Alto Hospicio seems to find noteworthy the fact that most young people who participate are from families who consider themselves within a racially homogenous *mestizo*ness.

Similarly, the Wiphala, a multi-coloured patchwork flag that represents the native peoples of the Andes (including Colombia, Ecuador, Peru, Bolivia, Chile and Argentina), is often used as a visual marker of grassroots politics and community organisation. While ideally these politics are concordant with the interests of indigenous peoples, the symbol is used liberally – from Raquel's *Consejo Regional* campaign posters to its display at an earthquake relief concert put on by some of Chile's most prominent musicians. In these contexts it is not specifically associated with Andean indigeneity, but becomes a broader symbol of community solidarity. Through this usage, the flag effectively establishes an opposition between Northern Chile and northern Chileans' perceived antithesis of Santiago.

While critics (primarily speaking from Bolivia, Peru or the position of an indigenous spokesperson either in Santiago or representing the more prominent Mapuche group in Chile) suggest these examples of Altiplano dances and the Wiphala are improper appropriations of indigenous culture or symbolism, these debates do not happen publicly in Alto Hospicio. Instead Hospiceños see themselves as promoting the normativity of homogeneity in terms of both class and race. And when pictures of the Caporales dance or Wiphala appear on Facebook, they are understood as northern rather than indigenous, reinforcing social media as a de-politicised space.

During my first October in Alto Hospicio, Juan invited me to a daylong event for what is known in South American usually as Indigenous People's Day (celebrated as Columbus Day in North America). In Central and South America 12 October is observed in memory of the slaughter and colonisation of the indigenous peoples of the Americas, as well as the continuing imperialism experienced by citizens of the Americas from Mexico to the south at the hands of the United States, Canada and European countries. This celebration included a troupe of five-year-olds demonstrating the Chilean national dance of *La Cueca*, an Afro-Colombian singer performing a song from her native city, a Peruvian guitar player and several local activists speaking about community inclusion and social development. To close the programme they organised a group picture of all attendees, including myself. When Juan posted the photograph on Facebook he included the caption, 'We are all Americans'.[16] Indeed, even in this space of inclusiveness and multiculturalism, rather than highlighting indigeneity as a distinctive form of identifying, all Americans were brought together within a discourse of similarity.

International solidarity

While tensions remain between Hospiceños and the international migrants whom they perceive to be taking resources that are rightfully

Chileans', discourses of class solidarity at times overcome even the rifts between native Chileans and migrants. In January 2014 the international court of the United Nations at The Hague decided on a maritime dispute between Chile and Peru. The North is contested territory, even more than 130 years after the end of the War of the Pacific, in which the region of Tarapacá was transferred from Peru to Chile. The Hague's decision did not affect any coastline or cities, but gave Peru more territory for fishing rights.[17] Because fishing in Chile is controlled by a very limited number of oligarchic families, the decision changed very little in terms of economics and trade for most northern Chileans. Many wrote Facebook comments similar to 'All of the fishing industry here is owned by a few wealthy families. It doesn't really matter to me.' Both politically active and somewhat apolitical Chilean users asserted a similar view, but in different ways. Both groups seemed to be communicating that though perhaps the Chilean and Peruvian governments were in a dispute, the people were not.

Some friends did admit to me that they felt the decision to cede some water area to Peru was unfair, but they also acknowledged that avoiding conflict was important. Many said that the decision was irrelevant because economic gain from the sea territory only ends up in the hands of seven families of the oligarchy. However, these nuanced opinions were not published on Facebook, neither through original writing

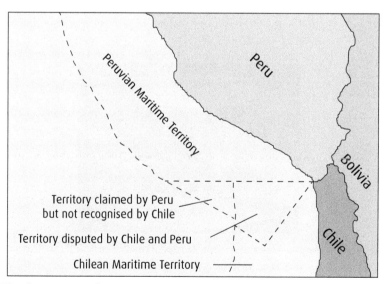

Fig. 6.10 Map of maritime territory

nor links to online sources. Instead solidarity between Peruvians and Chileans overwhelmingly dominated Facebook posts.

On the political side, Raquel and her friend Marcelo both shared a piece of text essentially thanking Peruvians and Bolivians for standing with Chileans during the Santa Maria School Massacre. The text explained:

> In the Santa Maria School Massacre of Iquique, together with Chilean workers, Bolivians and some Peruvians also died. When the consuls asked them to leave, they refused, saying 'We came with the Chileans and we will die with the Chileans. We are not Bolivians or Peruvians, we are workers.'

A local band known for their songs' political content posted a long piece of text from which I draw out some relevant parts:

> Patriots, fellow Chileans . . . Why do we not go to war against Monsanto? Why not fight to recover copper from your country? Why do you not wage war on Spanish companies that rob us when we pay for light and water? Why were you not in solidarity with artisanal fishermen when the Chilean government perpetually delivered the sea to the seven richest families? . . . Chileans and Peruvians, stop being so easily swayed by media sensationalism of the bourgeois press. We should continue fighting together against those that make our lives impossible!

Fig. 6.11   Meme about maritime border. Translation: 'Tell me, are we Chilean or Peruvian now?'
'I don't know, poh [typical Chilean filler word], or I don't know, peh [typical Peruvian filler word]!!!'

Most people who usually stay away from political discussion stuck to humour. Many memes declared sentiments such as 'The sea is neither Chilean nor Peruvian, it belongs to the fish!'

It seemed that everyone was paying attention, but no one really cared. Perhaps because the border dispute only affected the oligarchy, or perhaps because individuals believed an end to the dispute was more important than the particular division of sea rights, these individuals expressed their interest by enthusiastically posting and commenting. It seemed important to individuals to declare 'Yes, I am paying attention!', without taking sides on a matter that was 'supposed' to be important, but in their daily lives simply did not matter. They were communicating that authentic northern Chileans are simply not concerned about the oligarchy's successes or failures. These wealthy families are not part of the local community; like mining companies they extract resources and take the profits elsewhere. Instead, being local means being concerned about relationships with neighbours, whether metaphorical neighbours of the nation or the very individuals who have migrated from these countries and now live right next door.

For most Hospiceños class solidarity rises above international divisions, demonstrating that the wider community imagined by residents of Alto Hospicio may not include oligarchs and other cosmopolitan figures, but does include people like themselves – even if they are from across disputed borders. Because the Peruvians in question occupy a similar marginalised social class to Alto Hospicio residents, they fit a familiar form of normativity. When framed as class allies rather than exploitative indigenous people, Peruvians are easily incorporated into Hospiceño solidarity with other marginalised people.

Similarity, difference, community

Hospiceños use social media both to reflect their imagined notions of community – local, regional and national – and actively to construct these alliances. On social media Hospiceños promote forms of normativity, in this case by creating oppositions to some groups and alliances with others, often depending on the specific context. They affirm community affiliations by highlighting sameness, even in instances of pointing out similarities between the Peruvian working class and themselves, and effectively erasing discourses of difference, such as that of indigeneity, from public discussion.[18] Hospiceños define the boundaries of their community and the spaces and people with whom they identify through discourses of similarities. For those people they see as inherently different, and the discourses that highlight those differences, they use tactics of distinction to represent their distance. Both usually function along lines of class, at times overshadowing even racial and national differences.

These strategies work through highlighting and erasure. Though Hospiceños' 'Chileanness' is often highlighted through memes and texts, these social media posts focus on shared characteristics between all Chileans and obscure the sorts of exceptionalism and cosmopolitanism attributed to 'Santiago'. Similarly they use tactics of erasure to portray their own community as homogenous. These tactics indeed have the ability to frame some groups as legitimate or included while refusing to recognise others. Indigenous individuals in Alto Hospicio are a key example of this exclusion. As Yeh writes, 'People are not indigenous naturally, but rather by convention and recognition by others'.[19] In erasing this identity, normativity is valued above individual difference. Various forms of non-normative marginality are expected to be subsumed within the widely experienced form of marginality common to Hospiceños' experiences – marginality as defined by class experience.

It is in these tactics that we also see the use of exaggeration to highlight. When a meme refers to travel to Santiago as 'going abroad', it is not meant to be taken literally, but uses overstatement to make the distinction clear. A popular series of memes satirised the class difference felt between Hospiceños and cosmopolitan Chileans from the central region, and featured a character from a popular television *novella* (soap opera). Lita Achonda is the classist mother of the protagonist on the television series *Pituca sin Lucas* [Posh without Money] and the series of memes features her calling various annoyances 'so middle class'. In the meme featured below, she refers to an earthquake as middle class, thus distancing herself (very upper-class by upbringing) from something considered obtrusive in life. Referring to an earthquake as 'middle class' downplays its destructive power, waving it off as merely irritating. Yet framing this opinion as that of someone like the character Lita also distances those perceived as upper class from the realities of Chilean life – and so from the lived experience of Hospiceños, particularly after the 2014 earthquake.

In highlighting exaggerated forms Hospiceños also reveal similarities or differences with a humorous slant so that the message comes across in stark relief. Through humour, and other forms of highlighting and erasure, these imaginings of community serve to reinforce, and at

Fig. 6.12 Meme about class. Translation: 'But what earthquake could be more middle class?'

times wholly to create, discourses of normativity. This normativity is experienced as solidarity in the face of difficult circumstances.

Marginality forms the basis of Hospiceños, normativity as well as their claims to citizenship. Marginality is the standard by which an individual, or even a symbol, is considered to be part of (or excluded from) the Hospiceño notion of community. While the imagining of national communities has often drawn upon symbols, icons and print media in order to bring together people who could not know one another personally,[20] now, theoretically, technology such as social media may allow national citizens to know one another across geographic divides, as well as those of class and other social sector differences. Yet it is precisely social media where Hospiceños maintain these divisions, rather than overcome them. Performing distance from cosmopolitan Others online refocuses Hospiceños' citizenship on the local, so that they maintain emphasis on normativity, solidarity and marginality. Social media is key, not only to enacting Hospiceños' particular notions of community and politics, but also to shaping their imaginings of what constitutes solidarity.

7
Conclusion: The extraordinary ordinariness of Alto Hospicio

'*q wn*'

Three letters representing two words: '*que weon*'. Of course *weon* is one of those Chilean Spanish words which everyone understands, but which is not quite translatable. It may be used for greeting a good friend, or talking about an enemy – or even shouted when the national team scores a seemingly impossible goal. Twenty-three-year-old Tomás used this word to introduce a meme on his Facebook wall.

This meme, illustrated in Fig. 7.1, makes clear the ways in which everyday behaviours are performances. Included within these behaviours is social media use, where people perform in order to identify the self as a particular kind of person, claim certain kinds of affiliation and place oneself within the world. This meme acknowledges that many people create meaning through a mixture of bodily expression, purchasing particular symbolically laden brands and social media usage, but the density of symbols used within the text evokes exaggeration and sarcasm. The imagined character who writes this text is ridiculous. Tomás acknowledges this ridiculousness by using the word '*weon*', in this instance meaning something like 'what a jackass'.

Using '*weon*', Tomás distinguishes himself from this straw character who might write such a post on social media. Hospiceños usually strive toward an unassuming aesthetic associated with marginality, but this meme describes conspicuous aesthetics and behaviours associated with consumption and cosmopolitanism. Only a cosmopolitan Other would be so insincere as to construct such an image in conscious opposition to normative aesthetics, social identifications and attitudes. And though maybe Tomás and most Hospiceños would say that the types of

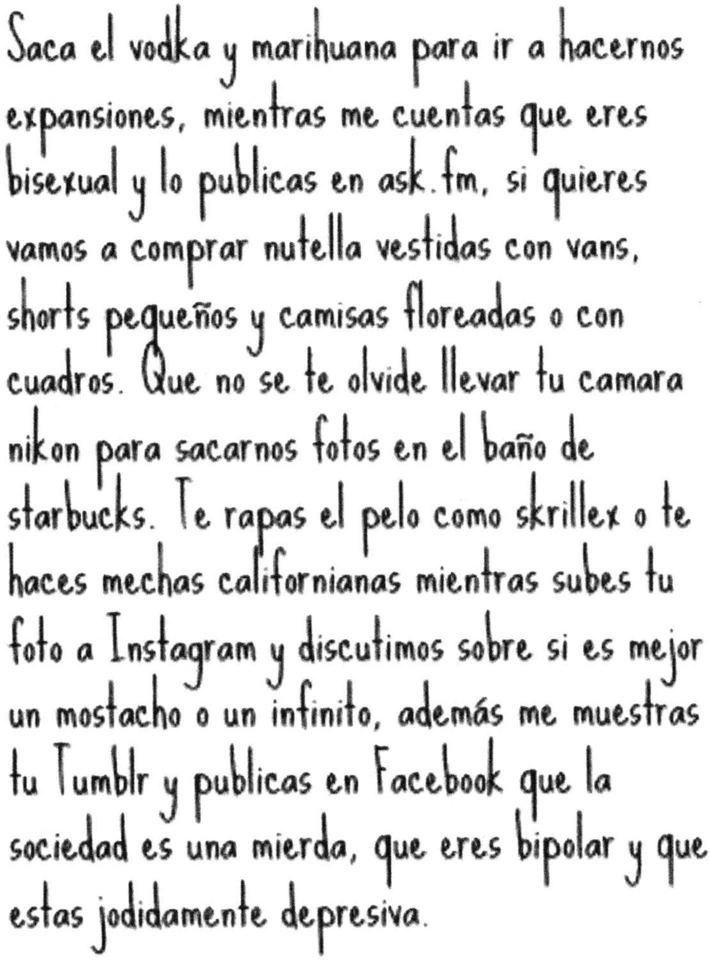

Saca el vodka y marihuana para ir a hacernos expansiones, mientras me cuentas que eres bisexual y lo publicas en ask.fm, si quieres vamos a comprar nutella vestidas con vans, shorts pequeños y camisas floreadas o con cuadros. Que no se te olvide llevar tu camara nikon para sacarnos fotos en el baño de starbucks. Te rapas el pelo como skrillex o te haces mechas californianas mientras subes tu foto a Instagram y discutimos sobre si es mejor un mostacho o un infinito, además me muestras tu Tumblr y publicas en Facebook que la sociedad es una mierda, que eres bipolar y que estas jodidamente depresiva.

Fig. 7.1   Meme about hipsters. Translation: 'Take the vodka and marijuana and let's go get expansions (ear stretchers), while you tell me that you're bisexual and you publish it on ask.fm. If you want, let's go buy nutella, dressed in Vans (brand shoes), short shorts and flowered or plaid blouses. And don't forget to take your Nikon camera to take pictures of ourselves in the bathroom of Starbucks. You can do your hair like Skrillex (American electronic music producer) or you put in a lot of highlights while you upload your photo to Instagram and we argue about if a (traditional) moustache or infinity (overly stylised moustache) is better, and you also show me your Tumblr and publish on Facebook that society is bullshit, that you're bipolar and that you're fucking depressed.'

performance described by the text are overt and excessive, the meme also reminds us of the ways in which social media usage is always a performance, even when the idea of conscious presentation is antithetical to the prevailing form of normativity. Indeed, the performances described in this meme are the antithesis of Hospiceños' normativity, in which the trick is to perform normativity on social media while seeming not to perform anything at all.

Social media ethnography in Alto Hospicio

Traditional ethnographies often focus on particular groups within the community in order to make visible broader local cultural expectations and norms. A group such as La Escuelita or the Red Foxes Motor Club might have provided such a focus for an ethnography of Alto Hospicio. By studying social media, however, the same cultural expectations and norms become clear on a larger scale. Because Hospiceños use social media precisely to negotiate these norms, it is an excellent window for understanding a Hospiceño world view: what is expected and what is not; what questions may be asked and which may not; who is allowed to question, or even to make their opinions heard, and who is not; and how individuals not only behave and interact within this worldview, but also how they understand their individual place within (or outside of) it.

Social media also reveals some of the ways in which social life is changing, in both Alto Hospicio and Chile's Great North in general, as a result of new communication technologies. In such a frontier space, often conceptualised by both those who live there and those in the cosmopolitan metropole as a hinterland, advances in communications technology do change daily life. Social media allows people to stay in better contact with family members who are absent, whether as a result of the mining industry or international migration. Social media provides ample forms of entertainment and is even used to organise activities such as dates and group outings.

However, social media has not changed everything. It is popular to praise the opportunities social media provides for bridging socioeconomic divides or empowering populations politically. Yet Hospiceños, who are comparatively marginalised in both respects, do not see these new advantages as major uses of social media. Whether new media truly has the potential to reduce global or national inequalities is a question that must be left to other populations. In Alto Hospicio social media remains an extension of the normative social life of the city, rather than a different realm in which new aspirations may be achieved.

Just as social media does not automatically bridge economic or political divides, individuals do not always use social media to seek new ways of connecting in the world, nor to find means of self-expression not available in the local context. In Alto Hospicio the kinds of identifications that are made visible on social media correspond to community values and the very social scripts which often guide behaviour. Certainly there are some young people (and perhaps older ones as well) who reach across divides – whether geographical or ideological – to encounter new ways of viewing the world, new possibilities or new aspirations as a result of their connection on social media. However, the overwhelming normativity of social media in Alto Hospicio makes it clear that using social media to reject prevailing forms of normativity is a result of the desires of individuals rather than inherent aspects of the media. Social media may facilitate newfound freedom for some – but there is every reason to believe that if social media was not available these individuals would seek this sort of freedom through other channels. Social media tends to reinforce ways of identifying that are highlighted in other arenas of social life (for instance family connections, regional affiliation and humour) and to erase those that are less important to the community (including indigeneity, overt politicisation or non-normative gender and sexuality identifications). Social media in Alto Hospicio is not a space for the proliferation of identifications. Indeed, even Hospiceños' use of aesthetics and visuality online illustrate that, even when a whole world of possibility is available, the visibility of interactions and the public nature of how community gatekeepers moderate others may transform social media into a conservative force.

The power of social media as a conservative force relies on its accessibility to a wide audience, in part because the necessary technology is reasonably affordable as a result of the tax-free import zone. Even in a place such as Alto Hospicio, smartphones and internet access are not considered luxury goods; they are practically necessary possessions for all but the poorest residents, even when refrigerators or stoves are not always deemed essential. Such electronic items are not associated with an extravagant lifestyle, but rather are indispensable for communication. Thus social media and its associated technology have quickly and almost seamlessly been subsumed within the unassuming normativity that dominates social life in Alto Hospicio.

Social media and social context

The central argument of this book is that, for residents of Alto Hospicio, social media acts as an arena in which normative modes of citizenship are not only performed, but also reinforced as important social values. Hospiceños use social media to express solidarity, test authenticity, maintain normativity, perform identifications and challenge conceptions of what true 'Chileanness' is, all from a marginalised position within the nation. Each of these aims of social media usage demonstrates the ways in which Hospiceños' online lives are inflected with expressing citizenship in relation to local, regional, national and global levels. The residents of Alto Hospicio position their own legal status, rights, public participation and sense of belonging precisely in the ways they perform marginalised identifications on social media.

In the first chapter of this book I provide a brief history of the processes (and violent acts) through which the Pinochet regime introduced a neoliberal economic model to Chile. These economic policies, carried forward by post-dictatorship democratic governments as well, have no doubt been instrumental in positioning Chile among the nations that benefit from a rapid and ideally free movement of material resources, people and ideas in the current global economic system. Chile receives immigrants seeking to perform manual labour and is a major exporter of natural resources, both major contributing factors to Chile's place among the world's strongest economies. The majority of Alto Hospicio's residents are caught up in this movement of people and resources, whether as immigrants, workers in importation and exportation or in mining the very resources whose exportation sustains the whole country's economy. Most Hospiceños also have the resources to participate in other types of global exchange using the internet to download music, read articles, watch films or interact with others. Yet within the nation and the world capitalist economic system, Hospiceños remain marginalised.

The marginalised position of Hospiceños has been produced through historical economic conditions, beginning with the War of the Pacific and nitrate mining and continuing to the violence and neoliberal economic shocks of the Pinochet regime. Though the northern region provides economic stability to the entire nation, it remains exploited and politically peripheral; the city of Alto Hospicio itself represents the most extreme case of these two conditions. The stigmas of poverty, crime and inhospitableness associated with Alto Hospicio have created conditions of suspicion that always already influence social life, including its enactment on social media.

These realities of social life in Alto Hospicio inform a situation in which individuals are more comfortable using social media to solidify local identifications than to imagine new possibilities of global connections. Hospiceños connect to the world through social media, but their aims are not new relationships, wider identifications, broadened self-understanding, proliferation of aesthetic styles or imagined new life possibilities. Rather their social media usage almost always corresponds to performing solidarity within their marginalised community. The peripheral location of Alto Hospicio within the nation serves as a context for the ways in which Hospiceños curate self-representations, identify core self-concepts and test one another's authenticity. In doing so, they imagine their marginalisation to be the quality that makes them authentically Chilean. Being working class and politically disenfranchised marks true cultural Chileanness, thus reversing the logic of centre and periphery.

Political economy and history deeply impact the ways in which Hospiceños understand their place within the nation, and indeed how they imagine their own local community. They contrast the homogeneity, solidarity and ordinariness of Alto Hospicio with the cosmopolitanism and political power they associate with the Chilean government and residents of more central metropolitan areas, specifically the national capital of Santiago. At the same time Hospiceños reproduce discourses of solidarity in connection to proletariat populations, even across a somewhat contested border with Peru. By contrasting their own lived experiences with those of populations more central to the nation, they strengthen their own communal sense of affiliation; Hospiceños believe themselves to be the true Chilean citizens in contrast to the imagined cosmopolitan Others. With these local investments in normativity in mind, it is then clear how social media becomes a mechanism for resisting larger issues and institutions of power – all while normativity remains a point of solidarity rather than a repressive force.

Neoliberalism, marginality and social media

This book takes on the subject of normativity in a neoliberal era – a time in which many assume notions of solidarity have been replaced with desires to distinguish the self from others on any possible level. While the 'freeing' of capital in some places also liberates individuals from traditional social structures such as the family, connects self-expression to consumption and encourages fantasy and aspiration as personal modes of imagining, almost the exact opposite results emerge in Alto Hospicio. Such consequences reveal that the individualism we often take as a natural outcome of neoliberalism is not always intrinsic to these sorts of economic policies. It is just one of the possible results, always dependent on context, that neoliberal ideologies may produce.[1]

Neoliberal economics beget a whole proliferation of cultural forms, which are always context dependent. For Hospiceños, being unassuming in one's aesthetics, life goals and even social media use marks one as belonging. Others – cosmopolitans, capitalists and politicians – generally are understood to hold more power, but Hospiceños discursively distance them as excessive, superficial and at times corrupt (particularly in the case of the last). In doing so they highlight their own similarity within the community, asserting their marginality through solidarity.

This marginality is closely associated with identification as workers. Rather than consumption it is labour, both in the home and outside for wages, that provides a foundation among Hospiceños for core self-understanding and representation. The socio-economic position of most Hospiceños becomes a source of solidarity, not just within the local community but also cutting across borders, As a result working-class- or proletariat-based normativity, rather than forms of distinction, are important cultural tropes.

Political economy, particularly the dominant industries in the area, do not affect individuals' sense of pride and self-identifications. However, they do impact more broadly upon the very ways in which normative understandings of familial relationships and gendered identifications are represented, performed, taught and usually taken up without resistance online. The family is strengthened as the centre of social life, as well as providing a trusted anchor in the seemingly endless possibilities of internet-based relationships.

Many more individual expressions of self rely on these social scripts about productive activity, which is highly gendered – from acceptable forms of creativity to discussions about sex. While men usually identify as family providers and express pride in the sacrifices they make in order to labour as wage earners for their families, women most often identify as the caretakers of family, expressing their own labour as that of emotion work. These marked divisions between men's and women's work often reinforce forms of normative gender identifications as well as notions of family. Even when lived realities differ from the norm, expressions of gendered self-understanding on social media serve to reinforce assumptions about gender rather than challenge them. Hospiceños both place importance on the visual representation of family connections on social media and use assumptions about naturalised gender differences as a base for gender-related humour. Through these proliferations of normativity, heterosexual familial structures become essential to Hospiceños' modes of performing and to the regulation of others' performances on social media.

The unassuming aesthetic

While neoliberal economic systems often produce a proliferation of consumer goods and advertising which expands aesthetic possibilities – often even compelling individuals to see aesthetics as central to ways of performing the self – Alto Hospicio has remained outside this formation. First glancing at both public and private spaces in Alto Hospicio, the prevailing form of normativity seems to have effectively erased any sense of aesthetics. Clothing styles, home architecture and decoration, construction of public space and indeed the curation of aesthetics on social media rarely stray from an entirely utilitarian appearance. In spite of the vast options of visual representations available on social media, aesthetics on Hospiceños' Facebook, Instagram and Tumblr pages largely correspond to the types of unassuming aesthetics they curate in their daily lives. This is apparent in the styles of selfies, footies and other sorts of Instagram photographs that Hospiceños upload, as well as in their sarcastic memes, such as that shared by Tomas above.

Yet it is not so much the functionality of items that defines aesthetics in Alto Hospicio, rather a sense of presentation of being inconspicuous and unassuming. When young people want to snap a picture, simply capturing their feet lounging in front of the television set will do. If an individual wants to relate a sentiment – expressing pride, sharing philosophical outlooks or even commenting on politics – a humorous meme works without individual nuance or heightened risk of negative feedback. Yet this seeming lack of aesthetics in Alto Hospicio is indeed a consciously curated form. Hospiceños, particularly those whose families are relatively well off because of involvement in the mining industry, have the option to purchase the latest fashions and add balconies, landscaping or other forms of adornment to their homes. Perhaps even more easily, young people could put on their finest clothing and arrange their bedroom to take a highly stylised selfie, or could curate collections of beautiful scenes on Instagram. Instead they choose to represent themselves aesthetically on social media within the bounds of normative unassuming aesthetics. By making this conscious choice, Hospiceños develop their unassuming styles as a particular aesthetic, rather than a lack thereof.

This aesthetic in many ways refuses class distinction. While the economy is dominated by prosperous mining and importation industries, the people of Alto Hospicio are by and large the manual labourers rather than owners of these resources. Both the history of labour movement solidarity as well as current experiences of the production process (at times characterised by workers as exploitation) lead to a refusal of class distinction – despite the fact that these workers earn reasonably good salaries and at a basic level are capable of purchasing goods or acquiring other sorts of cultural and social capital that could very well be used in creating distinctions. The conditions of Alto Hospicio demonstrate the overgeneralisation inherent in assumptions that modern capitalism inevitably generates incessant aspirations for greater material wealth or the proliferation of consumption-based class distinction.

Networks, normativity and boundaries

The global and semi-public nature of social media also provides for expansive social fields, in which connections across all kinds of social and geographic boundaries become possible. Yet Hospiceños prefer to connect with people they know, using as a guide the visibility of their social networks inherent in certain forms of social media. Just as I aroused suspicion at first when trying to connect with Hospiceños online, residents of Alto Hospicio tend to be wary of newcomers until their connections within the community become visible. Hospiceños' choices of which social media to use for various purposes often rely in part on the visibility of social networks provided by the platform. New relationships become validated through connections to existing relationships with family, long-term friends, neighbours and work-mates. The fact that young Hospiceños prefer using Facebook as a dating site, rather than applications such as Tinder or Grindr, makes their preference for visible relationships clear. Equally, the practice of making new friends through commenting on mutual acquaintances' Facebook posts demonstrates how visible social connections do the work of authenticating individuals as trustworthy, and thus worthy of time and communication. These communications strategies are indeed quite logical within the context of historical and political economic processes that have fed discourses of suspicion in Alto Hospicio.

The visibility of networks and communications on social media also makes it an ideal place for performing the boundaries of the expected and expanding the traditional mechanisms of 'keeping people in their place', such as through gossip and indirect language. Social media allows users to prick the bubbles of pretension that they see while maintaining distance from direct confrontation – which would indeed be antithetical to the solidarity which Hospiceños also value.

To act within normativity is to be sensitive to the possibility of diverging from it. As a result it pervades almost all aspects of life for Hospiceños – what they eat, what they wear, what they talk about and how they dream of the future. Individuals express their own personal preferences, styles and ambitions, but the range in which those self-expressions fall is much more limited than might have been expected, particularly given the size of the city[2] and the numbers of migrants from various cultural backgrounds. Those who are not sensitive to this type of divergence are challenged for their boundary crossing on social media at times, by those who feel a stronger interest in maintaining boundaries. Those who challenge in this way, either consciously or unconsciously, highlight the normative ways in which they expect others to express themselves. Social media, as a semi-public space, becomes an ideal stage on which normativity is both reproduced and redefined through these sanctions.

Alto Hospicio, then, helps to explain a core component of social media itself. These shared and group-focused media are an ideal conduit for normativity – but this is also a property of social media that allows it to be taken up easily, without disrupting daily life. Within a very short time social media has become taken for granted and integrated into quotidian forms of communication and presentation of the self in everyday life. Indeed, normativity may explain both what is extraordinary about Alto Hospicio as well as what is ordinary about social media. Social media is an ideal technology for establishing and extending normativity to the rest of social life. In turn it is also subject to the pressures of normativity, so that everyone knows what should and should not be posted, where the limits of obscenity are and in what ways politics may be approached without raising eyebrows.

In many instances humour is key both to testing and maintaining the boundaries of acceptability. Humour ranges from funny status messages and sarcastic comments to ridiculous forms of exaggeration and visual puns exemplified by memes. When someone acts unacceptably, humour provides a means of chastising such activity without causing shame. But humour also marks the space as informal, and often works to strengthen, reaffirm or even begin new friendships. This type of playfulness allows for commentary on social structure without direct articulation, and acts as a barrier to accountability for sincere forms of social commentary. Humorous memes are used to test the boundaries of the appropriate and possible in a safe way, and thus are integral to notions of normativity. In fact humour may be the key to the ways in which individuals view normativity as desirable rather than repressive.

Humour also reinforces Hospiceños' sense that social media is an authentic form of interacting with friends and acquaintances. Much of the humour on their social media pages works through interaction in comments. Hospiceños even respond to memes by posting corresponding memes in the comment area afforded by Facebook. As Sherzer contends, humour may be used as a test of local knowledge, and when successful constitutes a collective achievement.[3]

In Alto Hospicio the implicit decision not to flaunt wealth and material goods, build striking houses nor express individual personality in self style work all work in order to serve community cohesion. There is little impulse to inspire jealousy. Instead Hospiceños exert effort to maintain a status quo which is obtainable by everyone. Yet this norm requires that individuals define the boundaries of normativity as a public project. These boundaries become clear in gossip, and in resistance to those who appear to cross them. As such, social media becomes integral to maintaining normativity. While the production of normativity is an important aspect of daily social life on the street, in civic society and in personal conversations with neighbours, the project is furthered and made more visible when Hospiceños use social media to perform 'sameness'.

Performing social scripts

Throughout this book I use the concept of social scripts to explain the ways in which normativity makes some behaviours seem 'natural' and expected, while other behaviours are construed as weird, out of place or inappropriate. The idea of social scripts draws on the notion that people are always performing; though they may improvise, basic cultural narratives serve as a platform for these performances. Interaction on social media makes clear the ways in which these scripts are not preexisting, but are constantly constructed by those acting within them. Not all Hospiceños always live within the bounds of what the larger group might consider appropriate – but it is these very ruptures in naturalised assumptions that make the assumptions visible. Examples of these ruptures demonstrate how those who hold more stake in maintaining normativity often actively reassert the prevailing social norms when they are challenged.

The idea of social scripts also acknowledges the importance of the audience in interaction. Both actors and audiences constantly interpret and redefine the social scripts in the context of their specific history and political economy. Everyday performances on social media tell stories of self-understanding and affiliation, both to the self and others, creating the 'socially real' through the telling.[4] As Dwight Conquergood contends, performance does not necessarily begin with experience, but performance often realises the experience.[5]

Above all, the idea that social media platforms are a stage for performing social scripts to an audience reminds us that social media is indeed 'social'. The interactive nature of social media is key to the popularity of certain platforms and applications as opposed to others. Because Hospiceños conceive of Twitter as unidirectional, they consider it boring. Conversely Facebook, WhatsApp, and Instagram provide ample opportunity for 'liking', commenting, conversing and engaging in other forms of interaction (such as posting a link or photograph on a friend's Facebook wall); they are consequently ingrained in daily communications. But more deeply, the interactive nature of social media is important because it provides a platform on which social scripts are not only acted out, but also actively negotiated. So while normativity does structure much of Hospiceños' daily lives, this is not a unidirectional process. Like all forms of hegemony,[6] normativity is negotiated by individuals within a larger structure. The social scripts certainly exist, and they do provide an outline for social life in Alto Hospicio, but many Hospiceños value their ability to improvise as well.

It is precisely because of the centrality of community that social media is important to Hospiceños and takes the specific forms that it does. Social media, rather than alienating individuals from their neighbours, families, or friends, creates new inroads to interaction in Alto Hospicio, at times even fostering the creation of new social relationships. There is no reason to believe these relationships are any less sincere or any more mediated than relationships that begin or develop any other way. Hospiceños use social media to seek out people with mutual interests, similar backgrounds and human networks in common; in so doing they simply supplement their social lives, rather than replace them or make them less authentic.

Performing the ordinary in an extraordinary place

These social networks are important to the community because of the unique set of existing circumstances and neoliberal ideologies that structure the space of Alto Hospicio. The absence of both state intervention and large private businesses often leaves the residents to their own devices. Within this context social networks and community become important resources, and thus identifications with sameness rather than difference are important to highlight. Discourses of normativity may repress, erase or obscure some forms of identification, but they serve to provide community cohesion, often seen as necessary for individuals who feel marginalised within broader structures. While some Hospiceños say that the range of expression in Alto Hospicio makes life boring, none outwardly convey that they feel personally repressed or unable to express their individuality. Instead the bounding of expression happens at an unconscious level in which the range of 'natural' options is circumscribed through social scripts. Individuals do not therefore experience a loss of options; rather they simply do not consider certain options in the first place.

Normativity is closely connected to notions of citizenship, and particularly strands of citizenship that highlight belonging. By remaining within the bounds of expected and naturalised ways of performing, interacting and expressing the self, Hospiceños communicate that they are 'good citizens'. They abide by the prevailing social scripts rather than challenging them, and overall contribute to a cohesive community. But this normativity is also closely connected to the ways in which Hospiceños conceive of citizenship in relation to the nation-state. Maintaining local normativity allows Hospiceños to conceive of their marginality in contrast to the imagined excesses and cosmopolitanism of sites more physically and figuratively central to the nation. By maintaining unassuming aesthetics, close community ties, traditional family forms and a focus on the local, Hospiceños represent themselves as the real Chilean citizens – marginalised by government and business interests and peripheral to political participation, legal status and rights, but nonetheless those who truly belong.

In identifying as marginalised citizens, individuals highlight their modes of self-understanding that correspond to Hospiceño normativity. However, when certain aspects of the self are highlighted, others are erased, obscured or left unmentioned. Work and family are both usually highlighted, and often used to place the self within broader social worlds. While men often take pride in providing for their families, adult women take pride in caring for them. Non-heteronormative relationships are downplayed at times in favour of identification with one's natal family. Other connections within the community are also highlighted, whether through affiliations such as neighbourhood, childhood friendship, extended family or through more formal organisations, including community groups or municipal government. While highlighting local community is almost always an important way of performing citizenship associated with belonging, Hospiceños' attitudes toward nationalism are more complex. In the context of P/politics, regionalism and localism are highlighted over the national. Yet when associated with cultural forms such as food, sport or heritage, they identify closely and enthusiastically with being Chilean.

With such identifications Hospiceños attempt to reverse understandings of centre and periphery, representing themselves as the true Chileans; conversely those in the cosmopolitan centres of the nation are positioned as inauthentic. This conception of citizenship is closely associated with social and economic class – areas almost always highlighted by Hospiceños in claiming solidarity with working-class and non-cosmopolitan lifestyles. At times this even leads to cross-border identifications in which perceptions of common class and proletarian ideals supersede national identification. Similarly differences in race and, particularly, indigeneity are often erased in order to highlight a broader sense of marginality in which most Hospiceños can claim a part, rather than compartmentalising or hierarchising forms of disadvantage.

Overall these forms of highlighting and erasure create a strong sense of solidarity among most Hospiceños, frequently directed against such structures as the state, neoliberal capitalism or notions of cosmopolitan Otherness. However, these tactics also tend to erase forms of difference that otherwise could be important to peoples' self-understanding: for example identification as an indigenous person, sexual or gender non-normativity or life aspirations that include goals associated with cosmopolitanism or other 'alternative' lifestyles. These erasures are not only reflected in individuals' posts on social media; they are also actively maintained through sanctioning certain kinds of posting through negative feedback. Thus the discursive structures of social media not only express forms of normativity in Alto Hospicio; they are key to mobilising and maintaining them.

In essence, social media is what users make it. In Alto Hospicio, where normativity and solidarity are important social values, social media is oriented towards those aims. New media circulate old stories, and are both the products and producers of the social scripts to which its users are subject. Hospiceños reproduce their normativities through social media even without realising it. They highlight their marginalised citizenship and erase forms of distinction, creating their own particular community identification in the process.

Appendix 1 – Social Media Questionnaire

In June, July and August 2014, together with field work assistant Jorge Castro Gárate of the department of Social Work at Universidad Arturo Pratt in Iquique, I surveyed 100 Hospiceños about their use of social media. The survey took place in two parts. Part One took about one hour and the second part only 10 minutes.

The first part of the survey began with questions regarding basic demographics: gender, age, domestic situation, occupation, ethnic or racial identification and longevity in Alto Hospicio. It then asked about family attributes and indicators of wealth. The majority of the survey was made up of questions regarding use of social media: which media the respondent used, how long had accounts been held, with what frequency were these social media used, what sort of devices were used to access the media, with whom did the respondent communicate using the media, how many 'friends' did the respondent have and where were these other people located.

The second part of the survey asked questions related to communication with family members on social media, differences between social media friends known face-to-face and those known only online, fake profiles, use of photographs online and the relationship between social media usage and business or commerce. This survey also asked for assessments of happiness, popularity, social obligations and interpersonal tensions as a result of social media usage.

These surveys were both quantitative and qualitative in nature, and were replicated in all nine field sites of the Global Social Media Impact Study. Quantitative cross-field site analyses are available in Chapter 4 of the edited volume *How the World Changed Social Media*, which explores various themes of the study as a whole.

Notes

Chapter 1

1   Bosniak, L. S. 2001. 'Denationalizing Citizenship.' In Aleinikoff, T. A. and D. Klusmeyer, eds. *Citizenship: Comparison and Perspectives.* Carnegie Endowment For International Peace. Washington DC. See also Bloemraad, I., Korteweg, A. and Yurdakul, G. 2008. 'Citizenship and Immigration: Multiculturalism, Assimilation, and Challenges to the Nation-State.' *Annual Review of Sociology* 34: 153–79, 154.

2   Anderson, B. 1983. *Imagined Communities.* London: Verso.

3   Lukose, R. 2009. *Liberalization's Children: Gender, Youth, and Consumer Citizenship in Globalizing India.* Durham, NC: Duke University Press. 9.

4   Habermas, J. 1962. *The Structural Transformation of the Public Sphere: An Inquiry into a Category of Bourgeois Society.* Cambridge: Polity Press. 105.

5   See Castles, S. 2002. 'Migration and community formation under conditions of globalization.' *International Migration Review* 36(4): 1143–68; Castles, S. and Davidson, A. 2000. *Citizenship and Migration: Globalization and the Politics of Belonging.* New York: Routledge; Vertovec, S. 2004. 'Migrant transnationalism and modes of transformation.' *International Migration Review* 38(3): 970–1001.

6   See Pêcheux, M. 1982. *Language, Semantics, and Ideology.* New York: St. Martin's Press. 157; Muñoz, J. 1999. *Disidentifications: Queers of Color and the Performance of Politics.* Minneapolis: University of Minnesota Press. 157–60.

7   Alto Hospicio sits in Chile's Region I of Tarapacá. These administrative divisions, created in 1974, are numbered from I–XIV, from North to South along the length of the country. The Santiago metropolitan region is excluded from this numbering system. Region XV of Arica and Parinacota, to the north of Region I, was created in 2007, splitting the former Region I in two. The Great North of Chile is one of five natural regions of Chile, created in 1950 by the Corporación de Fomento de la Producción de Chile, a governmental organisation that promotes economic growth. This region spans Chile's border with Peru in the North to the city of Antofagasta, encompassing the Atacama Desert. When referring to regionalism in this book I mean the area encompassed by the Great North, and use this distinction to indicate the similarity of lifestyles, driven by the common natural resources and industries in this natural region.

8   'Copper solution: The mining industry has enriched Chile. But its future is precarious.' *The Economist,* 27 April 2013. Available online at http://www.economist.com/news/business/ 21576714-mining-industry-has-enriched-chile-its-future-precarious-copper-solution.

9   'Indice de Calidad de Vida Urbana.' 2014. Núcleo de Estudios Metropolitanos, Instituto de Estudios Urbanos y Territoriales Santiago: Pontificia Universidad Católica de Chile y la Cámara Chilena de la Construcción. Available online at http://www.estudiosurbanos.uc.cl/ component/zoo/item/indice-de-calidad-de-vida-urbana-icvu.

10 Frazier, L. J. 2007. *Salt in the Sand: Memory, Violence, and the Nation-State in Chile, 1890 to the Present.* Durham, NC: Duke University Press. 34.

11 'Copper solution.' 2013. *The Economist.*

12 Frazier, 2007. *Salt in the Sand.* 34.

13   Figures for 2005–11, Library of Congress Country Studies, 'Chile: Mining'. Available at http://countrystudies.us/chile/71.htm.

14   Frazier, 2007. *Salt in the Sand.* 25.

15   Frazier, 2007. *Salt in the Sand.* 25.

16   Brown, K. W. 2012. *A History of Mining in Latin America: From the Colonial Era to the Present.* Albuquerque, NM: University of New Mexico Press.

17   Klein, N. 2007. *The Shock Doctrine.* New York: Picador. 93–4.

18   These policies correspond to measures called 'structural adjustment' in countries which pledge such reforms in exchanges for loans from the International Monetary Fund. However, in the Chilean example Pinochet enthusiastically adopted such measures absent of a loan from the IMF.

19   The system is based on a direct payment to the schools based on daily attendance. 'Public' schools are those owned by the municipality of the commune in which the school is located. 'Private' schools often receive government subsidies, and may be organized as either for profit or not for profit. In order to receive public funding, private schools must reserve 15% of seats in each class to students classified as "vulnerable" (based on family income and mother's level of education). Schools receive extra funding for each "vulnerable" student they enroll.

20   Collier, S. and Sater, W. F. 2002. *A History of Chile, 1808–2002.* Cambridge: Cambridge University Press. 366–75.

21   Purchasing power parity converts gross domestic product to international dollars (an international dollar has the same purchasing power over GDP as the US dollar has in the United States). For comparison, PPP during the same time frame was $53,042 in the United States, $38,259 in the United Kingdom, $15,037 in Brazil, $11,774 in Peru and $6,131 in Bolivia. See 'GDP per capita, PPP (current international $)', World Bank, International Comparison Program database, World Development Indicators (2011). Available at http://data.worldbank.org/indicator/ NY.GDP.PCAP.PP.CD.

22   Harvey, D. 2005. *A Brief History of Neoliberalism.* New York: Oxford University Press. 1.

23   Frazier writes, 'The neoliberal model put in place by the military and deepened under civilian rule called for the redefinition of citizenship through consumption and the prioritization of market relations over former political cultures'. See Frazier, 2007. *Salt in the Sand.* 72.

24   Ong, A. 1991. 'The Gender and Labor Politics of Postmodernity.' *Annual Review of Anthropology* (1991): 279–309.

25   Larrain, T. A. 2009. 'Moving Home: The Everyday Making of the Chilean Middle Class.' Ph.D. thesis, Department of Sociology of the London School of Economics.

26   Lancaster, R. 2008. 'Preface.' Collins. J. L., Leonardo, M. Di and Williams, B., eds. *New Landscapes of Inequality.* Santa Fe: School for Advanced Research Press.

27   Jofré, D. 2007. 'Reconstructing the Politics of Indigenous Identity in Chile.' *Archaeologies* 3(1): 16–38.

28   In fact in May 2010 Chile joined the Organization for Economic Cooperation and Development, which consists of the world's 34 economically strongest countries.

29   About 30 per cent of young people aged between 18 and 24 matriculate in Chilean higher education, including traditional universities, non-traditional universities, technical schools and professional institutes. In 2014 the Region of Tarapacá had about 28 per cent of individuals aged 18–24 enrolled in tertiary education while the central provinces of Valparaíso and Santiago had 43 per cent and 35 per cent respectively. See Ministerio de Educación, Gobierno de Chile, *Bases de Datos de Matriculados.* Available online at http://www.mifuturo.cl/index.php/bases-de-datos/matriculados.

30   Larraín, J. 2006. 'Changes in Chilean Identity: Thirty Years after the Military Coup.' *Nations and Nationalism* 12(2): 321–38.

31   The fact that the Candela Project reports that Chilean genetics are approximately 44 per cent Native American, 52 per cent European, and 4 per cent African, the 2011 Latinobarómetro survey found that about 66 per cent of Chileans considered themselves to be 'white', while only 25 per cent said '*mestizo*' and eight per cent self-identified as 'indigenous' (the 2012 census, which was later de-certified, reported that more than ten per cent of the population identified as indigenous). See 'Latinobarómetro', Corporación Latinobarómetro (2011). Available online at http://www.latinobarometro.org/lat.jsp; Gänger, S., 'Conquering the Past: Post-War Archaeology and Nationalism in the Borderlands of Chile and Peru, c. 1880–1920.' 2009. *Comparative Studies in Society and History* 51(4): 691–714.

32 Larraín. 'Changes in Chilean Identity.' 2006.

33 Organization for Economic Cooperation and Development. 2015. OECD Income Distribution and Poverty Database. Available at www.oecd.org/els/social/inequality.

34 Within the contemporary context of global neoliberal capitalism, many nation-states find it difficult to reach ideals of order, prosperity and peace within modernity. As these governments increasingly lose control to international organisations and banks over regulating their own money supplies, credit ratings and labour supplies, they often concentrate on regulating markets, attracting foreign investment, repaying foreign debt and maintaining stable environments for the operations of transnational capital. Yet as they focus on these seemingly foundational aspects of maintaining a stable economy, their ability to provide adequately for the needs of their citizens suffers. See Goldstein, D. 2004. *The Spectacular City: Violence and Performance in Urban Bolivia*. Durham, NC: Duke University Press. 21.

35 Frazier, 2007. *Salt in the Sand*. 57.

36 See Larsen, J. E. and Andersen, J. 1998. 'Gender, Poverty and Empowerment.' *Critical Social Policy* 18(2): 241–58; Brodwin, P. 2001. 'Marginality and Cultural Intimacy in a Trans-national Haitian Community.' Occasional Paper No. 91, October. Department of Anthropology, University of Wisconsin-Milwaukee, USA; Sommers, L. M., Mehretu, A. and Pigozzi, B. W. M. 1999. 'Towards Typologies of Socio-economic Marginality: North/South Comparisons.' *Marginality in Space – Past, Present and Future: Theoretical and Methodological Aspects of Cultural, Social and Economical Parameters of Marginal and Critical Regions*. Jussila, H., Majoral, R. and Mutambirwa, C. C., eds. London: Ashgate Publishing Ltd. 7–24.

37 Structural violence describes high rates of disease and death, unemployment, homelessness, paucity of educational opportunities, limited political power, hunger, thirst, and bodily pain, particularly as magnified by racism, sexism, and other forms of discrimination. See Kleinman, A. 2000. 'The Violences of Everyday Life: The Multiple Forms and Dynamics of Social Violence.' In Kleinman, A. and Das, V., eds. *Violence and Subjectivity*. Berkeley, CA: University of California Press. 226–41; Farmer, P. 1997. *Infections and Inequalities: The Modern Plagues*. Berkeley, CA: University of California Press. 263.

38 Darden, J. T. 1989. 'Blacks and other Racial Minorities: The Significance of Colour in Inequality.' *Urban Geography* 10: 562–77; Davis, B. 2003. 'Marginality in a Pluralistic Society.' *Eye On Psi Chi* 2(1): 1–4; Gans, H. J. 1996. 'From Underclass to Under-caste: Some Observations about the Future of the Post-Industrial Economy and its Major Victims.' In *Urban Poverty and the Underclass: A Reader*. Mingione, E. M., ed. Oxford: Blackwell; Leimgruber, W. 2004. *Between Global and Local: Marginality and Marginal Regions in the Context of Globalization and Deregulation*. Burlington, VT: Ashgate Publishing Limited.

39 Goldstein, 2004. *The Spectacular City*. 12. This conflation of individuals and places within a framework of morality also corresponds to Modan's notion of 'moral geography'. See Modan, G. 2007. *Turf Wars: Discourse, Diversity, and the Politics of Place*. New York: Blackwell; Thomann, M. 2016. 'Zones of Difference, Boundaries of Access: Moral Geography and Community Mapping in Abidjan, Côte d'Ivoire.' *Journal of Homosexuality* 63(3): 426–36.

40 See Tsing, A. L. 1993. *In the Realm of the Diamond Queen: Marginality in an Out-of-the-Way Place*. Princeton, NJ: Princeton University Press.

41 See Gutkind, P. C. W. 1974. *Urban Anthropology: Perspectives on 'Third World' Urbanization and Urbanism*. Assen, The Netherlands: Van Gorcum; Hardoy, J. 1972. *El Proceso de Urbanización en America Latina*. La Habana, Cuba: Oficina Regional de Cultural para America Latina y el Caribe; Roberts, B. R. 1978. *Cities of Peasants: the Political Economy of Urbanization in the Third World*. London: Edward Arnold.

42 Albó, X., Greaves, T. and Sandoval, G. Z. 1981. *Chukiyawu: La Cara Aymara de La Paz*, Vol. 4 (Cuadernos de investigacion No. 29). La Paz: CIPCA; Lomnitz, L. A. 1977. *Networks and Marginality: Life in a Mexican Shantytown*, New York: Academic Press; Peattie, L. R. 1974. 'The Concept of "Marginality" as applied to Squatter Settlements.' Cornelius, W. A. and Trueblood, F. M., eds. *Latin American Urban Research* 4: Anthropological Perspectives on Latin American Urbanization. Beverly Hills: Sage. 101–9; Smith, G. 1989. *Livelihood and Resistance: Peasants and the Politics of Land in Peru*. Berkeley: University of California Press; Ibañez, C. G. V. 1983. *Rituals of Marginality: Politics, Process, and Culture Change in Urban Central Mexico 1969–1974*. Berkeley, CA: University of California Press.

43 Auyero, J. 1999. 'The Hyper-Shantytown: Ethnographic Portraits of Neo-liberal Violence(s).' *Ethnography* 1(1): 93–116.

44 I use the terms 'identify' and 'identification' in contrast to the more common term, 'identity', as a processual, active term derived from a verb. While Goffman popularised the term 'identity', Brubaker and Cooper argue this word is over-endowed with meaning, and extrapolating the different senses of the word allows for more useful analysis. They suggest, 'Identification lacks the reifying connotations of identity. It invites us to specify the agents that do the identifying. And it does not presuppose that such identifying (even by powerful agents, such as the state) will necessarily result in the internal sameness, the distinctiveness, the bounded groupness that political entrepreneurs may seek to achieve'. See Brubaker, R. and Cooper, F. 2000. 'Beyond "Identity".' *Theory and Society* 29:1–47.

45 Brubaker and Cooper, 2000. "Beyond "Identity".'

46 Brubaker and Cooper suggest that the term 'self-understanding' designates a 'situated subjectivity', or one's sense of who one is, of one's social location and how one is prepared to act. Self-understanding suggests ways in which individual and collective action can be governed by particularistic understandings of self and social location rather than by putatively universal, structurally determined interests, similar to what Pierre Bourdieu has called *sens pratique*, 'the practical sense—at once cognitive and emotional—that persons have of themselves and their social world'. See Brubaker and Cooper, 2000. "Beyond Identity." 17; Bourdieu, P. 1990. *The Logic of Practice*. Cambridge: Polity Press.

47 Bucholtz, M. and Hall, K. 2004. 'Theorizing Identity in Language and Sexuality Research.' *Language in Society* 33(4): 469–515. 493.

48 Bourdieu, P. 1984. *Distinction: A Social Critique of the Judgement of Taste*. New York: Routledge.

49 Larraín. 2006. *Changes in Chilean Identity*.

50 The 2012 national census suggests around 9,539 Mapuche live in the region of Tarapacá, but no precise results are recorded specifically for Alto Hospicio.

51 This contrasts starkly with the subjectivities of Mapuche in southern Chile, where they are racialised and often confront the national government. See Marino, M. E., Pilleux, M., Quilaqueo, D. and Martín, B. 2009. 'Discursive Racism in Chile: The Mapuche Case.' Van Dijk, T. A., ed. *Racism and Discourse in Latin America*. New York: Rowman and Littlefield. 95–130; Crow, J. 2010. 'Negotiating Inclusion in the Nation: Mapuche Intellectuals and the Chilean State.' *Latin American and Caribbean Ethnic Studies* 5(2): 131–52.

52 The United States's CIA Factbook ranks Bolivia as one of the poorest and least developed countries in the hemisphere. Bolivia's terrain, especially in the Altiplano, makes travel difficult, and after losing its coastal region to a Chilean military pursuit in 1879 it is now begrudgingly land-locked. This affects the ability of Bolivian industries to export, subjects imports to the taxes and regulations of other countries and reportedly requires Bolivia to pay Chile or Brazil for access to fibre optic cables, driving internet prices up and speed down. The 2001 National Census placed poverty rates at 59 per cent and extreme poverty at 24.4 per cent. As the 2011 UNICEF report on poverty in Bolivia suggests, 'With almost no productive investment, diminishing internal demand, lack of confidence, uncertainty, increasing lack of prestige of political parties and lack of credibility of the political system, conditions do not exist for economic reactivation in the short term.'

53 Vergara, J. I. and Gundermann, H. 2012. 'Conformación y Dinámica Interna del Campo Identitario Regional en Tarapacá y Los Lagos, Chile.' *Chungara, Revista de Antropología Chilena* 44(1): 115–34. Available at http://dx.doi.org/10.4067/ S071773562012000100009

54 Bosniak, 2001. 'Denationalizing Citizenship.'

55 Carruthers, D. and Rodriguez, P. 2009. 'Mapuche Protest, Environmental Conflict and Social Movement Linkage in Chile.' *Third World Quarterly* 30(4): 743–60; Richards, P. 2005. 'The Politics of Gender, Human Rights, and Being Indigenous in Chile.' *Gender & Society* 19(2): 199–220; Richards, P. 2010. 'Of Indians and Terrorists: How the State and Local Elites Construct the Mapuche in Neoliberal Multicultural Chile.' *Journal of Latin American Studies* 42: 59–90.

56 Some Chileans suggest that the word *flaite* comes from Michael Jordan's line of Nike 'Air Flight' shoes, which when pirated carried the mark, 'Flight Air'. However, the more widely cited origin of the word suggests that *flaite* comes from 'flyer', as in someone who is high on drugs.

57 According to the 2011 Casen survey, in the region of Tarapacá, family ownership of household goods were as follows: vehicle 32 per cent (28.7 per cent in Chile as a whole); washing machine 60.9 per cent (70.8 per cent), refrigerator 67.1 per cent (79.8 per cent), water

heater 34.5 per cent (59.8 per cent), mobile phone 93.3 per cent (94 per cent) and cable tele-vision connection 39.6 per cent (41 per cent), computer 42.9 per cent (44.5 per cent), inter-net access 34.6 per cent (33.4 per cent). See 'Encuesta de caracterizacion socioeconomica nacional.' 2011. Santiago: Casen. Available online at http://observatorio.ministeriodesar-rollosocial.gob.cl/ casen_obj.php

58 Bourdieu, P. 1984. *Distinction*. See also Barr-Melej, P. 1998. 'Cowboys and Constructions: Nationalist Representations of Pastoral Life in Post-Portalian Chile.' *Journal of Latin American Studies* 30(1): 35–61; Gramsci, A. 1971. *Selections from the Prison Notebooks of Antonio Gramsci*. Hoare, Q. and Nowell Smith, G., eds. New York: International Publishers.

59 Larrain, T. A. 2014. 'Housing Markets Performing Class: Middle Class Cultures and Market Professionals in Chile.' *The Sociological Review* 62(2): 400–20.

60 Bourdieu, P. 2005. *The Social Structures of the Economy*. Cambridge: Polity Press.

61 Savage, M., Bagnall, G. and Longhurst, B. 2001. 'Ordinary, Ambivalent and Defensive: Class Identities in the Northwest of England.' *Sociology* 35(4): 875–92.

62 Larraín, A. 2009. 'Moving Home.'

63 Aizura, A. Z. 2006. 'Of Borders and Homes: The Imaginary Community of (Trans)sexual Citizenship.' *Inter-Asia Cultural Studies* 7(2): 289–309; Smith, S. 1989. 'Society, Space and Citizenship Transactions.' *IBG* 14:144–56.

64 Horst, H. and Miller, D. 2012. *Digital Anthropology*. Oxford: Berg.

Chapter 2

1 Carvallo-Fernandini, R. and Lafuente, D. S. 2008. 'The History of CTC and Entel: Precursors of the Telecommunications in Chile.' Valparaíso: Universidad Católica de Valparaiso. Available online at http://www.ieeeghn.org/wiki/ images/0/08/Carvallo-Fernandini.pdf.

2 'Latin America Digital Future in Focus' report. 2013. Comscore. Available online at http:// www.comscore.com/ Insights/Blog/2013_Digital_Future_in_Focus_Series.

3 For more information see Appendix 1: Social Media Questionnaire.

4 Phatic communication refers to 'small talk' or 'grooming' which exists for the pur-poses of maintaining social relations without the subject matter or precise information exchanged being of particular importance. See Malinowski, B. 1923 'The Problem of Meaning in Primitive Languages.' Ogden, C. K and Richards, I. A., eds. *The Meaning of Meaning*. London: Routledge. 146–52; Miller, V. 2008. 'New Media, Networking and Phatic Culture.' *Convergence: The International Journal of Research into New Media Technologies* 14(4): 387–400.

5 See Velghe, F. 2015. 'Hallo hoe gaan dit, wat maak jy?: Phatic communication, the Mobile Phone and Coping Strategies in a South African Context.' *Multilingual Margins* 2(1): 10–30.

6 Miller, D., Costa, E., Haynes, N., McDonald, T., Nicolescu, R., Sinanan, J., Spyer. J., Venkatraman, S. and Wang, X. 2016. *How the World Changed Social Media*. London: University College London Press.

7 In my survey of 100 people between ages 16 and 55, only five have never had a Facebook account, and all 95 others continue to use Facebook regularly. Eighty-two of the 100 people check Facebook at least once a day and 45 say they are 'always connected'.

8 While in some locations around the world Facebook is losing hold with teens, as they migrate to platforms such as Whatsapp, Twitter or Snapchat, there is no such discernible movement in Alto Hospicio. Among Hospiceño teens over 70 per cent say that they are 'always connected' on Facebook. In fact, of the eight countries studied in the Global Social Media Impact Study, only the field site in England reported a trend away from Facebook. See Miller, D. 2016. *Social Media in an English Village*. London: UCL Press.

9 Habermas, 1962. *The Structural Transformation of the Public Sphere*. 105.

10 Though in many places sushi is associated with fine dining and international cuisine, the dish has become something of a staple in Chile in the last decade; it is fairly affordable with many delivery services offering 40 pieces for $10,000CLP ($16). Peruvian-Japanese food (call Nikkei) has a long history, given the large number of Japanese immigrants to Peru dat-ing back to the late 1800s. As Peruvian immigrants arrived in Chile they brought with them a love for sushi; this subsequently became popular among almost all Chileans, spanning class differences, in the early 2000s. Of course, it should be noted that Chilean 'sushi' differs

significantly from authentic Japanese sushi, usually featuring salmon, shrimp or cooked chicken combined with rice, cream cheese, avocado and often covered in panko bread crumbs and fried. It is usually served with soy sauce and also sweetened 'teriyaki' sauce.

11　In a survey of 100 Hospiceños 77 per cent of respondents used the application (in mid-2014). Of those two-thirds regularly communicated in groups on WhatsApp.

12　See Rubin, G. 1984. 'Thinking Sex: Notes for a Radical Theory of the Politics of Sexuality.' In Vance, C., ed. *Pleasure and Danger: Exploring Female Sexuality.* Boston: Routledge. 267–391. Rubin explains how sexual activity that is paid or pornographic falls within the same 'bad, abnormal, unnatural' classification as other forms of non-heteronormative sexuality, such as homosexuality or group sex.

13　The percentage of Twitter users represents a big decline from Facebook and WhatsApp, and the service is used primarily by teens and adults in their early twenties. Only 30 per cent of survey respondents said they used the medium, including 33 per cent of teens, 23 per cent of 20-somethings and 21 per cent of 30-somethings. Of those 40 and above, only eight per cent of survey respondents have an account. Even among those that do have accounts, only about half report tweeting or re-tweeting at least once a month.

14　Overall only 22 per cent of those surveyed said they use the application. Over 35 per cent of teens, 26 per cent of 20-somethings and 21 per cent of 30-somethings used Instagram; no one over 40 reported having an account.

15　This notion of social media aligns with Madianou and Miller's concept of 'polymedia'. See Madianou, M. and Miller, D. 2012. 'Polymedia: Towards a New Theory of Digital Media in Interpersonal Communication.' *International Journal of Cultural Studies* 16(2): 169–87.

16　In addition to these six highly used social media sites, several other platforms have a small following in Alto Hospicio. A few individuals use Viber and Line much like WhatsApp, sending pictures, videos and messages to other users, but with the added benefit of a calling feature that uses data rather than phone minutes, much like Skype (though since this time, WhatsApp has introduced a similar feature). Skype itself resonates with Hospiceños and most have used it, but do so very rarely – perhaps because, as Alvaro commented, 'the call just drops'. Some Hospiceños used dating applications such as Grindr and Scruff, which focus on gay men, and Tinder, which is aimed primarily at heterosexual dating, but allow any user to limit their matches to men or women. However, for reasons I discuss in Chapter 4, Facebook remains a much more important (if covert) platform for potential dates. Though YouTube is the most used platform for music-related social media activity, one Hospiceño man mentioned using Soundcloud, an application that allows users to record, upload, and share 'sounds' – usually some form of music. One survey respondent also mentioned Pinterest, a platform for searching and 'collecting' images on 'pin boards' for viewing later. This woman in her early fifties created a pin board of home craft ideas she would like to try, including crochet patterns, home-sewn throw pillows and ideas for wall art. Yet Pinterest is geared towards aesthetic aspirations of the type that generally conflict with the modes of normativity that prevail in Alto Hospicio. Thus it is not surprising that its use is quite limited.

17　While 66 per cent of all respondents say they watch at least one YouTube video a month, with the average being around 60 videos per month, only 17 per cent of survey respondents actually had a YouTube account. Only 11 per cent of those surveyed had left a comment on YouTube in the last month (the average being about one per week), and 12 per cent said they had posted a video to YouTube in the last month.

18　Overall, only six per cent of people surveyed use the platform. However, almost 20 per cent of teens have accounts and many 20-somethings said that they had accounts previously, but had recently closed them.

19　See Kristeva, J. 1980. *Desire in Language: A Semiotic Approach to Literature and Art.* New York: Columbia University Press; Fairclough, N. 2003. *Analysing Discourse: Textual Analysis for Social Research.* New York: Routledge.

20　See Bauman, R. and Briggs, C. L. 1990. 'Poetics and Performance as Critical Perspectives on Language and Social Life.' *Annual Review of Anthropology* 19: 59–88.

21　Leppänen, S., Kytölä, S., Jousmäki, H., Peuronen, S. and Westinen, E. 2013. 'Entextualization and Resemiotization as Resources for (Dis)identification in Social Media.' *Tilburg Papers in Cultural Studies,* 57. Tilburg University.

22　Dawkins, R. 1976. *The Selfish Gene.* Oxford: Oxford University Press.

23　See Turkle, S. 2010. *Alone Together.* New York: Basic Books.

24 Butler, J. 1999. *Gender Trouble: Feminism and the Subversion of Identity*. New York: Routledge. 33.

25 Wittgenstein, L. 1953. *Philosophical Investigations*, 3rd ed. Anscombe, G. E. M., trans. London: Macmillan.

26 These acts of identification do not simply express something that already exists, but constitute the relationships and categories as they are expressed. Because identification takes place in the context of social scripts, the repetition of culturally recognised symbols congeals over time to produce an appearance of naturalness. See Butler, 1999. *Gender Trouble*. 44.

27 Bourdieu, P. 1977. *Outline of a Theory of Practice*. Nice, R., trans. Cambridge: Cambridge University Press. 29.

28 Bourdieu discerns a difference between *knowing that* and *knowing how*. For example, a Hospiceño may not explicitly know that they should not wear expensive clothing; they just know how to dress themselves the way they always have – in used clothing from the market. They may not know that telling their friends about their exclusively Spanish and German ancestry is 'wrong'; they simply cultivate a sense of shared culture through discourses of racial homogeneity and *mestizaje*. See Bourdieu, P. 1977. *Outline of a Theory of Practice*.

29 Butler, 1999. *Gender Trouble*.

30 Bourdieu calls these mental schemata *habitus*. Habitus in a way sets limits to normativity, through sensibilities, dispositions and taste, which are based on the embodiment of social structures. See Bourdieu, P. 2006 'Structures and the Habitus.' Moore, H. L. and Sanders, T., eds. *Anthropology in Theory: Issues in Epistemology*. Malden, MA: Blackwell. 56.

31 Turner uses the term 'social scripts', which I contrast here with Durkheim's notion of 'social facts'. He describes social facts similarly, as the values, cultural norms and social structures which transcend the individual and are capable of exercising a social constraint. Yet these are generally institutions such as kinship and marriage, currency, language, religion and political organisation that individuals take into account in their everyday interactions with others. Deviating from the norms of these institutions often makes the individual an outlier in the group. However, social scripts are more subtle, working through 'structures of feeling' (as described by Williams) rather than formal institutions, so that nowhere is it formally suggested that flashy jewellery, clothing, housing or even showing off an advanced education is against a social code, but as Vicky's gossip makes clear, these behaviours go against the accepted social script. See Turner, V. 1982. *From Ritual to Theatre: The Human Seriousness of Play*. New York: Performing Arts Journal Publications; Durkheim, E. 2012. 'The Rules of Sociological Method.' Longhofer, W. and Winchester, D., eds. *Social Theory Re-Wired: New Connections to Classical and Contemporary Perspectives*. New York: Routledge. 33–50; Williams, R. 1977. *Marxism and Literature*. New York: Oxford University Press.

32 Turner, V. 1982. *From Ritual to Theatre*. 122.

33 Goffman, E. 1959. *The Presentation of Self in Everyday Life*. Garden City: Doubleday.

34 Schechner suggests that even though there are differences between heightened performances and ordinary daily action, 'Any behaviour, event, action or thing can be studied "as" performance, can be analysed in terms of doing, behaving, and showing. To consider a thing as performance is simply to regard it from a performance perspective or in performance terms.' Similarly, Turner defines 'performance' to include 'social dramas' or any action that is formed, understood and reiterated through cultural scripting. See Schechner, R. 2002. *Performance Studies: An Introduction*. New York: Routledge; Turner, V. 1986. *The Anthropology of Performance*. New York: PAJ Publications.

35 Bucholtz, M. and Hall, K. 2004. 'Theorizing Identity in Language and Sexuality Research.' *Language in Society* 33: 469–515, 491.

36 Brubaker and Cooper, 2000. 'Beyond "Identity."'

Chapter 3

1 See Debord, G. 1994. *The Society of the Spectacle*. New York: Zone Books; Jameson, F. 1991. *Postmodernism, or, The Cultural Logic of Late Capitalism*. New York: Verso; Benjamin, W. 1936. *The Work of Art in the Age of Mechanical Reproduction*. New York: Random House; Adorno, T. and Horkheimer, M. 2002 [1944]. 'The Culture Industry: Enlightenment as Mass Deception.' *Dialectic of Enlightenment*. Redwood City, CA: Stanford University Press.

2   Eagleton, T. 1990. *The Ideology of the Aesthetic*. Oxford: Oxford University Press; Laclau, E. and Mouffe, C. 1985. *Hegemony and Socialist Strategy*. London: Verso; Ranciere, J. 2002. 'The Aesthetic Revolution and its Outcomes.' *The New Left Review* 14: 133–51.

3   I define 'selfies' more loosely here than the standard definition. 'Selfies' are often considered to be photographs taken by a person who also appears in the picture. They may be alone or in a group, and are identified by the appearance of an arm that juts out to the side of the frame as if it is holding the camera, or by the use of a mirror so that the camera (or camera-equipped phone) is visible in the reflection of the subject of the photo. In my usage I consider a selfie to be any casual photograph that depicts the person who posts it on their own social media account. It may be taken by them in the classical 'selfie' style, but may also be taken by a friend on the subject's camera explicitly for uploading on their own profile page. I privilege function – a casual photograph presenting the self/self-image – rather than the method of capture in this definition. By contrast I do not include photographs that are taken by the subject but centre on body parts other than the face (such as feet or fingernails). Again, while these may fall under a strict definition of 'selfie' in terms of the method of photo capture, I argue that their use and meaning are different from a picture of the self which displays the face.

4   Most of the images of people in this chapter come from individuals under 35, because they post more frequently and are more likely to agree to have their images appear. Unless otherwise noted, however, these trends are also true for people aged 35–55.

5   Miller, D. and Sinanan, J. 2016. *Visualising Facebook: A Comparative Perspective*. London: University College London Press. 14.

6   In my survey of 100 people, over three-quarters said that they posted 20 per cent or less of the photographs they take on social media.

7   Dutton, D. 2002. 'Aesthetic Universals.' Gaut, B. and Dominic McIver Lopes, D., eds. *The Routledge Companion to Aesthetics*. New York: Routledge.

8   See Miller, D. 2016. *Social Media in an English Village*.

9   My explanation of this aesthetic draws on Koskinen's suggestion that camera phone imagery constitutes an 'aesthetic of banality'. But I further this notion to point out that the particular moments that Hospiceños portray through photography depict the unassuming aesthetics that in their environment are also ubiquitous outside of the camera phone. Almost any Hospiceño could access the resources to produce this aesthetic, but it is not the same as the 'accessible aesthetic' of folklore artistic production discussed by Kirchenblatt Gimblett. It is neither the 'ordinary aesthetic' that hooks attributes to the working class's replacement of beauty with consumerism, nor its contrast, the aesthetic of 'beautiful objects' created by the 'poor' on 'different continents'. My argument is neither that the predominant aesthetic of Alto Hospicio is nonexistent, nor is it entirely utilitarian – privileging form above function and the 'choice of the necessary', as Bourdieu calls the working-class aesthetic. While many Hospiceños clearly could afford to redecorate their homes or buy expensive clothing from Zofri or Iquique department stores, their aesthetic choices lean toward an appearance of what Bourdieu calls 'necessity' in order to remain within the normativity associated with working class. It is an aesthetic that is presented as if it were not one, because aspiring to a particular aesthetic would be performing something; a certain kind of pretension. Yet the aesthetic relies on deliberate choices to not be pretentious or striking: instead to be modest, to be unassuming. See Koskinen, I. 2007. 'Managing Banality in Mobile Multimedia.' *Peritierra*. R., ed. *The Social Construction and Usage of Communications Technology: Asian and European Experiences*. Philadelphia: University of Philippines Press. 60–81; Gimblett, B. K. 1983. 'An Accessible Aesthetic: The Role of Folk Arts and the Folk Artist in the Curriculum.' *New York Folklore: The Journal of the New York Folklore Society* 9(3–4): 9–18; hooks, b. 1995. 'Beauty Laid Bare: Aesthetics in the Ordinary.' Walker, R., ed. *To Be Real*. New York: Anchor Books. 157–65; Bourdieu, P. 1984. *Distinction*. 41, 372, 376.

10   Ritchie, D. 2005. 'Frame-Shifting in Humor and Irony.' *Metaphor and Symbol* 20 (4): 275–94, 288.

11   Yus calls this form of joking 'arousal-safety' in which the joke intends to elicit either excitement or offence, then quickly reverts to the expected. Yus suggests that humour is partially based on the audience's pleasure in discovering congruencies. 'The tension involved in searching for a solution may be released when the "meaning" of a joke is discovered.' See Yus, F. 2003. 'Humor and the Search for Relevance.' *Journal of Pragmatics* 35: 1295–1331, 1314.

12 Taylor, E. 2014. 'The Curation of the Self in the Age of the Internet.' Paper presented at IUAES/JASCA Conference, Tokyo, Japan. Available at http://erinbtaylor.com/the-curation-of-the-self-in-the-age-of-the-internet.

13 Geertz, C. 1976. 'Art as a Cultural System.' *MLN* 91(6): 1473–99, 1478.

Chapter 4

1   Strathern, M. 1988. *The Gender of the Gift: Problems with Women and Problems with Society in Melanesia*. Berkeley, CA: University of California Press.

2   The 'Anuario de Estadísticas Criminales Fundación Paz Ciudadana' reported on 2007 crime statistics (the most recent year available) that there were about 1,000 thefts without force or violence (the type of pickpocketing everyone assumed to be so common), meaning that the reported rate of victims was only just over one per cent (assuming a population of 100,000). This rate was consistent with other sizeable cities in Chile. Yet anecdotally most individuals had stories of personally experiencing theft, and very few reported the crimes, feeling that doing so had no outcome. This suggested that the official rates did not correspond with the actual theft rates. Scarpa, M. S., ed. 2008. 'Anuario de Estadísticas Criminales Fundación Paz Ciudadana.' Santiago: Fundacion Paz Ciudadana. Available online at http://www.pazciudadana.cl/wp-content/uploads/ 2013/07/2009-01-20_Anuario-de-estad% C3%83%C2%ADsticas-criminales-2008.pdf.

3   In academic literature authenticity often refers to values of cultural continuity and a sense of pristine, genuine and traditional cultural practices. See Hervik, P. 1999. 'The Mysterious Maya of National Geographic.' *Journal of Latin American Anthropology* 4(1): 166–97; Handler, R. 1986. 'Authenticity.' *Anthropology Today* 2(1): 2–4. My usage follows more closely notions of authenticity which focus on what counts as 'genuine' for a given purpose. See Bucholtz and Hall, 2005. 'Identity and Interaction.'

4   Bucholtz and Hall, 2005. 'Identity and Interaction.' 601.

5   See Venkatraman, S. Forthcoming. *Social Media in South India*. London: UCL Press; McDonald, T. Forthcoming. *Social Media in Rural China*. London: UCL Press.

6   Papacharissi, Z. 2009. 'The Virtual Geographies of Social Networks: A Comparative Analysis of Facebook, Linkedln and AsmallWorld.' *New Media and Society* 11(1–2): 199–220, 215.

7   See boyd, d. 2011. 'Social Network Sites as Networked Publics: Affordances, Dynamics, and Implications.' Papacharissi, Z., ed. *A Networked Self. Identity, Community, and Culture on Social Network Sites*. 39–58. New York: Routledge; Lee, C. K. M. 2011. 'Micro-Blogging and Status Updates on Facebook: Texts and Practices.' Thurlow, C. and Mroczek, K., eds. *Digital Discourse: Language in the New Media*. Oxford: Oxford University Press. 111–128; Hillewaert, S. 2015. 'Writing with an Accent: Orthographic Practice, Emblems, and Traces on Facebook.' *Journal of Linguistic Anthropology* 25(2): 195–214.

8   Strathern takes a relationship-based rather than society-based approach to anthropology, calling relationships the 'crux of social action'. She sees the visibility of the relationship as fundamental to its importance. Similarly, Jacobson's approach to research on friendship emphasises the situational aspect. He is not only concerned with constant friendship and its characteristics, but 'with the labelling process itself, that is, with the situations in which a person gives and takes away the label of "friend".' See Strathern, 1988. *The Gender of the Gift*; Jacobson, D. 1975. 'Fair Weather Friend: Label and Context in Middle Class Friendships.' *Journal of Anthropological Research* 31(3): 225–34.

9   Sixty-three per cent were friends with their mother on Facebook and 48 per cent with their father. For those who are not friends with their parents on Facebook, it is often because their parents do not yet have accounts.

10 Some scholars have criticised the notions of DNA and blood as icons of authenticity in relatedness and ancestry. See Nelkin, D. and Lindee, S. 1996. *The DNA Mystique: The Gene as a Cultural Icon*. Ann Arbor: University of Michigan Press; Sturm, C. 2002. *Blood Politics: Race, Culture, and Identity in the Cherokee Nation of Oklahoma*. Berkeley, CA: University of California Press.

11 Schneider, D. M. 1964. *A Critique of the Study of Kinship*. Ann Arbor: University of Michigan Press.

12 *Flaite* can also be used to describe a woman, but in common discourse the stereotypical *flaite* is imaged to be a young man.

13 Similarly McDonald writes that children are seen as 'little treasures' in northern China. McDonald, Forthcoming. *Social Media in Rural China*.

14 This family affection that is shared on social media is not always the same in other places. Miller writes that in The Glades teens began ignoring Facebook in favour of Twitter, precisely because they felt they could not escape the watch of their parents who had more recently joined Facebook. See Miller, 2016. *Social Media in an English Village*.

15 For a counter example see Venkatraman, S. Forthcoming. *Social Media in South India*.

16 For a similar case see Sinanan, J. Forthcoming. *Social Media in Trinidad*. London: UCL Press.

17 Bruess, C. J. S. and Pearson, J. C. 1993. '"Sweet Pea" and "Pussy Cat": An Examination of Idiom Use and Marital Satisfaction Over the Life Cycle.' *Journal of Social and Personal Relationships* 10(4): 609–15.

18 Hillewaert suggests that when users are mindful of the public nature of social media posts they feel encouraged to display creativity within their linguistic practices, to which audiences often respond through a display of their own creativity. Hillewaert, S. 2015. 'Writing with an Accent.' 198.

19 Florini, S. 2013. 'Tweets, Tweeps, and Signifyin': Communication and Cultural Performance on "Black Twitter."' *Television New Media* 15(3): 223–37.

20 See Goodwin, M. H. 1990. *He-Said-She-Said: Talk as Social Organization Among Black Children*. Bloomington, IN: Indiana University Press. 185–9; Heath, S. B. 1983. *Ways with Words: Language, Life, and Work in Communities and Classrooms*. Cambridge: Cambridge University Press; Labov, W. 1972. *Language in the Inner City: Studies in the Black English Vernacular*. Philadelphia, PA: University of Pennsylvania Press. 306; Smitherman, G. 2000. '"If I'm Lyin, I'm Flyin": The Game of Insult in Black Language.' *Talkin that Talk: Language, Culture, and Education in African America*. New York, NY: Routledge. 223–30, 225; Morgan. M. 2002. 'Language, Power, and Discourse in African American Culture.' *Studies in the Social and Cultural Foundations of Language 20*. Cambridge: Cambridge University Press. 56–7.

21 Bauman suggests that such verbal play is 'marked as subject to evaluation for the way it is done, for the relative skill and effectiveness of the performer's display of competence'. See Bauman, R. 1875. *Verbal Art as Performance*. Rowley: Newbury House Publishers. 293.

22 Viewing social media "as" performance points us to the importance of the ways audiences come to bear on what Facebook posts become. While Goffman defines performance as activities that have influence on observers, Hymes more specifically insists that performance must be instantiated by members of a community that have access to folk knowledge. Thus community takes on central importance in thinking of social media posting as performance, and the public nature of that performance is essential to the expression of social ties and social life. See Goffman, 1959. *The Presentation of Self in Everyday Life*; Hymes, D. 1981. *In Vain I Tried to Tell You*. Philadelphia: University of Pennsylvania Press.

23 Labov, 1972. *Language in the Inner City*. 304–6.

Chapter 5

1 In my survey, which accounted for 341 household members, only 46 per cent of adult women were employed outside the home. Women's employment outside the home is very generational. For women in the survey, those working outside the home accounted for 86 per cent of women aged 20–30, 72 per cent aged 30–40, and only 12 per cent above age 40. In contrast only one man over the age of 25 did not work, and he was over 50 and retired.

2 In this analysis I rely in part on Connell's concept of gender regimes, or the institutionalised power relations between women and men where gender is a property of institutions and historical processes as well as individuals and their self-expression. This conception allows for viewing heteronormativity as a system in which gendered expectations place men and women into seemingly naturalised, distinct and complementary categories, based on heterosexual family structures. While a system of heteronormativity may recognise that not all people fall into this pattern, it takes binary genders linked to heterosexuality as a naturalised norm, thus bases other assumptions on this division. See Connell, R. W. 1987. *Gender*

and *Power: Society, the Person and Sexual Politics.* Stanford, CA: Sanford University Press; Lovaas, K. and Jenkins, M. M. 2006. 'Charting a Path through the "Desert of Nothing".' *Sexualities and Communication in Everyday Life: A Reader.* Thousand Oaks, CA: Sage.

3   'Copper Solution.' 2013. *The Economist.*

4   Jofré, 2007. 'Reconstructing the Politics of Indigenous Identity in Chile'; Babidge, S. 2013. '"Socios": The Contested Morality of "Partnerships" in Indigenous Community–Mining Company Relations, Northern Chile.' *The Journal of Latin American and Caribbean Anthropology* 18(2): 274–93.

5   Martin, E. 1997. 'Managing Americans: Policy and Changes in the Meanings of Work and the Self.' Shore, C. and Right, S., eds. *Anthropology of Policy: Critical Perspectives on Governance and Power.* London: Routledge. 183–200; Dunn, E. 2005. *Privatizing Poland: Baby Food, Big Business, and the Remaking of Labor.* Ithaca, NY: Cornell University Press; Yanagisako, S. 2002. *Producing Culture and Capital: Family Firms in Italy.* Princeton, NJ: Princeton University Press.

6   Ashforth, B. E. and Kreiner, G. E. 1999. '"How Can You Do It?": Dirty Work and the Challenge of Constructing a Positive Identity.' *The Academy of Management Review* 24(3): 413–34. 419; Lynch, G. 1987. *Roughnecks, Drillers, and Tool Pushers: Thirty-three Years in the Oil Fields.* Austin: University of Texas Press; Moodie, D. and Ndatshe, V. 1994. *Going for Gold: Men, Mines, and Migration.* Berkeley, CA: University of California Press.

7   Hospiceños, like most Chileans, see the importance of presenting themselves as enlightened citizens, and part of that is being *'bien educado'* [well educated]. Rather than applying specifically to formal education, being 'well educated' is better demonstrated through good manners, using the formal *'Usted'* [you] instead of the informal *'tú'* and in general using good grammar. One widely shared pop-culture article from *Opinza* lists such acts as avoiding gossip, not expressing irrelevant opinions and acting with deference when meeting new people as 'habits of very well educated people'. See Conlin, L. '10 hábitos de la gente muy bien educada.' *Opinza,* 2 January 2015. Available at http://opinza.com/2015/01/10-habitos-de-la-gente-muy-bien-educada/

8   Most of the people who work in high schools, or as managers for medium-sized or large businesses in Alto Hospicio, live in Iquique and commute to Alto Hospicio daily.

9   Chile's 2012 census did not specify marriage and divorce rates by city. For the region of Tarapacá as a whole, however, 45 per cent of people age 30–44 reported being single, 51 per cent were married, and about four per cent were divorced. For the same population 40.5 per cent reported that they lived with their (legal) spouse and 28.4 per cent lived with a partner of another gender to whom they were not legally married. For those aged 15–29 about nine per cent lived with a spouse, while 21.9 per cent lived with a partner to whom they were not married, suggesting that co-habitation was far more common than legal marriage as a form of making a family with a partner.

10 However, it is also essential to note that a number of men I spoke with complained that when they came home from work (either at the end of the day or the end of a mining shift) they were expected to contribute to labour in the home. These complaints suggested that they felt that their wage labour exempted them from participation in necessary labour to keep the home organised and clean, children cared for and the family fed.

11 Di Leonardo, M. 1987. 'The Female World of Cards and Holidays: Women, Families, and the Work of Kinship.' *Signs* 12(3): 440–53; James, N. 1989. 'Emotional Labour: Skill and Work in the Social Regulation of Feelings.' *The Sociological Review* 31(1): 15–42.

12 See Butler 1999. *Gender Trouble*; Kessler, S. J. and McKenna, W. 1978. *Gender: An Ethnomethodological Approach.* New York: Wiley; West, C. and Zimmerman, D. H. 1987. 'Doing Gender.' *Gender and Society* 1(2). 125–51.

13 Leidner, R. 1991. 'Serving Hamburgers and Selling Insurance: Gender, Work, and Identity in Interactive Service Jobs.' *Gender and Society* 5(2): 154–77, 155.

14 Milkman, R. 1987. *Gender at Work: The Dynamics of Job Segregation by Sex during World War II.* Urbana: University of Illinois Press. 50.

15 Beechey, V. 1988. 'Rethinking the Definition of Work: Gender and Work.' Jenson, J., Elisabeth Hagen, E. and Ceallaigh Reddy, C., eds. *Feminization of the Labor Force: Paradoxes and Promises.* New York: Oxford University Press; Fenstermaker Berk, S. 1985. *The Gender Factory: The Apportionment of Work in American Households.* New York: Plenum.

16 Leidner, 1991. 'Serving Hamburgers and Selling Insurance.' 155.

17   Gelber, S. M. 1997. 'Do-It-Yourself: Constructing, Repairing and Maintaining Domestic Masculinity.' *American Quarterly* 49 (1): 66–112.

18   Gagnon and Simon argue that men often use sexual conduct, or expressions and discourse relating to it, in order to appear 'masculine'. This claim was later supported by empirical work by Holland et al. See Gagnon, J. H. and Simon, W. 1973. *Sexual Conduct: The Social Sources of Human Sexuality.* Chicago: Aldine; Holland, J., Ramazanoglu, C., Sharpe, S. and Thomson, R. 1998. *The Male in the Head: Young People, Heterosexuality and Power.* London: Tufnell Press.

19   This stands in contrast to Halberstam's contention that masculinity is usually less performative then femininity, as well as de Beauvoir's famous contention that 'one is not born, but becomes a woman'. Within this context, as well as many others recorded in Latin America, masculinity is always already in jeopardy until proven, whereas femininity requires less explicit performance. See Halberstam, J. 1998. *Female Masculinity.* Durham, NC: Duke University Press; De Beauvoir, S. 2009. *The Second Sex.* New York: Vintage Books; Gutmann, M. 1997. 'Trafficking in Men: The Anthropology of Masculinity.' *Annual Review of Anthropology* 26: 385–409.

20   Wright, T. 2000. 'Gay Organizations, NGOs, and the Globalization of Sexual Identity: The Case of Bolivia.' *The Journal of Latin American Anthropology* 5(2): 89–111.

21   Haynes, N. 2016. 'Kiss with a Fist: The Chola's Humor and Humiliation in Bolivian Lucha Libre.' *Journal of Language and Sexuality* 5(2).

22   Pascoe, C. J. 2011. *Dude, You're a Fag: Masculinity and Sexuality in High School.* Berkeley, CA: University of California Press.

23   Richardson suggests that the dominant Western understanding of the relationship between gender and sexuality posits a natural order that relies on the gender dualism/binaries of male/female; heterosexual/homosexual; masculine/feminine. 'Within this epistemological frame sexuality is a property of gender, a gender that is pre-given and located in the gendered/sexed body.' Richardson, D. 2007. 'Patterned Fluidities: (Re)Imagining the Relationship between Gender and Sexuality.' *Sociology* 41:457–74, 461.

24   Both Seidman and Chauncy have argued in various contexts that gender often serves as a 'master code' of sexuality, wherein gender expression is understood as a chief sign of one's sexuality. In some cases then men could have sex with other men and still be thought of as 'normal' (heterosexual) by virtue of their masculinity, whereas gender non-conforming individuals were considered to be the only 'real' homosexuals. This corresponds in part to widely cited Latin American views of masculinity in which the active or penetrating partner is considered to retain masculinity while only the passive or penetrated partner is considered to be feminine, gay or a 'fag'. See Seidman, S. 2002. *Beyond the Closet. The Transformation of Gay and Lesbian Life.* New York: Routledge; Chauncey, G. 1994. *Gay New York.* New York: Basic Books; Wright, 2000. 'Gay Organizations, NGOs, and the Globalization of Sexual Identity'; Lancaster, R. N. 1997. '"That We Should All Turn Queer?": Homosexual Stigma in the Making of Manhood and the Breaking of a Revolution in Nicaragua.' Herdt. G. H, ed. *Same Sex, Different Cultures: Gays and Lesbians Across Cultures,* Boulder, CO: Westview Press. 97–115; Parker, R. 1999. *Beneath the Equator: Cultures of Desire, Male Homosexuality, and Emerging Gay Communities in Brazil.* New York: Routledge; Gutmann, M. 2003. *Changing Men and Masculinities in Latin America.* Durham, NC: Duke University Press.

25   While many individuals obviously deviated from certain aspects of normativity, for the most part they remained within what Rubin calls the 'charmed circle' of the sexual value system. See Rubin, 1984. 'Thinking Sex.'

26   Hennessy, R. 2006. 'The Value of a Second Skin.' Richardson, D., McLaughlin, J. and Casey, M. E., eds. *Intersections between Feminist and Queer Theory.* Basingstoke: Palgrave. 116–35; Kirsch, M. H. 2000. *Queer Theory and Social Change.* London: Routledge; McLaughlin, J., Casey, M. E. and Richardson, D. 2006. 'At the Intersections of Feminist and Queer Debates.' Richardson, D., McLaughlin, J. and Casey, M. E., eds. *Intersections between Feminist and Queer Theory.* Basingstoke: Palgrave.

27   Richardson, 2007. 'Patterned Fluidities.' 470.

28   Leidner, 1991. 'Serving Hamburgers and Selling Insurance,' 175.

29   Marshall, T. H. 2009 [1950]. 'Citizenship and Social Class.' Manza, J. and Sauder, M., eds. *Inequality and Society.* New York: W. W. Norton and Co. 148–54.

30 Mort, F. 1995. 'Archaeologies of City Life: Commercial Culture, Masculinity, and Spatial Relations in 1980s London.' *Environment and Planning D: Society and Space* 13: 573–90; Zukin, S. 2004. *Point of Purchase: How Shopping Changed American Culture.* New York: Routledge.
31 Leitner, H. and Ehrkamp, P. 2003. 'Beyond National Citizenship: Turkish Immigrants and the (Re)construction of Citizenship in Germany.' *Urban Geography* 24(2): 127–46.
32 Lukacs, G. 1968. *History and Class Consciousness: Studies in Marxist Dialectics.* Livingstone, R., ed. Cambridge, MA: The MIT Press.
33 Ashforth and Kreiner, 1999. 'How Can You Do It?'.

Chapter 6

1 For comparison, the 2010 earthquake in Haiti registered 7.0 on the Richter scale. However, the Chilean earthquake caused far less damage and death due to the better infrastructure.
2 Gregory, S. 1998. *Black Corona: Race and the Politics of Place in an Urban Community.* Princeton, NJ: Princeton University Press.
3 Valentine, drawing on Anderson, suggests that 'whether geographically bounded or not, community is not a natural fact but an achievement, a process that does not happen without the exercise of agency and power'. See Valentine, D. 2007. *Imagining Transgender: An Ethnography of a Category.* Durham, NC: Duke University Press. 73; Anderson, 1983. *Imagined Communities.*
4 Frazier, 2007. *Salt in the Sand.* 3.
5 Druttman, B. and McHugh, E. 'Candidates Look to Chile's Outlying Regions to Boost Votes.' *The Santiago Times,* 2 December 2013. Available at http://santiagotimes.cl/candidates-look-chiles-outlying-regions-boost-votes/
6 The Socialist Party of Chile is centre-left; it was Salvador Allende's party and is now part of the *Nueva Mayoria.* The Independent Democratic Union is centre-right, founded in 1983 by Pinochet collaborators. It was the party with the most congressional representation between 2010–14. Both parties today are considered quite mainstream.
7 Given the history of labour movements in the region it was not surprising to find that 'Politics' (as defined by Hospiceños) were polarised, not between 'conservative' and 'liberal', but between what could be described as left-wing socialist politics and apathy about national politics in general. Thus I addressed apathy in the previous section and I discuss young left-wing activists here: discussions of conservative politics remain absent to reflect the fact that among Hospiceños active involvement in conservative political organizations was minimal if it existed at all.
8 See the video at https://www.youtube.com/watch?feature=player_embedded&v=sQyHcrq1F2U
9 See Han, C. 2012. *Life in Debt: Times of Care and Violence in Neoliberal Chile.* Berkeley, CA: University of California Press.
10 Because of the difference I perceived in local definitions of politics with my own broader definition, in this chapter I use Politics (with a capital P) to indicate the sorts of national issues and institutions that most Hospiceños considered political and politics (with a small p) to indicate a broader notion of politics as local, regional, national or international discussions and wielding of power that have to do with governance, law and negotiations between individual freedoms and government regulations.
11 Mendez, M. L. 2008. '"Middle Class Identities in a Neoliberal Age: Tensions between Contested Authenticities.' *Sociological Review,* 56(2): 220–37.
12 Regional GDP for Tarapacá is less than $9 billion, while that of Santiago is over $173 billion. See 'GDP per capita, PPP (current international $)', World Bank (2011).
13 Yeh, E. T. 2007. 'Tibetan Indigeneity: Translations, Resemblances, and Uptake.' De la Cadena, M. and Starn, O., eds. *Indigenous Experience Today.* New York: Berg. 69–97; Tsing, A. L. 2003. 'Agrarian Allegory and Global Futures.' Greenough, P. and Tsing, A., eds. *Nature in the Global South: Environmental Projects in South and Southeast Asia.* Durham, NC: Duke University Press. 124–69.
14 Frazier, 2007. *Salt in the Sand.*

15 Whether the specific migrants work in the industry or not, the economic opportunities of the region are based on the prosperity of mining.

16 'America', in South America, refers to the whole of the American continent (usually North and South America are conceptualised as a single land mass); it is often a political statement, reclaiming the word from a specifically North American usage.

17 "Chile–Peru Border defined by UN Court at The Hague.' *BBC News* (28 January 2014). Accessed 29 January 2014, http://www.bbc.com/news/world-europe-25911867.

18 These tactics of highlighting similarity and difference correspond to Bucholtz and Hall's notions of 'adequation and distinction'. As they explain, affirming affiliation often works through expressing sameness or difference, both of which are effective tactics of identification. See Bucholtz and Hall, 2005. 'Identity and Interaction.' 599.

19 Yeh, 2007. 'Tibetan Indigeneity.' 76.

20 Anderson, 1983. *Imagined Communities.*

Chapter 7

1 Also see Ong's discussion of 'neoliberalism as exception' and 'exceptions to neoliberalism'. Ong, A. 2006. *Neoliberalism as Exception: Mutations in Citizenship and Sovereignty.* Durham, NC: Duke University Press.

2 Redfield suggests that smaller 'folk' communities exhibit homogeneity, solidarity and fellowship, while urban areas exhibit a loss of these characteristics. See Redfield, R. 1955. *The Little Community and Peasant Society and Culture.* Chicago: University of Chilcago Press.

3 Sherzer, J. 2002. *Word Play and Verbal Art.* Austin: University of Texas Press. 51.

4 See Butler's discussion of performativity and identity. Butler, 1999. *Gender Trouble.* 146.

5 Conquergood, D. 1986. 'Between Experience and Meaning: Performance as a Paradigm for Meaningful Action.' *Renewal and Revision: The Future of Interpretation.* Colson, T., ed. Austin: Omega. 6–7.

6 Gramsci, 1971. *Selections from the Prison Notebooks.* 216.

References

Adler Lomnitz, L. 1977. *Networks and Marginality: Life in a Mexican Shantytown*. New York: Academic Press.

Adorno, T. and Horkheimer, M. 2002 [1944]. 'The Culture Industry: Enlightenment as Mass Deception.' *Dialectic of Enlightenment*. Redwood City, CA: Stanford University Press.

Aizura, Aren Z. 2006. '*Of Borders and Homes: The Imaginary Community of (Trans)sexual Citizenship.*' *Inter-Asia Cultural Studies* 7(2): 289–309.

Albó, X., Greaves, T. and Sandoval Z. G. 1981. *Chukiyawu: La Cara Aymara de La Paz*, vol. 4 (Cuadernos de investigacion No.29). La Paz: CIPCA.

Anderson, B. 1983. *Imagined Communities*. London: Verso.

Ariztia Larrain, T. 2009. 'Moving Home: The Everyday Making of the Chilean Middle Class.' Ph.D. thesis, Department of Sociology of the London School of Economics, London.

Ariztia Larrain, T. 2014. 'Housing Markets Performing Class: Middle Class Cultures and Market Professionals in Chile.' *The Sociological Review* 62(2): 400–20.

Ashforth, B. E. and Kreiner, G. E. 1999. '"How Can You Do It?": Dirty Work and the Challenge of Constructing a Positive Identity.' *The Academy of Management Review* 24(3): 413–34.

Auyero, J. 1999. 'The Hyper-Shantytown: Ethnographic Portraits of neo-liberal violence(s).' *Ethnography* 1(1): 93–116.

Babidge, S. 2013. '"Socios": The Contested Morality of "Partnerships" in Indigenous Community–Mining Company Relations, Northern Chile.' *The Journal of Latin American and Caribbean Anthropology* 18(2): 274–93.

Barr-Melej, P. 1998. 'Cowboys and Constructions: Nationalist Representations of Pastoral Life in Post-Portalian Chile.' *Journal of Latin American Studies* 30(1): 35–61.

Bauman, R. 1975. *Verbal Art as Performance*. Rowley: Newbury House Publishers.

Bauman, R. and Briggs, C. L. 1990. 'Poetics and Performance as Critical Perspectives on Language and Social Life.' *Annual Review of Anthropology* 19: 59–88.

Beechey, V. 1988. 'Rethinking the Definition of Work: Gender and Work.' In Jenson, J., Hagen, E. and Reddy, C., eds. *Feminization of the Labor Force: Paradoxes and Promises*. New York: Oxford University Press.

Benjamin, W. 1936. *The Work of Art in the Age of Mechanical Reproduction*. New York: Random House.

Bloemraad, I., Korteweg, A. and Yurdakul, G. 2008. 'Citizenship and Immigration: Multiculturalism, Assimilation, and Challenges to the Nation-State.' *Annual Review of Sociology* 34: 153–79.

Bosniak, L. S. 2001. '"Denationalizing Citizenship.' *Citizenship. Comparison and Perspectives*. Aleinikoff, T. A. and Klusmeyer, D., eds. Carnegie Endowment For International Peace.

Bourdieu, P. 1977. *Outline of a Theory of Practice*. Nice, R., trans. Cambridge: Cambridge University Press.

Bourdieu, P. 1984. *Distinction: A Social Critique of the Judgment of Taste*. Nice, R., trans. New York: Routledge.

Bourdieu, P. 1990. *The Logic of Practice*, Nice, R., trans. Cambridge: Polity Press.

Bourdieu, P. 2005. *The Social Structures of the Economy*. Malden, MA: Polity Press.

Bourdieu, P. 2006. 'Structures and the Habitus.' Moore, H. L. and Sanders, T., eds. *Anthropology in Theory: Issues in Epistemology*. Malden, MA: Blackwell.

boyd, danah. 2011. 'Social Network Sites as Networked Publics: Affordances, Dynamics, and Implications.' Papacharissi, Z., ed. *A Networked Self. Identity, Community, and Culture on Social Network Sites*. New York: Routledge. 39–58.

Brice Heath, S. 1983. *Ways with Words: Language, Life, and Work in Communities and Classrooms.* Cambridge: Cambridge University Press.

Brodwin, P. 2001. 'Marginality and Cultural Intimacy in a Trans-national Haitian Community.' Occasional Paper No. 91, October. Department of Anthropology, University of Wisconsin-Milwaukee, USA.

Brown, K. W. 2012. *A History of Mining in Latin America: From the Colonial Era to the Present.* Albuquerque, NM: University of New Mexico Press.

Brubaker, R. and Cooper, F. 2000. 'Beyond "Identity".' *Theory and Society* 29:1–47.

Bruess, C. J. S. and Pearson, J. C. 1993. '"Sweet Pea" and "Pussy Cat": An Examination of Idiom Use and Marital Satisfaction Over the Life Cycle.' *Journal of Social and Personal Relationships* 10(4): 609–15.

Bucholtz, M. and Hall, K. 2004. 'Theorizing Identity in Language and Sexuality Research.' *Language in Society* 33: 469–515.

Bucholtz, M. and Hall, K. 2005. 'Identity and Interaction: A Sociocultural Linguistic Approach.' *Discourse Studies* 7(4): 585–614.

Butler, J. 1999. *Gender Trouble: Feminism and the Subversion of Identity.* New York: Routledge.

Carruthers, D. and Rodriguez, P. 2009. 'Mapuche Protest, Environmental Conflict and Social Movement Linkage in Chile.' *Third World Quarterly* 30(4): 743–60.

Carvallo-Fernandini, R. and Saavedra Lafuente, D. *The History of CTC and Entel: Precursors of the Telecommunications in Chile.* 2008. Universidad Católica de Valparaiso. Available at http://www.ieeeghn.org/wiki/images/0/08/Carvallo-Fernandini.pdf

Castles, S. 2002. 'Migration and Community Formation under Conditions of Globalization.' *International Migration Review* 36(4): 1143–68.

Castles, S. and Davidson, A. 2000. *Citizenship and Migration: Globalization and the Politics of Belonging.* New York: Routledge.

Chauncey, G. 1994. *Gay New York.* New York: Basic Books.

'Chile-Peru Border defined by UN Court at The Hague.' BBC News, 28 January 2014. http://www.bbc.com/news/world-europe-25911867. Accessed 29 January 2014

Collier, S. and Sater, W. F. 2002. *A History of Chile, 1808–2002.* Cambridge: Cambridge University Press.

Conlin, L. '10 hábitos de la gente muy bien educada.' *Opinza,* 2 January 2015. Available at http://opinza.com/2015/01/10-habitos-de-la-gente-muy-bien-educada/

Connell, R. W. 1987. *Gender and Power: Society, the Person and Sexual Politics.* Stanford, CA: Stanford University Press.

Conquergood, D. 1986. 'Between Experience and Meaning: Performance as a Paradigm for Meaningful Action.' Colson, T. ed. *Renewal and Revision: The Future of Interpretation.* Austin: Omega. 36–7.

'Copper solution: The mining industry has enriched Chile. But its future is precarious.' *The Economist,* 27 April 2013. Available online at http://www.economist.com/news/ business/ 21576714-mining-industry-has-enriched-chile-its-future-precarious-copper-solution.

Crow, J. 2010. 'Negotiating Inclusion in the Nation: Mapuche Intellectuals and the Chilean State.' *Latin American and Caribbean Ethnic Studies* 5(2): 131–52.

Darden, J. T. 1989. 'Blacks and other Racial Minorities: The Significance of Colour in Inequality.' *Urban Geography* 10: 562–77.

Davis, B. 2003. 'Marginality in a Pluralistic Society.' *Eye On Psi Chi* 2(1): 1–4.

Dawkins, R. 1976. *The Selfish Gene.* Oxford: Oxford University Press.

De Beauvoir, S. 2009. *The Second Sex.* New York: Vintage Books.

Debord, G. 1994. *The Society of the Spectacle.* New York: Zone Books.

di Leonardo, M. 1987. 'The Female World of Cards and Holidays: Women, Families, and the Work of Kinship.' *Signs* 12(3): 440–53.

Druttman, B. and McHugh, E. 'Candidates Look to Chile's Outlying Regions to Boost Votes.' *The Santiago Times,* 2 December 2013. Available at http://santiagotimes.cl/ candidates-look-chiles-outlying-regions-boost-votes/

Dunn, E. 2005. *Privatizing Poland: Baby Food, Big Business, and the Remaking of Labor.* Ithaca, NY: Cornell University Press.

Durkheim, E. 2012. 'The Rules of Sociological Method.' Longhofer, W. and Daniel Winchester, D., eds. *Social Theory Re-Wired: New Connections to Classical and Contemporary Perspectives*. New York: Routledge.

Dutton, D. 2002. 'Aesthetic Universals.' Gaut, B. and Dominic McIver Lopes, D., eds. *The Routledge Companion to Aesthetics*. New York: Routledge.

Eagleton, T. 1990. *The Ideology of the Aesthetic*. Oxford: Oxford University Press.

Encuesta de caracterizacion socioeconomica nacional. 2011. Santiago: Casen. Available at http://observatorio.ministeriodesarrollosocial.gob.cl/casen_obj.php

Fairclough, N. 2003. *Analysing Discourse: Textual Analysis for Social Research*. New York: Routledge.

Farmer, P. 1997. *Infections and Inequalities: The Modern Plagues*. Berkeley, CA: University of California Press. 263.

Fenstermaker Berk, S. 1985. *The Gender Factory: The Apportionment of Work in American Households*. New York: Plenum.

Florini, S. 2013. 'Tweets, Tweeps, and Signifyin": Communication and Cultural Performance on "Black Twitter."' *Television New Media* 15(3): 223–7.

Frazier, L. J. 2007. *Salt in the Sand: Memory, Violence, and the Nation-State in Chile, 1890 to the Present*. Durham, NC: Duke University Press.

Gagnon, J. H. and Simon, W. 1973. *Sexual Conduct: The Social Sources of Human Sexuality*. Chicago: Aldine.

Gänger, S. 2009. 'Conquering the Past: Post-War Archaeology and Nationalism in the Borderlands of Chile and Peru, c. 1880–1920.' *Comparative Studies in Society and History* 51(4): 691–714.

Gans, H. J. 1996. 'From Underclass to Under-caste: Some Observations about the Future of the Post-Industrial Economy and its Major Victims.' Mingione, E., ed. *Urban Poverty and the Underclass: A Reader*. Oxford: Blackwell.

'GDP per capita, PPP (current international $)'. 2011. World Bank, International Comparison Program database, World Development Indicators. Available at http://data.worldbank.org/indicator/NY.GD

Geertz, C. 1976. 'Art as a Cultural System.' *MLN* 91(6): 1473–99.

Gelber, S. M. 1997. 'Do-It-Yourself: Constructing, Repairing and Maintaining Domestic Masculinity.' *American Quarterly* 49 (1): 66–112.

Goffman, E. 1959. *The Presentation of Self in Everyday Life*. Garden City, NY: Doubleday.

Goldstein, D. 2004. *The Spectacular City: Violence and Performance in Urban Bolivia*. Durham, NC: Duke University Press. 21.

Gramsci, A. 1971. Hoare, Q. and Nowell Smith, G., eds. *Selections from the Prison Notebooks of Antonio Gramsci*. New York: International Publishers.

Gregory, S. 1998. *Black Corona: Race and the Politics of Place in an Urban Community*. Princeton, NJ: Princeton University Press.

Gutkind, P. C. W. 1974. *Urban Anthropology: Perspectives on "Third World" Urbanization and Urbanism*. Assen, The Netherlands: Van Gorcum.

Gutmann, M. 2003. *Changing Men and Masculinities in Latin America*. Durham, NC: Duke University Press.

Gutmann, M. 1997. 'Trafficking in Men: The Anthropology of Masculinity.' *Annual Review of Anthropology* 26: 385–409.

Habermas, J. 1962. *The Structural Transformation of the Public Sphere: An Inquiry into a Category of Bourgeois Society*. Cambridge: Polity Press. 105.

Halberstam, J. 1998. *Female Masculinity*. Durham, NC: Duke University Press.

Han, C. 2012. *Life in Debt: Times of Care and Violence in Neoliberal Chile*. Berkeley, CA: University of California Press.

Handler, R. 1986. 'Authenticity.' *Anthropology Today* 2(1): 2–4.

Hardoy, J. 1972. *El Proceso de Urbanización en America Latina*. La Habana, Cuba: Oficina Regional de Cultural para America Latina y el Caribe.

Harness Goodwin, M. 1990. *He-Said-She-Said: Talk as Social Organization Among Black Children*. Bloomington, IN: Indiana University Press. 185–9.

Harvey, D. 2005. *A Brief History of Neoliberalism*. New York: Oxford University Press.

Haynes, N. 2016. 'Kiss with a Fist: The Chola's Humor and Humiliation in Bolivian Lucha Libre.' *Journal of Language and Sexuality* 5(2).

Hennessy, R. 2006. 'The Value of a Second Skin.' Richardson, D., McLaughlin, J. and Casey, M. E., eds. *Intersections between Feminist and Queer Theory*. Basingstoke: Palgrave. 116–35.

Hervik, P. 1999. 'The Mysterious Maya of National Geographic.' *Journal of Latin American Anthropology* 4(1): 166–97.

Hillewaert, S. 2015. 'Writing with an Accent: Orthographic Practice, Emblems, and Traces on Facebook.' *Journal of Linguistic Anthropology* 25(2): 195–214.

Holland, J., Ramazanoglu, C., Sharpe, S. and Thomson, R. 1998. *The Male in the Head: Young People, Heterosexuality and Power.* London: Tufnell Press.

hooks, b. 1995. 'Beauty Laid Bare: Aesthetics in the Ordinary.' Walker, R., ed. *To Be Real.* New York: Anchor Books.

Horst, H. and Miller, D. 2012. *Digital Anthropology.* Oxford: Berg.

Hymes, D. 1981. *In Vain I Tried to Tell You.* Philadelphia: University of Pennsylvania Press.

'Indice de Calidad de Vida Urbana.' 2014. Núcleo de Estudios Metropolitanos, Instituto de Estudios Urbanos y Territoriales. Santiago: Pontificia Universidad Católica de Chile y la Cámara Chilena de la Construcción. Available at http://www.estudiosurbanos.uc.cl/component/zoo/ item/indice-de-calidad-de-vida-urbana-icvu

Jacobson, D. 1975. 'Fair Weather Friend: Label and Context in Middle Class Friendships.' *Journal of Anthropological Research* 31(3): 225–34.

James, N. 1989. 'Emotional Labour: Skill and Work in the Social Regulation of Feelings.' *The Sociological Review* 31(1):15–42.

Jameson, F. 1991. *Postmodernism, or, The Cultural Logic of Late Capitalism.* New York: Verso.

Jofré, D. 2007. 'Reconstructing the Politics of Indigenous Identity in Chile.' *Archaeologies* 3(1): 16–38.

Kessler, S. J. and McKenna, W. 1978. *Gender: An Ethnomethodological Approach.* New York: Wiley.

Kirchenblatt Gimblett, B. 1983. '"An Accessible Aesthetic: The Role of Folk Arts and the Folk Artist in the Curriculum.' *New York Folklore: The Journal of the New York Folklore Society* 9(3–4): 9–18.

Kirsch, M. H. 2000. *Queer Theory and Social Change.* London: Routledge.

Klein, N. 2007. *The Shock Doctrine.* New York: Picador. 93–4.

Kleinman, A. 2000. 'The Violences of Everyday Life: The Multiple Forms and Dynamics of Social Violence.' Kleinman, A. and Das, V., eds. *Violence and Subjectivity.* Berkeley, CA: University of California Press. 226–41, 227.

Koskinen, I. 2007. 'Managing Banality in Mobile Multimedia.' Peritierra, R., ed. *The Social Construction and Usage of Communications Technology: Asian and European Experiences.* Philadelphia: University of the Philippines Press. 60–81.

Kristeva, J. 1980. *Desire in Language: A Semiotic Approach to Literature and Art.* New York: Columbia University Press.

Laclau, E. and Mouffe, C. 1985. *Hegemony and Socialist Strategy.* London: Verso.

Labov, W. 1972. *Language in the Inner City: Studies in the Black English Vernacular.* Philadelphia, PA: University of Pennsylvania Press.

Lancaster, R. N. 1997. '"That We Should All Turn Queer?": Homosexual Stigma in the Making of Manhood and the Breaking of a Revolution in Nicaragua.' Herdt, G. H., ed. *Same Sex, Different Cultures: Gays and Lesbians Across Cultures.* Boulder, CO: Westview Press. 97–115.

Lancaster, R. N. 2008. 'Preface.' Collins, J. L., di Leonardo, M. and Williams, B., eds. *New Landscapes of Inequality.* Santa Fe: School for Advanced Research Press.

Larraín, J. 2006. 'Changes in Chilean Identity: Thirty Years after the Military Coup.' *Nations and Nationalism* 12(2): 321–38.

Larsen, J. E. and Andersen, J. 1998. 'Gender, Poverty and Empowerment.' *Critical Social Policy* 18(2): 241–58.

Latin America Digital Future in Focus report. Comscore. 2013. Available online at http://www.comscore.com/Insights/Blog/2013_Digital_Future_in_Focus_Series.

'Latinobarómetro.' 2011. Corporación Latinobarómetro. Available at http://latinobarometro.org/.

Lee, C. K. M. 2011. 'Micro-Blogging and Status Updates on Facebook: Texts and Practices.' Thurlow, C. and Mroczek, K., eds. *Digital Discourse: Language in the New Media.* Oxford: Oxford University Press. 111–28.

Leidner, R. 1991. 'Serving Hamburgers and Selling Insurance: Gender, Work, and Identity in Interactive Service Jobs.' *Gender and Society* 5(2): 154–77.

Leimgruber, W. 2004. *Between Global and Local: Marginality and Marginal Regions in the Context of Globalization and Deregulation.* Burlington, VT: Ashgate Publishing Ltd.

Leitner, H. and Ehrkamp, P. 2003. 'Beyond national citizenship: Turkish immigrants and the (re)construction of citizenship in Germany.' *Urban Geography* 24(2): 127–46.

Leppänen, S., Kytölä, S., Jousmäki, H., Peuronen, S. and Westinen, E. 2013. 'Entextualization and Resemiotization as Resources for (Dis)identification in Social Media.' *Tilburg Papers in Cultural Studies*, no. 57. Tilburg University.

Lovaas, K. and Jenkins, M. M. 2006. 'Charting a Path through the "Desert of Nothing".' In *Sexualities and Communication in Everyday Life: A Reader.* Thousand Oaks, CA: Sage.

Lukacs, G. 1968. Livingstone, R., ed. *History and Class Consciousness: Studies in Marxist Dialectics.* Cambridge MA: The MIT Press.

Ritty, L. 2009. *Liberalization's Children: Gender, Youth, and Consumer Citizenship in Globalizing India.* Durham, NC: Duke University Press.

Lynch, G. 1987. *Roughnecks, Drillers, and Tool Pushers: Thirty-three Years in the Oil Fields.* Austin: University of Texas Press.

Madianou, M. and Miller, D. 2012. 'Polymedia: Towards a New Theory of Digital Media in Interpersonal Communication.' *International Journal of Cultural Studies* 16(2): 169–87.

Malinowski, B. 1923. 'The Problem of Meaning in Primitive Languages.' Ogden, C. K. and Richards, I. A., eds. *The Meaning of Meaning.* London: Routledge. 146–52.

Marino, M. E., Pilleux, M., Quilaqueo, D. and San Martín, B. 2009. 'Discursive Racism in Chile: The Mapuche Case.' Van Dijk, T. A., ed. *Racism and Discourse in Latin America.* New York: Rowman and Littlefield. 95–130.

Marshall, T. H. 2009 [1950]. 'Citizenship and Social Class.' Manza, J. and Sauder, M., eds. *Inequality and Society.* New York: W. W. Norton and Co. 148–54.

Martin, E. 1997. 'Managing Americans: Policy and Changes in the Meanings of Work and the Self.' *Anthropology of Policy: Critical Perspectives on Governance and Power.* Shore, C. and Right, S., eds. London: Routledge.

McDonald, T. Forthcoming. *Social Media in Rural China.* London: UCL Press.

McLaughlin, J., Casey, M. E. and Richardson, D. 2006. 'At the Intersections of Feminist and Queer Debates.' Richardson, D., McLaughlin, J. and Casey, M. E., eds. *Intersections between Feminist and Queer Theory.* Basingstoke: Palgrave.

Mendez, M. L. 2008. 'Middle Class Identities in a Neoliberal Age: Tensions between Contested Authenticities.' *Sociological Review* 56(2): 220–37.

Milkman, R. 1987. *Gender at Work: The Dynamics of Job Segregation by Sex during World War II.* Urbana: University of Illinois Press.

Miller, D. 2016. *Social Media in an English Village.* London: UCL Press.

Miller, D. and Sinanan, J. Forthcoming. *Visualising Facebook: A Comparative Perspective.* London: UCL Press.

Miller, D., Costa, E., Haynes, N., McDonald, T.,Nicolescu, R., Sinanan, J., Spyer, J., Venkatraman, S. and Wang, Xinyuan. 2016. *How the World Changed Social Media.* London: UCL Press.

Miller, V. 2008. 'New Media, Networking and Phatic Culture.' *Convergence: The International Journal of Research into New Media Technologies* 14(4): 387–400.

Ministerio de Educación, Gobierno de Chile, *Bases de Datos de Matriculados.* Available online at http://www.mifuturo.cl/index.php/bases-de-datos/matriculados.

Modan, G. 2007. *Turf Wars: Discourse, Diversity, and the Politics of Place.* New York: Blackwell.

Moodie, D. and Ndatshe, V. 1994. *Going for Gold: Men, Mines, and Migration.* Berkeley: University of California Press.

Morgan, M. 2002 'Language, Power, and Discourse in African American Culture.' *Studies in the Social and Cultural Foundations of Language 20.* Cambridge: Cambridge University Press. 56–7

Mort, F. 1995. 'Archaeologies of City Life: Commercial Culture, Masculinity, and Spatial Relations in 1980s London.' *Environment and Planning D: Society and Space* 13: 573–90.

Muñoz, J. 1999. *Disidentifications: Queers of Color and the Performance of Politics.* Minneapolis: University of Minnesota Press. 157–60.

Nelkin, D. and Lindee, S. 1996. *The DNA Mystique: The Gene as a Cultural Icon.* Ann Arbor: University of Michigan Press.

Ong, A. 1991. 'The Gender and Labor Politics of Postmodernity.' *Annual Review of Anthropology* 20: 279–309.

Ong, A. 2006. *Neoliberalism as Exception: Mutations in Citizenship and Sovereignty.* Durham, NC: Duke University Press.

Organization for Economic Cooperation and Development. 2015. OECD Income Distribution and Poverty Database. Available at www.oecd.org/els/social/inequality

Papacharissi, Z. 2009. 'The Virtual Geographies of Social Networks: A Comparative Analysis of Facebook, LinkedIn and A Small World.' *New Media and Society* 11(1–2): 199–220.

Parker, R. 1999. *Beneath the Equator: Cultures of Desire, Male Homosexuality, and Emerging Gay Communities in Brazil.* New York: Routledge.

Pascoe, C. J. 2011. *Dude, You're a Fag: Masculinity and Sexuality in High School.* Berkeley: University of California Press.

Peattie, L. R. 1974. 'The Concept of "marginality" as Applied to Squatter Settlements.' Cornelius, W. A. and Trueblood, F. M., eds. *Latin American Urban Research* 4: Anthropological Perspectives on Latin American Urbanization. Beverly Hills: Sage. 101–9.

Pêcheux, M. 1982. *Language, Semantics, and Ideology.* New York: St. Martin's Press. 157.

Ranciere, J. 2002. 'The Aesthetic Revolution and its Outcomes.' *The New Left Review* 14: 133–51.

Richards, P. 2005. 'The Politics of Gender, Human Rights, and Being Indigenous in Chile.' *Gender & Society* 19(2): 199–220.

Richards, P. 2010. 'Of Indians and Terrorists: How the State and Local Elites Construct the Mapuche in Neoliberal Multicultural Chile.' *Journal of Latin American Studies* 42: 59–90.

Richardson, D. 2007. 'Patterned Fluidities: (Re)Imagining the Relationship between Gender and Sexuality.' *Sociology* 41: 457–74.

Ritchie, D. 2005. 'Frame-Shifting in Humor and Irony.' *Metaphor and Symbol* 20(4): 275–94.

Roberts, B. R. 1978. *Cities of Peasants: The Political Economy of Urbanization in the Third World.* London: Edward Arnold.

Rubin, G. 1984. 'Thinking Sex: Notes for a Radical Theory of the Politics of Sexuality.' Vance, C., ed. *Pleasure and Danger: Exploring Female Sexuality.* Vance, C., ed. Boston: Routledge. 267–391.

Savage, M., Bagnall, G. and Longhurst, B. 2001. 'Ordinary, Ambivalent and Defensive: Class Identities in the Northwest of England.' *Sociology* 35(4): 875–92.

Schechner, R. 2002. *Performance Studies: An Introduction.* New York: Routledge.

Schneider, D. M. 1964. *A Critique of the Study of Kinship.* Ann Arbor: University of Michigan Press.

Sherzer, J. 2002. *Word Play and Verbal Art.* Austin: University of Texas Press.

Seidman, S. 2002. *Beyond the Closet. The Transformation of Gay and Lesbian Life.* New York: Routledge.

Sepúlveda, M., ed. 2008. *Anuario de Estadísticas Criminales Fundación Paz Ciudadana.* Santiago: Fundacion Paz Ciudadana. Available online at http://www.pazciudadana.cl/wp-content/uploads/2013/07/2009-01-20_Anuario-de-estad%C3%83%C2%ADsticas-criminales-2008.pdf

Sherzer, J. 2002. *Word Play and Verbal Art.* Austin: University of Texas Press.

Sinanan, J. Forthcoming. *Social Media in Trinidad.* London: UCL Press.

Smith, G. 1989. *Livelihood and Resistance: Peasants and the Politics of Land in Peru.* Berkeley: University of California Press.

Smith, S. 1989. 'Society, Space and Citizenship Transactions.' *IBG* 14: 144–56.

Smitherman, G. 2000. '"If I'm Lyin, I'm Flyin": The Game of Insult in Black Language.' *Talkin that Talk: Language, Culture, and Education in African America.* New York, NY: Routledge. 223–30.

Sommers, L. M., Mehretu, A. and Pigozzi, B. W. M. 1999. 'Towards Typologies of Socio-economic Marginality: North/South Comparisons.' Jussila, H., Majoral, R. and Mutambirwa, C. C., eds. *Marginality in Space – Past, Present and Future: Theoretical and Methodological Aspects of Cultural, Social and Economical Parameters of Marginal and Critical Regions.* London: Ashgate Publishing Ltd. 7–24.

Strathern, M. 1988. *The Gender of the Gift: Problems with Women and Problems with Society in Melanesia.* Berkeley: University of California Press.

Sturm, C. 2002. *Blood Politics: Race, Culture, and Identity in the Cherokee Nation of Oklahoma.* Berkeley: University of California Press.

Taylor, E. 2014. 'The Curation of the Self in the Age of the Internet.' Paper presented at IUAES/JASCA Conference, Tokyo, Japan. Available at http://erinbtaylor.com/the-curation-of-the-self-in-the-age-of-the-internet.

Thomann, M. 2016. 'Zones of Difference, Boundaries of Access: Moral Geography and Community Mapping in Abidjan, Côte d'Ivoire.' *Journal of Homosexuality* 63(3): 426–36.

Tsing, A. L. 2003. 'Agrarian Allegory and Global Futures.' Greenough, P. and Tsing, A., eds. *Nature in the Global South: Environmental Projects in South and Southeast Asia*. Durham, NC: Duke University Press. 124–69.

Tsing, A. L. 1993. *In the Realm of the Diamond Queen: Marginality in an Out-of-the-Way Place*. Princeton, NJ: Princeton University Press.

Turkle, S. 2010. *Alone Together*. New York: Basic Books.

Turner, V. 1982. *From Ritual to Theatre: The Human Seriousness of Play*. New York: Performing Arts Journal Publications.

Turner, V. 1986. *The Anthropology of Performance*. New York: PAJ Publications.

Valentine, D. 2007. *Imagining Transgender: An Ethnography of a Category*. Durham, NC: Duke University Press.

Velez Ibañez, C. G. 1983. *Rituals of Marginality: Politics, Process, and Culture Change in Urban Central Mexico 1969–1974*. Berkeley: University of California Press.

Velghe, F. 2015. 'Hallo hoe gaan dit, wat maak jy?: Phatic communication, the Mobile Phone and Coping Strategies in a South African Context.' *Multilingual Margins* 2(1): 10–30.

Venkatraman, S. Forthcoming. *Social Media in South India*. London: UCL Press.

Vergara, J. I. and Gundermann, H. 'Conformación y Dinámica Interna del Campo Identitario Regional en Tarapacá y Los Lagos, Chile.' In *Chungara, Revista de Antropología Chilena* 44, no. 1 (2012): 115–34. Available at http://dx.doi.org/10.4067/ S0717-73562012000100009

Vertovec, S. 2004. 'Migrant Transnationalism and Modes of Transformation.' *International Migration Review* 38(3): 970–1001.

West, C. and Zimmerman, D. H. 1987. 'Doing Gender.' *Gender and Society* 1(2): 125–51.

Williams, R. 1977. *Marxism and Literature*. New York: Oxford University Press.

Wittgenstein, L. 1953. *Philosophical Investigations*, 3rd ed. Anscombe, G. E. M., trans. London: Macmillan.

Wright, T. 2000. 'Gay Organizations, NGOs, and the Globalization of Sexual Identity: The Case of Bolivia.' *The Journal of Latin American Anthropology* 5(2): 89–111.

Yanagisako, S. 2002. *Producing Culture and Capital: Family Firms in Italy*. Princeton, NJ: Princeton University Press.

Yeh, E. T. 2007. 'Tibetan Indigeneity: Translations, Resemblances, and Uptake.' De la Cadena, M. and Starn, O., eds. *Indigenous Experience Today*. New York: Berg.

Yus, F. 2003. 'Humor and the Search for Relevance.' *Journal of Pragmatics* 35: 1295–1331.

Zukin, S. 2004. *Point of Purchase: How Shopping Changed American Culture*. New York: Routledge.

Index

Lightning Source UK Ltd.
Milton Keynes UK
UKOW07n2007101116

287355UK00003B/15/P